RECLAIMING HAMILTON

RECLAIMING HAMILTON

ESSAYS FROM THE NEW AMBITIOUS CITY

EDITED BY
PAUL WEINBERG

James Street North Books is an imprint of Wolsak and Wynn Publishers.

Cover and interior design: Marijke Friesen
Cover image: *Hammerbot* by Mike Kukucska
Typeset in Scala
Printed by Rapido Books, Montreal, Canada

The publisher gratefully acknowledges the support of the Ontario Arts Council, the Canada Council for the Arts and the Government of Canada.

James Street North Books
280 James Street North
Hamilton, ON
Canada L8R 2L3

Library and Archives Canada Cataloguing in Publication

Title: Reclaiming Hamilton : essays from the new ambitious city / edited by Paul Weinberg.
Names: Weinberg, Paul, 1950- editor.
Identifiers: Canadiana 20190165081 | ISBN 9781989496008 (softcover)
Subjects: LCSH: Hamilton (Ont.)—Anecdotes.
Classification: LCC FC3098.3 .R43 2019 | DDC 971.3/52—dc23

TABLE OF CONTENTS

Introduction:
A City Reinvents Itself

Paul Weinberg

Sometime in the past ten years or more Hamilton discovered it had become "cool." What that means is of course open to interpretation. Once derided as retro for its so-called lunch-bucket industrial demeanour, Hamilton is now viewed both as a cutting-edge and a less stressful place to live. But what does this mean for the city and those who have long been fighting for it and writing about it?

New restaurants, art galleries, bookstores and independent coffee shops are popping up, along with two repertory movie theatres – the new Playhouse Cinema and reopened Westdale – to boot. The Supercrawl music and arts festival planted itself firmly in the downtown core in 2009 and has reappeared every fall with its closed streets and open music stages plus stalls selling a multitude of arts and crafts. Further to the east, there is the conversion of the Cotton Factory, an old and gargantuan factory complex, into a creative hub of small businesses and creative activity. It is part of a larger trend to preserve and repurpose the aging and empty industrial structures that dot the city.

A major development has been the influx of former Torontonians (such as myself) who have bought homes at prices unimaginable in an overpriced GTA housing market. They are either retirees or people still working, commuting daily by car, bus or train to Toronto and back, making ties to their new urban environment rather tenuous at times. Of course, the inevitable attention from real estate investors has led to higher prices for homes and climbing apartment rents. Hamilton is becoming less affordable for people of modest incomes, in contrast to what the city was like just a decade ago.

As early as 2005, when retired management consultant Graham Crawford returned to his hometown, he detected a new "vibrancy" in downtown Hamilton, centred around James Street North. The street had been a largely Portuguese strip with shops operating during the day, selling distinct ethnic foods like salted cod, before shutting down for the evening. An Art Crawl was starting to happen on the second Friday of every month. New art galleries had sprung up, but the restaurants – including the street's first coffee shop, the Mulberry, along with the building's upstairs consulting offices – had not yet opened their doors. It was the hospitality shown by Dave Kuruc, who was already operating the Mixed Media arts supply shop at the corner of James North and Cannon, which galvanized Crawford to start his own outlet, HIStory + HERitage, devoted to the life and history of the city.

Bounce forward to 2020 and the original galleries on James Street North have closed and moved elsewhere in the downtown as commercial rents have shot up in the inevitable transformation of a destination street in a capitalistic market. Real estate investors are buying up buildings that, in a little over fifteen years, have gone up in price from $180,000 to $800,000, according to one owner of a building on the street.

One of the early adopters of James North, Dave Kuruc, has now sold his building and relocated his arts supply business to Westdale, where he and his family live. He has combined his existing business with a new bookstore, King W. Books, in a commercial space once occupied by another bookseller, Bryan Prince. If you ask him about the revitalization of Hamilton, he'll tell you flatly that it's over. Graham Crawford has also sold his three-storey building on James North.

Furthermore, the Artword Artbar on Colbourne Street, a hub for jazz in the city for about a decade, has closed after the owning couple decided it was time to retire and sold their property just off James North to an architectural firm. They still remain active in the cultural scene, holding events in different locations. Meanwhile, other changes are in store for James North with new condos and offices being planned in refurbished buildings and assuredly even more sophisticated eating places.

Such things happen all the time in a vital urban centre like Hamilton and we can expect more to occur. What is certain is that a revival is continuing in Hamilton unabated and involves more than just the fate of James North or the similarly gentrified Locke Street further west. On other streets like Barton and Ottawa Street North, in other small but growing pockets like Cannon/Kensington and King East near Tim Hortons Field and even on Kenilworth there are credible signs that the reclaiming of Hamilton is ongoing and is not neighbourhood specific.

I agree with Graham Crawford that some of the words and phrases used to describe a revival in Hamilton – now taken up primarily by the city's economic development department and the real estate industry – are frankly over-the-top. The one he "hates" the most is *the new Brooklyn*. It is arguable that Hamilton's American rust boom-bust parallel is more likely to be Pittsburgh, which also had a thriving steel industry.

Revitalization is also problematic because there is an implication that before the 2000s there was nothing of value in Hamilton. This discards the sense of solidarity among steelworkers in the 1946 Stelco strike, the preservation of natural areas and parks by Thomas McQuesten and Thomas Beckett, and the majestic heritage buildings downtown, which were foolishly torn down for urban renewal on what is now the Jackson Square mall starting in the early 1970s. James North in the 1920s was a lively Italian strip where people were out and about, according to Crawford.

Crawford is a Hamilton booster par excellence but he is also realistic about his city's shortcomings, especially with the majority of elected politicians and the bureaucracy down at city hall whom he sees as isolated in their own bubble, separate from the rest of local citizens. So, to start talking about "an urban renaissance" there is enough to make him protest. Name the issue and this local activist will speak at length on the persistence of one-way streets, the failure of city council to inform the public or the stewards of sensitive natural areas about a massive four-year sewage spill in the billions of litres into Chedoke Creek and Cootes Paradise, the intolerance of the police towards LGBTQIA+ people, the hateful characters parading in front of city hall on Saturday mornings and the general secretive atmosphere and top-down attitudes at city hall, among other festering matters at hand.

Perhaps the most suitable label for the city is *City of Waterfalls*, another marketing term that has emerged. The Niagara Escarpment – with a hundred different waterfalls, hiking trails and a wooded forest – runs right through Hamilton. This is something that nature-challenged Torontonians lack and so they come here in droves to experience it.

The term *Ambitious City* has also returned to Hamilton. It was originally a mocking pejorative by a Toronto newspaper in the nineteenth century directed against Hamilton, which then decided to own the name in an ongoing competition between the two rival cities.

Reclaiming is the word we prefer to use in this anthology because it accurately portrays a bottom-up approach by a smaller number of artists, creative people, urbanists and activists in conjunction with like-minded citizens to make Hamilton a more livable place. When that effort began is open to debate. One possibility is that the original inspiration came from the environmentalists who opposed the building of the Red Hill expressway. And while that campaign failed, it helped spawn organizations like Environment Hamilton and other kinds of activism that have achieved greater success later on.

In the early 2000s, grassroots pressure coupled with help from the province led to the restoration and opening of the heritage building at the Lister Block on James Street North in 2012, for instance. "When [owner] LiUNA decided to renovate the Lister rather than tear it down, that was a tipping point about how the developer-backed politicians/ elite saw downtown," says political scientist Peter Graefe.

McMaster University geographer Richard Harris suggests that a city's renaissance, which he agrees is a vague term, can happen without the encouragement or awareness of the city government.

In the case of Hamilton, the city was offering various incentives for developers but it was not until the early 2000s that this started to bear fruit, he observes. Harris emphasizes that what is happening now is not purely a real estate phenomenon, although it can appear that way. "Maybe to put it another way. The real estate thing could not happen or would not be happening unless there was more to it than that."

Harris is also somewhat cautious about the rebranding of Hamilton. "I think you could say, certainly, there is a revitalization, and you could say it is a renaissance, but it certainly implies rather more than what has happened so far. But obviously change has been happening."

Meanwhile, the promised funding of an east-west light rail transit system in the lower city where the population has dropped is cited as key to revitalization for Hamilton. But the late 2019 decision by the provincial Progressive Conservative government in Ontario to halt its $1 billion financial support casts a shadow on the revival. The concern is that developers will start rethinking their plans along the path where the new line was slated to follow. At publication time, this issue is still in flux.

Decades ago, Hamilton's economic development department sold Hamilton as a "great place" primarily for those living in the new suburbs.

Today the new focus is on a "quality of life" in the hipper and revived lower city where young people and small entrepreneurs will want to congregate.

"I don't know how much city branding works, although I am sure there is an academic literature trying to address that question. Certainly, cities believe that it does because they all invest money in doing it. But maybe they are running hard just to stay in the same place," says Peter Graefe. He also speculates that what is happening specifically in Hamilton's lower city stems from the establishment of a greenbelt and the Places to Grow policy under a previous Liberal government that emphasized higher density growth in established urban areas. "Hamilton faced a new set of incentives to develop downtown holdings as opposed to simply building out the suburbs to the city limits."

What is ultimately exciting about Hamilton is the current level of political activism, reflected in an active social media and the existence of organizations like Environment Hamilton, the Hamilton Roundtable for Poverty Reduction, the Hamilton Centre for Civic Inclusion and the various tenant rights groups. There is less deference towards authority and whatever city hall or our various elites dish out. With this in mind we asked a few prominent Hamilton non-fiction writers to make a contribution to this collection.

- Newspaper columnist Margaret Shkimba looks at how geography and history inform and explain Hamilton's political and social landscape.
- Anthropologist Kevin MacKay reveals what happened after he and his colleagues bought a building on King William Street during the difficult economic times experienced by the downtown and sought to turn it into a model for ethical development.
- Raise the Hammer editor Ryan McGreal provides a blow-by-blow account of the LRT project that has polarized the city's population.

- Independent journalist Joey Coleman, a man quite conscious and unapologetic about his modest socio-economic roots, shares his experience covering the volatile and sometimes nasty display of politics down in Hamilton City Hall.
- McMaster professor Sarah V. Wayland investigates how Hamilton has always been a receiving point for waves of immigration, back to the beginning of colonialism.
- Community historian Shawn Selway reports on the current rush of investors for a piece of Hamilton real estate downtown and its impact on tenants and small merchants.
- Urban planner Rob Fiedler explores how divisions between an older denser inner city and the spread-out suburbs within an urban setting like Hamilton are not always clear-cut.
- Novelist Matthew Bin shares how the Tiger-Cats have been a key part of Hamilton's industrial and working-class civic culture.
- Freelance writer Paul Weinberg parses the decades-old debate surrounding the construction of the Red Hill Valley expressway and the introduction of one-way streets to get a full picture of Hamilton's unique car culture.
- Culture journalist Seema Narula looks critically at the lack of diversity in Hamilton's much acclaimed arts boom.
- Freelance editor Kerry Le Clair writes of her efforts to broaden the possibility of public art in Hamilton and to raise the awareness of the city's unappreciated Indigenous past with a mural project.
- Freelance writer Jessica Rose explores the personalities behind the projects, ranging from environmental to cultural, that make Hamilton a more human environment.
- McMaster university professors Nancy B. Bouchier and Ken Cruikshank celebrate the history of a working-class community, Brightside, which once thrived in the shadow of a larger Stelco operation close to the harbour.

Reclaiming Hamilton covers a broad range of subjects including culture in all of its aspects. This book also examines a more confident and transformative urban centre in the twenty-first century, which explains the return of the Ambitious City moniker. Yes, there is still tension between the Old Hamilton and the New Hamilton – whatever those categories mean. The city remains a work in progress.

All Happy Cities Are Alike; Each Unhappy City Is Unhappy in Its Own Way

Margaret Shkimba

When I was asked to contribute to this volume, Paul Weinberg, the editor, said I could pick my own topic. Uh-oh, I thought. At the time, I was wondering why it is that over the last fifty years (conveniently the span of my lifetime) there have been many times when Hamilton appeared to be on the cusp of something big, but never fully realized the dream or maybe any benefit at all, because of – something. What exactly it is I'm not sure. But when I look around at other municipalities, in Canada and around the world, and I see innovation and creativity expressing itself in architecture, in the accessibility of community spaces, in the remediation and reuse of old and degrading properties, and in the adoption of daring and bold environmental initiatives, I wonder, Why can't we do that here? What are we missing and what is getting in our way of becoming more than what we are?

There are those who think Hamiltonians have a tendency to shoot themselves in the foot, maybe even feet, or that we suffer, collectively and unconsciously, from imposter syndrome. With the mega-metropolis of Toronto an hour away on the highway, it's not hard to see why. But on an unconscious level, as a community, we don't really believe we deserve our "big chance," or we believe that we have an inherent ability to screw up due to a history of past mistakes and bad decisions, of which there have been several. The constant rebuilding of Gore Park comes to mind. This central marker of the downtown core has from its beginnings posed a contentious issue. Its odd shape is due to whatever disagreement or shift of fortunes that caused Nathaniel Hughson to rescind the offer of his half of the proposed park; the other half offered up by George Hamilton, the city's eponym. Over the years, and particularly the last thirty, the park has undergone several overhauls. If we can't come together on a consistent treatment of a central park with statuary and a fountain, how can we tackle the important issues that face us as a city of multiple communities, each with its own needs and diverse populations?

What marks Hamilton unique is the Niagara Escarpment, which Hamiltonians call "the Mountain," a sharp, tree-covered craggy cliff that runs east-west through the city, creating an upper-lower division of interests. I wondered how much our geography dictated progress and development and what it had to do with the creation of our identity as Hamilton both in how we see ourselves and in how others see us, particularly our neighbours around the lake, Toronto. It's as though we carry a chip, maybe of escarpment limestone, on our collective shoulders that contributes to a sense of "less than" that makes getting things done just that much more difficult. A sense of exceptionality pervades our politics and our populace; not exceptionality that exudes excellence, but one that breeds contempt: "That won't work in Hamilton" or "That might fly in Toronto, but Hamilton is different." How did we get here?

LOCATION, LOCATION, LOCATION

Thinking about how geography informs identity led me to theoretical musings concerning geography and a sense of "place." It's not uncommon for people to feel connected to geography, either through a spiritual or visceral feeling, or through the lived memories of friends, family and good times that resonate with certain environments. Carl Sauer, an American geographer credited with revolutionizing the field, defined cultural landscapes as the impact of culture on the physical landscape. The natural landscape is altered through the actions of a cultural group resulting in the creation of a cultural landscape. What does our cultural landscape say about Hamilton and Hamiltonians?

Richard Harris is a professor of geography at McMaster University and I met with him to talk about Hamilton, geography and identity. We sat down in a busy, yet relaxed and welcoming coffee shop on Locke Street, an area that has undergone considerable redevelopment over the last thirty years. Once a strip of second-hand shops and junk dealers, Locke has transformed into a street with restaurants, coffee shops and boutique shopping. Like James Street with its art galleries and Ottawa Street with its textile and antiques stores, Locke Street is part of lower city regeneration, particularly with its drinking and dining establishments.

Despite my convoluted attempt to explain my topic, Dr. Harris took my meaning, and although he thought *identity* might be too strong a word, he thought it was appropriate in the case of Hamiltonians. He told me:

> The physical geography of the place is very distinctive...the Mountain
> ...is a really important feature. It's visible from anywhere in the lower
> city. It's also helped shape the social geography of the city historically
> because for the longest while until roughly speaking the Second World
> War the east-west divide was still very much there and always had been
> to some extent defined against the Mountain. The existence of the

Mountain paradoxically pushed or exacerbated the east-west divide. But there was also a north-south, and that's why areas just underneath the escarpment were always perceived to be more desirable even in the east side versus the west side, just that little bit of elevation, a little bit less pollution, a little bit further away from industry.

He went on to say that it was fundamental to the way that Hamiltonians think of or distinguish themselves. And although attitudes may be changing, Dr. Harris said, "The physical divide really underlines the social divide."

The physical divide is one I know well, having grown up in the shadow of the escarpment in the east-end Rosedale area, bordered on the east by the Red Hill Valley and south and west by King's Forest and the escarpment. As a child, I looked forward to taking the bus up and down any of the Mountain access routes for the view of the lower city and the harbour and lake beyond. On night trips, I imagined the lights of the city must be what Hollywood looked like. What a wonderful city I live in, I marvelled as I pressed my face to the bus window.

The Red Hill Valley Parkway (RHVP) was first proposed in 1954, five years before I was born. Opposition to the parkway dominated neighbourhood politics my entire childhood. It wasn't until I moved away that I came to care less and, indeed, even see the benefit of another mountain access. Over the span of fifty years the city pursued development until eventually opposition was overcome through compromise and an election in 2003 that centred on the Red Hill question. The city agreed to a partnership with Six Nations of the Grand River to manage a portion of the green space. Six Nations became involved to protect further degradation of the archaeological significance of the Red Hill Valley, an area important to understanding the history and heritage of early Indigenous people in the area. It wasn't only the First Nations who mounted opposition to the RHVP. Environmentalists also had an interest in protecting the Red Hill Valley ecosystem from overexploitation. They were supported in their actions by anti-oil and anti-car activists. Some doubted the population projections of planners who were over-optimistic about growth in the face of declining industrial activity and commuter traffic.

The debate over the RHVP brought a spotlight to the area and demonstrated its value as a transportation route for the whole city rather than being conserved or otherwise left to nature. Yet the discourse was coloured for some of those in the east end with a sense of classism; it was seen as another concrete, industrial "thing," in this case a highway, paving over the last natural environment in an area with more than its share of the industrial landscape. It was viewed through the perspective of loss: the east end was losing a key natural recreation area because people from the Mountain needed a faster way to the highway. The project was polarizing, as evidenced by the length of time it took for realization, just over fifty years, and the millions of dollars spent in fighting and defending indefensible positions have only fed the lawyers and cost the taxpayers. While it hasn't brought untold increased prosperity and commercial success to the city, the RHVP provides faster access for those living on the escarpment to the transportation networks in the lower city and by all accounts is well travelled. It remains controversial ten years later as flooding and road safety have become significant issues. In the summer of 2017, it was discovered that the city had "lost" the results of surface tests that were taken in the wake of a number of tragic accidents that claimed the lives of several Hamiltonians. Civic outrage over what people perceived to be institutional incompetence at best and a cover-up at worst led to calls for a judicial inquiry to determine how it is that such important documents could go astray at city hall. The inquiry proceeds as I write this essay.

A similar dynamic, only reversed, emerged with the Light Rail Transit (LRT) project, which advocates championed not only as a mass transit project that the city needed, but also as a catalyst for urban development along a corridor desperate for redevelopment.

The proposed line, from Eastgate Square on Centennial Parkway in the east to McMaster University in the west, a major destination for current transit users, was to run through the city along King Street. The route allowed for much needed infrastructure improvements to piggyback onto LRT construction. Apart from the opponents to the project who lived along the route and who would see their businesses suffer through construction, and the mostly low-income, marginalized people who lost their homes due to project land needs, opposition was mounted by Mountain residents who felt left out of the billion dollar gift the province had promised for the project. The Hamilton Street Railway (HSR) has failed to keep pace with either amalgamation or the new developments springing up on the south Mountain. Addressing the disparities in area rating, a side effect and lingering issue of amalgamation, has been put off by one council after another for almost twenty years, with the result that transit is starved in newer areas and absent altogether in some amalgamated communities. Council voted over seventy times to support the LRT, the first leg of its BLAST network, and the 2018 mayoral run was a de facto referendum on the issue with the only serious contender to pro-LRT Mayor Eisenberger's run for re-election an LRT opponent, Vito Sgro. Donna Skelly, a short-term Mountain city councillor and vocal LRT opponent, stepped into the Conservative seat for Flamborough-Glanbrook in the 2018 provincial election. Despite pre-election promises by the Ford government, indeed by Premier Ford himself, the LRT was abruptly cancelled citing cost overruns. The decision of what to do with a billion dollars in transit money was removed from council's control and given to a small group of appointed deliberators. It was a play of politics and a condemnation of Hamilton's inability to breach the escarpment divide. Such an imperious decision could only be deployed on a deeply dysfunctional council.

The LRT debacle is reminiscent of what happened with the Sky-Train proposal put before council in 1981. The Coalition on Sane

Transit, founded by Mountain resident Lorna Kippen, fought against the project that would link Jackson Square in the core to Lime Ridge Mall on the south Mountain. Kippen is quoted in a CBC news report as saying the line would have destroyed any neighbourhood it went through. It was a project before its time for the people of Hamilton. Indeed, opponents said it wouldn't be needed for decades – the ridership wasn't there – resulting in the project's rejection by council. Vancouver picked it up and had it completed for the 1986 World Exposition where it became the Expo Line, the first line of their LRT system. It's only speculation as to who was right or wrong in the long run. Had Hamilton adopted the SkyTrain and provided mass transit up and down the Mountain back in 1981, the east-west LRT line would have had one less argument against it, that is, what about the Mountain?

WHO ARE WE?

Hamilton did not grow organically from a little village that, over time, possibly generations, became a city. According to Hamilton historian John Weaver, it was the "first speculative townsite to evolve into a major Canadian city." This speculation was fuelled by the almost fifty thousand people, mostly of British origin, but many of varied ethnic and racial identities, who assisted the British in the American Revolution. These Loyalists, as they were called, were transported first to locations on the east coast where overcrowded conditions created a need for more settlement space. The British government responded by acquiring the rights to settle the area east of Niagara from the Mississaugas in 1784. Persons who could prove themselves true to the Loyalist cause and particularly those whose fathers, sons and brothers fought for the British received substantial land grants. Those land grants became the beginnings of Wentworth County, consisting of Beverly, Ancaster, East and West Flamborough, Barton, Glanbrook, Binbrook and Saltfleet Townships. This is now called the Greater Hamilton Area, which was created in 2001 with the process that came to be known as amalgamation.

I'm writing this essay in the shadow of the work of the Truth and Reconciliation Commission, which exposed the horrific and traumatizing experience of many Indigenous people at the hands of the Canadian government, several religious institutions and, by extension, the Canadian people. Despite the assertion in our historical texts and popular histories that the area was deserted, "virgin" even, an Indigenous trail cut through the land beneath the escarpment along the high ground through the marsh. King Street is the old Iroquois Trail. Another Indigenous trail, the Mohawk Trail, travelled along Burlington Heights at the top of the Iroquois Bar or Terrace, a sandbar created by the waters of the old Lake Iroquois. The sandbar traverses the lower city from Burlington Heights in the west to the base of the escarpment at the top of James Street. It was well travelled, if not permanently settled, by the Indigenous people who lived in the surrounding areas. When we talk about settlement in Canada, we must recognize that First Nations have a vibrant, rich and continuous existence in the area that stretches back for thousands of years. We need to acknowledge that the land on which Hamilton was founded is the traditional territory of the Haudenosaunee and Anishinabek. This territory is covered by the Upper Canada treaties and directly adjacent to Haldimand Treaty territory and is acknowledged in the Dish with One Spoon wampum belt.

We're not taught much local history in our schools. There's the War of 1812, where the Battle of Stoney Creek was a decisive event and is re-enacted each year on the weekend closest to June 6 at Battlefield Park. I went one year with my children. The mosquitos were relentless. However, the War of 1812 was a big deal for the nascent town of Hamilton. Loyalist refugees had been on the move for almost thirty years, displaced from their homes by the American Revolution and transported to overcrowded settlements in the Maritimes before moving again to settle finally in Hamilton. The conviction of fifteen neighbours as traitors at the Bloody Assize of 1814 and the subsequent hanging of eight of them at Burlington Heights is a testament to the threat they felt to their security. The particularly gruesome verdict detailed that the prisoners would be "hanged by the neck but not until you are dead, for you must be cut down alive, and your bowels taken out and burned before your face (on your being still alive). Then your head must be severed from your body which must be divided into four parts, and your head and quarters to be at the King's disposal." The cry against such a barbarous verdict was loud and calls for leniency poured in throughout the appeal. Seven of the fifteen were released, eight were hung on a single gallows. It stands as an early claim to fame, or is it infamy? Beware, Hamilton hangs traitors.

John Weaver, professor of history at McMaster University and author of *Hamilton: An Illustrated History*, states, "The early history of the scattered communities which preceded the emergence of Hamilton consists of a meeting between a unique natural environment and men of ambition." This is true. Loyalist families settled on and farmed the land. Some of it, anyway. Most of it was sold to speculators who sold it to developers who parcelled the land into lots and sold it off to landless settlers and immigrants. It was sold so quickly the paperwork lagged the handshake by a considerable period of time and perhaps several transactions. By the time Hamilton became a city in 1846 the population had gone from zero to over ten thousand. Hamilton the city was created when George Hamilton petitioned the government at York to recognize the Gore District (1816), then the Gore as a police village (1833) and finally the city of Hamilton (1846). He donated land he purchased from James Durand, United Empire Loyalist and member of the British legislative assembly, for the construction of a courthouse and jail and was a tireless city booster. That was a whirlwind history, but the gist of it is that Hamilton was a city built by land speculators. Perhaps the greatest of these was Sir Allan Napier MacNab, of Dundurn Castle fame, who had his own brush with bankruptcy. Hamilton was promoted and sold, part and parcel of the international world, raising and crashing the fortunes of many early families.

To understand how Hamilton saw itself, I consulted several key texts in Hamilton history beginning with the anniversary publication *The Hamilton Centennial, 1846–1946* produced by the Hamilton Centennial Committee and which claimed to present "One Hundred Years of Progress." This volume of essays serves as a record of Hamilton achievements, but it also provides a snapshot in time, a landscape view of the image Hamilton chose to project into the world. It was a year after the end of World War II. Contributors to the edited collection included McMaster University professors, as well as leaders in education, public health, recreation and the arts, who authored chapters on the past, industrial and commercial development, churches, arts, education, health, sport and civic leaders. It ends with the chapter entitled "Hamilton, Youth's City of Opportunity." A poem by Marjorie Freeman Campbell, "The Loyalist City," opens the book and is opposite a colour plate of a painting, *The Landing of La Salle* by George Emarton, a Hamiltonian who died four years earlier at Dieppe. The reader is introduced to Hamilton as an integral part of the international world, the result of steady, sure progress, a hundred years of it. Hamilton, the message reads, is equipped to boldly go into the second half of the twentieth century, a city built on industry and commerce, and sustained by faith.

In his essay on industry and commerce, J.W. Watson, Ph.D., Department of Geography, McMaster University, claimed Hamilton "as the most industrialised city in Canada, with the greatest concentration of heavy industries." He phrased the statement as a question at the outset of his essay, which was chapter two, signifying the importance of industry to the city's growth. Dr. Watson focused on Hamilton's unique geography and access to raw materials and markets along with cheap energy and abundant skilled labour in building Hamilton's success. Hamilton's railways were a credit to industry, opening up access to territory beyond the waterways, long the traditional method of transportation. The back of the volume carries twenty-nine pages containing messages of congratulations from thirty-seven major corporations, sadly, some of them no longer operating in the Hamilton area. The year 1946 also witnessed a defining moment in Hamilton's history that goes against the narrative offered by J.W. Watson and the members of the Centennial Committee when the workers at the Steel Company of Canada, Stelco, went on strike demanding better wages, a forty-hour workweek and the right for the union to collect dues. The strike lasted a long, drawn-out, bitterly fought eighty-one days, and spread to other industries, but is considered by historians to be decisive in shaping labour-management issues in Canada. And, too, in shaping how Hamiltonians were seen by themselves and others. Hamilton emerged proudly as a blue-collar working town, its identity forged during the strike, and forcefully injecting the contributions of the worker into a narrative long focused on the activities of great men.

Jump forward twenty years, to 1966, the year before Canada's centennial celebrations. Marjorie Freeman Campbell, whose poem opened the centennial publication, published *A Mountain and a City: The Story of Hamilton*. Prime Minister Lester B. Pearson wrote the preface, reminiscing of his time in Hamilton as a schoolboy in the years 1910–1914. The tone of Campbell's tome is celebratory: Loyalist families, who lost so much when they fled America, who saw their homesteads burned, their children suffer and die, as, newly homeless and unwelcome by their neighbours, they made the trek from New York, Pennsylvania and Ohio to Niagara, before settling in the "virgin territory," the area that is now Hamilton. Campbell is a compelling storyteller and her history is an exhaustive record of the relevant details of civic life, a celebration of the great men and women, industrialists, politicians and civic-minded citizens who built the city. Campbell closes her history with a chapter on "Today." The year before, in 1965, a bold vision was put before city council to transform the core, from Main Street to York Boulevard, "a hodge-podge of unassorted, time-stained buildings, shabby streets and drab parking lots" according to Campbell. Looking at the rendering included in her book, only city hall is distinguishable today. The board of education building, with its distinctive round frontage, was built but then demolished when the board decided to move to a location on the Mountain, a decision not welcome among urban supporters who saw it as a loss of consumers in the core to more parking spots at a Mountain location. But back to the plan. Council was thrilled with the proposal and voted unanimously in support. Looking back, some point to the building of Jackson Square and the subsequent development of the area with the Art Gallery of Hamilton; sports, convention and entertainment facilities; a new library and the Eaton Centre, now called the City Centre, as furthering the decline of the core. That the area today doesn't look anything like the rendering approved by city council points to the fact that there were problems with the plan. What those problems were is beyond the scope of this essay. Important to consider is the unanimous support of city council, it may have been the last big project to get such glowing support, and the opposite effect it brought about. After a brief burst of prosperity when Jackson Square opened, the downtown began a slow and steady decline, in part fuelled by the new mall on the Mountain, Lime Ridge Mall.

Hamilton celebrated its quasquicentennial in 1971 and while not really a history of Hamilton, the publication *Pardon My Lunch Bucket* presents Hamilton at another point in time, 125 years after incorporation. It's another celebration marker, one designed to counter the negative picture that had emerged in the postwar period, one that painted Hamilton as grimy, stinky and dangerous. The opening of the Burlington Skyway Bridge in 1958 presented travellers with a view of Hamilton dominated by the steel mills and their smokestacks of billowing pollution. In 1967, the National Film Board production *Steeltown* was not received well by Hamiltonians, in fact, many were outraged. To add insult to injury, an Ottawa columnist referred to Hamilton as "Ontario's ugly duckling community." In this environment, the city council commissioned *Pardon My Lunch Bucket,* a beautiful coffee-table book replete with pictures and dripping with optimism. One reviewer writing in the *Hamilton Spectator* called it an "unrepentant love song to the city of Hamilton." It, too, ends on a futuristic note, looking forward to the year 2000, to a Hamilton still industrial, but with automated factories and a three-day workweek. Skybuses and monorails traverse the city, east-west and up and down the escarpment. There are movable homes and moving sidewalks; the vision is amazing. Hamilton is the centre of the Niagara region with a projected population of over eight hundred thousand. Well, it's now 2020 and we know that didn't happen.

The previously mentioned history by John Weaver, *Hamilton: An Illustrated History*, serves as a cold shower to the celebratory anniversary volumes of the past or the passion of Campbell's poetic prose. Weaver puts Hamilton in its place. He examines the stages of Hamilton's development, from a glimmer in George Hamilton's imagination to the early 1980s, and comes to the conclusion that Hamilton can be seen as both unique and typical. According to Weaver, Hamilton's struggles are much like the struggles of any mid-sized North American city. And indeed, he singles out the merging of municipalities – amalgamation – all along the Golden Horseshoe, from Niagara Falls to Oshawa, as problematic for each of the individual towns and cities along the route, their identity and interests in threat of being swallowed up by the larger metropolitan areas of Toronto and Hamilton. In terms of what makes Hamilton unique, Dr. Weaver highlights, in addition to our geography, is our relationship with Toronto and the rivalry that it entails. He states: "No Canadian city has had to endure comparable rivalry from a nearby metropolis." It's relentless. We are reminded of it in a lighthearted way with the traditional Toronto Argos vs. Hamilton Tiger-Cats football rivalry. The relationship has become more complicated as Torontonians fleeing an out-of-reach housing market relocate to Hamilton, pushing up property values and pushing the economically marginalized into a rental market far beyond their means.

The People and the Bay: A Social and Environmental History of Hamilton Harbour by Nancy Bouchier and Ken Cruikshank was published in 2016 and examines the relationship between Hamiltonians and the waterfront: Cootes Paradise, Hamilton Harbour and Lake Ontario. The unspoiled beauty discovered by the early colonialists had, by the mid-twentieth century, "become the largest and most beautiful septic tank in the world" due to the unfettered use of the lake for industrial purposes. Randle Reef, a toxic sludge of coal tar, a by-product of the steel-making process, lies just west of the Stelco docks, and has the distinction of being the "most toxic area in the harbour and the worst site of its kind in the Great Lakes." Once a pristine natural environment, Hamilton Harbour had become "an artefact of human design," its shoreline altered by the demands of industry, yet influenced by the needs of the people and communities that settled on the shores and subject to the unpredictable forces of nature. Bouchier and Cruikshank detail the importance of the waterfront both for recreation and industry, and explore its impacts on Hamiltonians, particularly those living in the North End and along the Beach Strip.

It's clear from these studies that Hamilton is inextricably linked to industry, it is who we are: Hamilton is Steeltown and will be long after the factories are gone. What is also clear is the pride with which Hamiltonians wear that label, or rather wore that label. The movement now is toward remediation of industrial lands and a rebranding from physical to intellectual labour in transitioning from a manufacturing to a knowledge-based economy. I wonder if that's a mission impossible. Even for Randle Reef, oozing out into Hamilton Harbour, the solution is containment not cleanup. Hamilton has a long way to go to shed the toxic image that is presented along the waterfront. This has become even more difficult with the news in the fall of 2019 that over a four-year period an open sewer gate leaked billions of sewage sludge into Cootes Paradise in what has become known as Sewergate. Hamiltonians became united in their outrage not only over the magnitude and duration of the leak, but also city council's decision to keep information from the public. While Hamiltonians have long endured the reputation as the "Armpit of Canada" due to our industrial pollution, Hamilton was being compared to another orifice, one lower down on the human body.

ONE BIG HAPPY FAMILY

Much like Dr. Weaver, I don't believe that Hamilton is different from any other municipality in that it exists as an amalgamation of smaller communities, settlements that grew into towns that became either cities themselves, or were annexed to another for a greater municipal area. Rarely are these entities renamed as a result; they are, instead, subsumed into the whole and become communities. The pace of population expansion and the voracious need for land to develop into housing, suburbs and shopping centres to service the population means the disappearance of the distinct markers of spatial identity; space itself being the most obvious disappearance. Winona blends into Stoney Creek blends into Hamilton with only a sign noting any difference among them. The markers are more pronounced leaving town as the sun sets, with the Ancaster and Dundas boundaries marked by the geographical characteristics of the Niagara Escarpment and the Dundas Valley. It makes sense to say you're leaving Hamilton and entering Dundas as you descend and ascend the valley along King Street or climb the escarpment as it veers south and up Wilson Street to Ancaster. It's more difficult to see the distinction at Centennial Parkway between east Hamilton and Stoney Creek.

Amalgamation of the region of Hamilton-Wentworth into the City of Hamilton was legislated by the provincial Conservative government under Mike Harris and brought together Ancaster, Flamborough, Waterdown, Stoney Creek, Binbrook and Glanbrook in the Greater Hamilton Area, the GHA or, for short, Hamilton. This was not well received by many in the amalgamated communities. People in these communities have historically defined themselves against Hamilton. It wasn't that the property value increase drove the migration to the suburbs, but the belief that a better life awaited them there, that the negatives of old, urban Hamilton could be avoided, most notably the environmental pollution that permeated the north and east ends, and the depression that seemed to settle on the downtown core during the 1980s. The people left for greener landscapes and they vowed never to come back.

On a rainy day in the mid-2000s, I found myself standing in the doorway of a downtown high-end restaurant. It had been years since I was in the neighbourhood, but when my girls were younger, we lived just a few streets over from the restaurant in the second floor of a house. The area was what people could call "sketchy" when I moved in with the girls. The house next door often held a porch full of men, recovering, I'm sure, from something, either a bad addiction or a raucous evening. One night, there was a stabbing in the parking lot across the street. My youngest was convinced we had moved to the poor part of town, although in truth, I thought it was a step up from the east-end neighbourhood we had moved from. At our new place, when I stepped out and turned left, the escarpment, a welcome touchstone with its ever-changing coat of many colours, loomed on the horizon. For a time before she was born, we lived just east of Kenilworth Avenue and when I stepped out and turned left, I was greeted with a smokestack at the bottom of the street, its grey plume billowing industrial pollutants carried off by the wind. When they say Hamiltonians have "grit," I know exactly what they mean. I was never quite sure what mission the minister was on who owned the house, but after it was badly damaged in a late-night fire, the men moved away and an older couple bought it to renovate. It was a beautiful old house, big and spacious. They turned it into apartments – its fate an early example of the gentrification crisis that continues to threaten the socio-economic diversity of our communities.

But back to the restaurant. As I stood in the doorway watching the rain fall, I got talking to a man who had a business in the community and we chatted about the improvements that were clearly evident, a result of an interest in cheap, affordable houses that only needed tender loving care to shine. He grew up in the community and was happy to see it prosper. He lives in Ancaster now, he said, but when he left, he left Hamilton, and the impoverishment that was beginning to settle in areas around the core was a thing to escape. I pointed out that he and those like him, who moved off to greener pastures in the Ancaster suburbs, fuelled the property decline in the inner core as they took their high-earning incomes to brand new homes and left the area to decay. I was pretty hard on him, but his attitude was patronizing – "oh look how the peasants have cleaned themselves up" seemed to be the subtext of his opening line. But how can you blame people for wanting what's best for their families, especially young children? He thought he was doing the best by his family, moving out of his childhood neighbourhood, which was undeniably urban, concrete and, for the most part, grey, and up the ladder to a better community in any one of the small towns surrounding Hamilton.

In my conversation with Dr. Harris, we discussed the perception versus the reality of the dangerous city/safe suburbs story that's often told. In light of the murder of Hamilton mobster Angelo Musitano in the driveway of his Waterdown home in May 2017, and the arrest and extradition to the US of hacker Karim Baratov from his Ancaster home earlier that same year, what was really happening? Despite the perception of a dangerous downtown core, the reality is that Hamilton is close to the provincial average for violent crime, the kind people are afraid of, as opposed to white-collar crime, which is more distant from their person. But now, as Dr. Harris says, "politics everywhere is becoming increasingly polarized regardless of facts or evidence, people believe what they want to believe." If it feeds the stereotype, it gets traction; if it doesn't, it disappears from our radar.

BRANDING AND BOOSTERISM

Over the years Hamilton has tried many things to bolster its reputation. The Ambitious City was our first attempt at branding and, in true Hamilton nature, it was serendipitous and in response to a snide comment made in a Toronto newspaper in 1847 soon after Hamilton attained city status. Hamilton intercepted the pass and carried it up the field for a marketing touchdown, ignoring the sneer of the Toronto crowd and capitalizing on the Ambitious City label for years, taking it all the way to the Steel City, or Steeltown, with a side detour to Lunchbox City for, well, lunch I guess. At the end of the nineteenth century, Hamilton became the Electric City, the first city to get AC electricity largely owing to the investment in hydroelectric power at DeCew Falls, which attracted industries such as Westinghouse, International Harvester and Otis Elevator among others to town. Nikola Tesla, the Serbian-American inventor who was integral in the creation of the modern electrical supply system, is said to have attended project construction. A section of Burlington Street was renamed Nikola Tesla Boulevard in the summer of 2016 to underscore Hamilton's historic connection to the industrial developments that built our modern economies, even though many of those companies no longer exist or have moved to other cities, in part, for cheaper electricity rates.

Hamilton is also known as the City of Waterfalls. It may have seemed a stretch at first with Niagara Falls just down the highway, but the dedicated work by Chris Ecklund, a Hamilton entrepreneur and philanthropist, in highlighting, literally with coloured lights at night, the numerous streams that pour over the escarpment, brought the public's attention to the natural beauty hidden along the escarpment. Social media helped spread the word and before long Tourism Hamilton was promoting the tagline. The City of Waterfalls campaign was so successful the claim to fame appeared on Smithsonianmag.com, declaring Hamilton as the "True Waterfall Capital of the World" in summer 2017. Unfortunately, tourist attention caught on and created chaos at several sites, and the summer of 2017 witnessed the death of an errant hiker as well as numerous rope rescues performed by firemen. Popularity has contributed to parking problems; transit routes haven't caught up. A clear example of the "be careful what you wish for" warning.

In the early 2000s Hamilton was becoming known as a haven for artists and all types creative with the unofficial town tag "Art is the New Steel" popping up on posters throughout the core as James Street transformed into gallery alley. The monthly Art Crawl, held on the second Friday of every month, with a Supercrawl in September, was the brainchild of a small group of local artists seeking a way to increase public accessibility to the art happening in the small galleries along James Street North. It began with the simple idea of staying open later one night of the month and Art Crawl was born. It quickly became the must-do hip event, especially during the summer months when artists/vendors lined the sidewalks with their wares. Supercrawl was added as the September event and focused on music, attracting big sponsors and name acts along the way. Of course, the city came late to the party but has been supportive of the changes to the street scene. The newfound attention has brought higher property values and all that entails. The sale in 2019 and subsequent closing of the Artword Artbar, a staple on the downtown arts scene, is an indication of, in the words of *Spectator* reporter Mark McNeil, the "shifting landscape driven by changing economics." It's not just the creatives who found themselves a victim of their own success, but also the poor and marginalized who lived above and behind the storefronts, innocent victims of the golden rule of supply and demand. Hamilton is now attracting young professionals who find themselves priced out of the Toronto market, a decided shift from when I was a young professional in the late 1970s, when leaving Hamilton seemed our only option. Hamilton's reputation is becoming less lunch bucket and more Uber Eats.

TROUBLES IN PARADISE

Hamilton became a sanctuary city in early 2014, the second city in Canada to declare itself such. Second, of course, to Toronto. Hamilton has a long history of attracting immigrants into the workforce and to settle throughout the city. Hamilton also has a history that includes racism. The Westdale housing development gained notoriety for its Black and Jewish exclusionary clauses in purchasing documents from the mid-twentieth century. After 9/11, it took twelve years of investigation before Hamilton police laid charges against the people responsible for firebombing a Hindu temple they had mistaken for a mosque. The firebombing was the catalyst for the city to reflect upon itself and resulted in the creation of the Hamilton Centre for Civic Inclusion and a declared civic commitment to fostering inclusivity. It could be this awareness, this commitment to a better world that saw Hamilton welcome almost one thousand refugees in response to the Syrian refugee crisis in 2016. But our self-congratulation rests on a shaky foundation. In the summer of 2019, Hamilton exploded on the national scene as the most hate-filled city in Canada, with the measure being police-reported hate crimes, which clocked in at three times the rate of Toronto, a shameful statistic to claim. To those marginalized and minority communities involved this came as no surprise, simply evidence of the experiences many felt living in Hamilton. The report reflected the debacle of Pride 2019, which was marred by political grandstanding as Mayor Eisenberger refused to support the city's own Pride Committee recommendations to not fly the Pride flag during Pride Week, a sorry indictment of the city's response to the problems facing the LGBTQ+ community. The Pride march turned into chaos as right-wing and fundamentalist Christian protestors clashed with Pride marchers. The police response was totally inadequate and coloured by long-standing animosities toward local anarchists. This came after months of Yellow Vest (YV) protests in the forecourt of city hall, a supposedly welcoming, civic space. The YV movement in

Canada holds extremist views regarding anti-immigration and white supremacy, particularly troubling to a multicultural community. So, to recap: Hamilton is a sanctuary city; we welcome immigrants and refugees from around the world. The YV protestors were prominent in the large forecourt of city hall, waving their anti-immigration signs and creating an atmosphere of fear and intimidation. This is what people travelling along the five lanes of Main Street saw every Saturday, for months.

Outrage over the continued presence of the YV protestors prompted a grassroots response from the community to retaliate and the community counter protester group PLAID was founded. Peace, Love, Acceptance, Inclusion, Diversity became the watchwords of those who gathered every Saturday to counter-protest the YV protestors. This grassroots attempt at a solution came after months of inaction by the city council to formally address the problem. The altercation at Pride 2019 prompted citizens to demand an inquiry into the police response, which is under way as I write this. City council was pushed to address the issue of hate speech vs. free speech and who gets to say what in public space. Like deer in the harsh headlights of virulent anti-immigration and white supremacist ideology, the mayor and council seemed to be caught unawares, leaving it to the PLAID protestors to project a counter image of Hamilton as welcoming diversity and community engagement.

Hamilton community and grassroots organizations came together at the invitation of the Hamilton Roundtable for Poverty Reduction to create a grand vision; one that was buoyed on a wave of optimism fuelled by unprecedented cooperation across all partners. Everybody was on board with the branding of Hamilton as "the best place to raise a child." This was later amended to "the best place to raise a child and age successfully"; a bit of a mouthful, but how to can you argue with the sentiment? Particularly given the growing number of elderly as the baby boomers reach the end of their demographic bulge, creating challenges for many municipal services. From cradle to grave, Hamilton is the place to be. The logic was simple and cost nothing, well except for the lunches and meetings to hash it all out among Hamilton agencies, businesses and anyone who wanted to sign the declaration. But there was no "thing" that would be established, no "office" or mechanism to ensure accountability to the vision was apparent, just a vague "feel-good" commitment to consider the kiddies, and later the elderly, in policy development and service provision. The idea was that every decision would be made through the prism of child welfare and aging. What's good for parents, jobs, housing, recreation is good for kids. What's good for kids is good for community, for the present and for the future. How could Hamilton lose? But it was a kind of Field of Dreams endeavour, promote it and they will come was the thinking. There was no checkup, no status report of markers or milestones met on the yellow brick road to a wonderland for kids and their parents. A CBC report by Adam Carter in 2015 concluded that Hamilton was perhaps not the best place to raise a child: children are still living in poverty, going hungry and falling behind in school.

Hamilton was part of the 2015 Pan Am Games that saw events taking place in locales around the Golden Horseshoe. It was a grand proposal for a new stadium to replace the aging Ivor Wynne Stadium and to build a velodrome to capitalize on Hamilton's growing reputation as a cycling centre after the success of the 2003 National Road Cycling Championships and the establishment of one of five Canadian National Cycling Centres in Ancaster. Hamilton was an ideal cycling location – with the escarpment to climb and the country roads beyond the suburbs, there is something for everyone and we were gaining a reputation. However, the stadium debate, which saw council dither endlessly over where to build the new stadium only to end up reorienting it in its current location, dominated Pan Am Games discussions. In the end, Hamilton council voted against the velodrome, despite strong community support. It was ours to lose and we gave it away to Milton.

Coming full circle and filed under the rubric "all old things are new again," in the summer of 2017 the Hamilton Chamber of Commerce took up the Ambitious City banner once more in their marketing campaign, Ambitious Again, to raise the profile of Hamilton as a destination for investment and business interests. While Hamilton was clearly on the radar for Toronto real estate agents looking to satisfy their residential clients, Toronto businesses and corporate interests remained for the most part in the dark about the opportunities that lay just down the highway in Hamilton. Enter Hamilton Economic Development and the pop-up consulate they established on Queen Street West in the spring of 2017. The *Globe and Mail* began their coverage of the two-day event with their customary snark: "No one can accuse Hamilton of not trying hard enough."

I met with Keanin Loomis, the chair of the Hamilton Chamber of Commerce, to talk about the Hamilton Consulate idea, and whether selling Hamilton as an investment opportunity to Toronto businesses and investors worked as planned. Loomis has no problem selling Hamilton to anyone. He first had to sell the idea of living in Hamilton to his wife, who was born and raised in Hamilton but who left for university and vowed never to return. So selling Hamilton to curious investors or businesses is easy, says Loomis, they just have to come to Hamilton – it sells itself. "I can go toe to toe with TO anytime," he grinned. He described the consulate idea as a radical one, and credited Glen Norton, the director of Economic Development, with the idea, an example of the ambition the chamber hoped to rekindle.

The campaign Ambitious Again is a reflection of Hamilton's return to prosperity, to finding itself after wallowing in misery for decades, a misery Loomis attributes to a host of causes: the one-way streets, the urban renewal projects of the 1970s that only lead to further decline, vehicle-centred development, economic shifts brought about through NAFTA and other trade deals – the causes are legion. But now it's 2017 and it's time for Hamilton to be Ambitious Again.

SIGN, SIGN, EVERYWHERE A SIGN

Bill Manson, writing in *Getting Around Hamilton: A Brief History of Transportation In and Around Hamilton*, pins the decline in the downtown core to the decision to widen Beach Road and connect Burlington Street to Highway 8, therefore allowing drivers travelling from Toronto to the United States to bypass Hamilton completely. With the completion of the Queen Elizabeth Highway (QEW), which provided a shorter, faster trip to the border, the fate of Hamilton's downtown centre was sealed. And when the Skyway Bridge was built in 1958, which took care of the problem traffic had with the canal lift bridge, the highway around Hamilton, rather than through it, was the way to go. And what do we see when we drive that highway as opposed to driving through town? How has the fact that our industrial landscape is the face we present to those travelling past affected how people view Hamilton and the people who live there?

Over time, the Chedoke Expressway (Hwy 403), the Lincoln Alexander Parkway and the Red Hill Valley Parkway combined with the QEW to create a ring road around Hamilton, providing drivers with the option of a higher speed alternative to the stop-and-go of inner-city traffic. Well, stop-and-go except for Hamilton, which has a reputation across Canada for its timed traffic lights through the city, creating a freeway at fifty km/h along the King and Main Street corridors, leaving motorists with no time to look, no time to stop and certainly no time to shop along the mainly commercial route. Hamilton: the fastest city to drive through and around. Maybe we could put that on a sign if we had one?

Hamilton debated the erection of a sign for years. The city underwent a public competition and a design was chosen in 2008. Although council voted to erect the sign before the 2015 Pan Am Games, the project was subsequently shelved when councillors balked at the price tag of $230,000. Laura Babcock, a Hamilton-based public relations consultant, resurrected the issue of a sign in the summer of 2013 when she realized that of all the small towns and big cities she travelled to throughout Canada, Hamilton was conspicuous in its absence of a sign. Any kind of sign. She created the #time4sign hashtag on Twitter in support of the project and presented before city council to advance the idea. She was quoted in a CBC report saying, "We're missing out on thousands of brand impressions every day." It was a clear opportunity to counter our negative "armpit" reputation, at the least. But the sign wasn't to be. Of the experience Babcock says, "I wish I hadn't gone in front of council. It probably could have gotten private funding and support faster. It became a political football in the election." Once that happened, it was the kiss of death.

A month after our conversation, in summer 2017, city council approved a proposal to install a sign in the forecourt of city hall. The initiative was guided through council approval by Mayor Fred Eisenberger, and involved private sector interests, including Power-Group, Babcock's PR firm. The design and construction would be funded entirely by private interests. The sign, which is derivative of the popular signs erected in Amsterdam, Brisbane, Nice, Los Angeles and, wait for it ... Toronto, drew sharp comments on social media. Critics were quick to draw attention to private advertising on public space, as the sign would carry the advertising of the sponsors. Others advocated for a more innovative design. And yet others complained about the selection process. For something we got for free, our collective gratitude was wanting. In the time since, it has become an identifying marker in the urban landscape, part of the attempt to brand Hamilton as a friendly, accessible city as people engage with it, posing in the letters and sharing images on social media.

WHAT IS TO BE DONE?

City councillor Maureen Wilson currently represents Ward 1, which happens to be the ward in which I live. I spoke with Wilson before her run for city council, intrigued by her involvement with the Useful

Knowledge Society of Hamilton (UKS), an online group of civic-minded Hamiltonians. The UKS sponsored several community information events designed to increase the level of community awareness and engagement around key issues of city planning and policy. Wilson, who holds degrees in political science and geography, was a key organizer of the group and I was interested in her thoughts on my dilemma. We met on a hot summer day in the cool air conditioning of the Locke Street branch of the Hamilton Public Library. Again, I fumbled badly in the explanation of my project, still struggling to articulate what it was I was looking for. In the 1990s, before coming to work in Hamilton, Wilson headed up the restructuring of Chatham-Kent and I wondered how the experience of amalgamation differed in the two communities. What, if anything, did amalgamation have to do with our inability to come together on big issues?

Rather than positioning the measure of amalgamation success as the happy creation of a shared civic identity, Wilson challenged me to consider the ways in which neighbourhood identities could coexist and even support the larger municipal effort. Wilson pointed to the constructive tension that exists between established neighbourhood associations, mostly in the lower city, and their respective city councillor. The relationship is one of information sharing, consensus building and accountability. Neighbourhood associations serve as a springboard to citizen engagement, a doorway to city building. Wilson attributes the increase in citizen engagement to a more politically sophisticated citizen, fuelled in part by social media. According to Wilson, tensions in land use have historically led to the creation of neighbourhood associations to represent local interests against encroaching commercialization or industrialization of neighbourhood space. In Hamilton, neighbourhood associations are not as prevalent in Mountain communities as they are in the lower city. She points to two reasons for this: the suburban nature of Mountain communities designed land-use conflict out of the equation and, more troubling perhaps for a healthy democracy, it's not convenient for local politicians to support the development of community hub or neighbourhood associations because it invites accountability. Yet, in the absence of any neighbourhood organization, how do politicians seek input or justify their decisions? How does politics give way to policy?

Wilson says that Hamilton politicians are out of practice with building community consensus. They have been for years. There's a "what's in it for me" attitude, a desire for immediate benefit that runs throughout our public works projects and she believes the answer lies in asking more not only of our elected officials but also of ourselves as engaged citizens. She advocates for increased citizen involvement in neighbour politics, for these groups to come together to increase awareness of both differences and similarities in order to make better decisions. It's not that we end up on the same page, says Wilson, but that we understand each other and respect our differences with civility. In terms of our elected officials, Wilson draws a distinction between politicians who focus on service provision, that is, answering constituents' requests about city operational issues, and politicians who are capacity builders, who focus on big picture policies and citizen building tools.

When I had asked Laura Babcock what she saw as an antidote to an intransigent council, she said, "Citizen-led efforts to build up parts of the city. Regardless of council."

Perhaps beginning with the Coalition on Sane Transit and their fight against the SkyTrain, citizens have pushed back on the dreams of developers and demanded their councillor's attention. In 2013, North End residents campaigned to stop people from speeding through their communities by getting the speed limit lowered to thirty km/h. In the time since, other community activists have succeeded in lowering the speed limit to thirty km/h from the city-wide standard of fifty km/h. Community groups in the core campaigned successfully for street conversion, that is, turning the one-way streets back into two-way streets.

Walkability is the buzzword in the city planning of people-friendly cities, communities that draw people out of their homes and into their neighbourhoods, bike lanes that encourage healthy living with a smaller carbon footprint. A gas plant was proposed for the industrial lands, in a community that would prefer environmental remediation to yet another heavy industry. The community successfully campaigned against the plant's construction. Communities and neighbourhood groups have been empowered, facilitated by social media and urgency for change.

I don't know that I'm any closer to understanding why Hamilton can't move ahead on major projects, but some of the power has shifted, it seems, to community groups and the engaged citizen. Social media demands attention, of citizens, of politicians; the discourse is instant and reactive, the repercussions can be swift and unforgiving. The voices of those previously without a formal forum now have one and it's being used to amplify issues that, in the past, would have relied on gatekeepers, such as the press or media outlets, to garner attention. Politicians are being held to a higher standard, their actions are under the microscope of a thousand eyes, at least. There has been more discussion around Hamilton and who Hamiltonians are than ever before as we struggle to define and rebrand ourselves for the twenty-first century. And that can't but be a good thing.

I would like to thank Drs. Richard Harris and John Weaver, Councillor Maureen Wilson, Keanin Loomis and Laura Babcock for taking the time to speak with me and help clarify my thoughts.

References

Bouchier, Nancy, and Ken Cruikshank. *The People and The Bay: A Social History and Environmental History of Hamilton Harbour.* Toronto: UBC Press, 2016.

Campbell, Marjorie Freeman. *A Mountain and a City: The Story of Hamilton.* Toronto: McClelland and Stewart, 1966.

Henley, Brian. *1846 Hamilton: From a Frontier Town to the Ambitious City.* Burlington: North Shore Publishing, 1995.

Loyalist Ancestors: Some Families of the Hamilton Area. Hamilton: United Empire Loyalists' Association of Canada, 1986.

Manson, Bill. *Getting Around Hamilton: A Brief History of Transportation In and Around
Hamilton*. Burlington: North Shore Publishing, 2002.

Weaver, John. *Hamilton: An Illustrated History*. Toronto: James Lorimer, 1981.

Wingfield, Alexander H., ed. *The Hamilton Centennial, 1846–1946*. Hamilton: Hamilton Centennial Committee, 1946.

Look on the Brightside, 1910–Present

Nancy B. Bouchier and Ken Cruikshank

After the publication of our book, *The People and the Bay*, in 2016, we gave many talks and presentations to a public keen to learn more about Hamilton Harbour and its social and environmental history, its remediation and future prospects.[1] On a number of occasions, audience members who had grown up in Brightside, a place neatly nestled between two inlets of Burlington Bay/Hamilton Harbour's eastern waterfront, approached us to chat.[2] Mostly in their seventies and eighties, they were eager to talk about their old neighbourhood, where they had grown up in the shadow of Stelco's factory site. Word had gotten out that our book devotes a few paragraphs to their old stomping grounds, which lay mostly on the north side of Burlington Street, between Birmingham and Plymouth Streets.[3]

The Brightsiders that we spoke with had vivid memories of their old neighbourhood, even though it's been gone for half a century. Many other Hamiltonians, however, are not even aware that a vibrant working-class neighbourhood existed where Industrial Drive and the Burlington Street Overpass diverge along the industrial waterfront in the east end of town. Save for Homer & Wilson Ltd., which since 1913 has been located on Lancaster Street, and for a few homes that remain along the south side of Burlington Street East and around the corner on Birmingham, few markers indicate that a thriving neighbourhood once stood on that land, nestled in the heart of Hamilton's industrial district.[4] As described by one former resident who had grown up there, "It was an oasis of homes in a desert of industry."[5] But it is long gone.

Just over fifty years ago, during Canada's centennial year of 1967, Brightsider John Michaluk fought for his hometown on the Grey Cup–winning Tiger-Cats team. It was a banner year for his team and his hometown. Yet that same year, Michaluk's family's home, along with almost every other house in his Brightside neighbourhood, was – by one means or the other – acquired and demolished to make way for the building of an arterial road in the city's Burlington Street Industrial Area Project. Stelco's growth then swallowed up whatever land remained.[6] Back in 1995, in the midst of Stelco's financial troubles, and with the hindsight enriched by a life's worth of experience, Michaluk reflected upon his old neighbourhood's destruction, lamenting its futility. Speaking to journalist Paul Palango for Hamilton's *Biz Magazine*, he remarked, "I speak as a little kid that came up and got expropriated from Brightside and now I go down and find there are no houses, there's no steel mill and there's no parking lots. Zero for three."[7]

Futile, indeed, when one considers that the fate of Stelco has been up in the air now for decades, and remains so even under its most recent owner, Bedrock Industries.[8] While the company struggles to survive, the City of Hamilton, too, struggles to grapple with the effects of deindustrialization, even as all of us face an environmental legacy that is daunting, to say the least.[9] Some Hamilton planners and visionaries point to a hopeful future, with what seems to be great potential for our adapting brownfield sites, such as the Stelco lands, for new uses. Hopeful dreamers envision myriad opportunities in the "wealth of industrial ruins" that remain, seeing them as places, for example, to create affordable housing to help redress the city's poverty and housing crises.[10] These effects are most evident in certain neighborhoods, as brought out in the week-long *Hamilton Spectator* series entitled "Code Red," which ran in the week of April 10, 2010, and was revisited a decade later, based on research carried out jointly by the *Hamilton Spectator* and McMaster University researchers.[11]

In taking a look at Brightside's mostly hidden history, we see some of the ways that Hamiltonians are remembering places that no longer physically exist, yet which live on in their hearts, minds and stories, and how new opportunities and new technologies have helped people both keep the past alive and bring it out to broader audiences. Brightside's story has much to offer those of us contemplating Hamilton's future. We ask, how did Brightside come to be and why and how did it disappear? For those of us who today wrestle with the major transformations that affect every part of our Hamilton community, this story raises issues of power, agency and voice. It provides a glimpse into how people can and have used the past to help understand the present and to express an informed vision for Hamilton's future. The fate of this working-class community offers a historical insight into how power shaped the development of the city of Hamilton.

≡

By the time that Brightside's developer, real estate man William Delos Flatt, turned his gaze to the development opportunities of land situated between Lottridge's and Stipes' Inlets along Hamilton's eastern waterfront in 1910, the City of Hamilton had experienced six decades of growth. No longer a small city on the southern shore of Burlington Bay, in 1846, it had become one of Canada's largest and most important industrial manufacturing urban centres. In 1911, it ranked sixth in the nation's urban hierarchy.[12] It had a growing population, good intra- and interurban transportation networks, and port and rail facilities that seemed second to none in Ontario.[13] The inlets of its eastern waterfront became home to big industry, with factories like Oliver Chilled Plow Works, International Harvester, Grasselli Chemical and the Hamilton Blast Furnace Company, a forerunner of Stelco.

Hamilton's industrial development happened because of local urban boosters, merchants and civic leaders, who anxiously sought to sustain and build a highly competitive business atmosphere for their city. They worked to fashion the sort of place that would attract industrialists and business leaders as Canada's revised national policy of protective tariffs and freight rate agreements created new opportunities for investment and industry.[14] Local supplies of electricity and generous concessions from Hamilton's city council, such as cash bonuses and tax relief, along with sustained Canadian economic growth helped to make Hamilton an attractive location for industry. The workers who flocked to Hamilton sought a better life, one with good opportunities for both work and home ownership.[15]

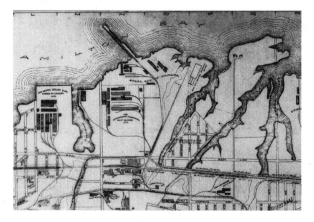

Figure 1: Brightside Development in the Middle of Inlets and Industries, 1912. The Brightside Development (centre), located directly below the city sewage treatment plant (top centre) in the midst of busy waterfront industry. Nestled between the Steel Company of Canada (left) and Grasselli Chemical (right) at the base of Lottridge's and Stipes' Inlets, just above the Hamilton Street Rail and Grand Trunk railway lines. Source: J.B. Nicholson, Map of the City of Hamilton (Hamilton: Canadian Records Company, 1912), 1:3,600 ft., MNC 15354, HI/440 Hamilton/1912 (4 sections), Courtesy of Library and Archives Canada.

W.D. Flatt aimed to make money while building homes for factory workers so they could pursue this good life. As the son of a member of the provincial parliament for nearby Millgrove, and as a member of the city's nascent real estate profession, he had wealth, good connections and a successful record of business activity before he turned to developing the Brightside neighbourhood. He had a varied career before then in lumber and timber-export industries and Shorthorn cattle breeding, working in the Muskoka, Hamilton and Burlington areas. In his spare time, Flatt wrote two books about his family and early settlement life in colonial Canada; they are tomes filled with tales about hardy pioneers and moral lessons about God and Empire.[16] Published in 1916 and 1918, they provide glimpses into his character, predilections and social pedigree. They also reveal Flatt's social connections to Hamilton's civic and business leaders of the day.[17]

Flatt's real estate developments, like his books, were typically aimed at a middle-class – not a working-class – audience, a fact that

reveals his focus on developing Brightside, a neighbourhood for workers, as being a bit unusual for him. In developing Brightside, Flatt took advantage of financial opportunities emerging in the days just preceding the industrial merger that created the Steel Company of Canada

Figure 2: Aerial View of Brightside and Industries Along the Sherman Inlet, 1919. This is one of our earliest photographs of the Brightside development taken from a different angle than figure 1. In its top right-hand corner, this aerial shot shows Brightside on the north (left-hand) side of Gilkison Street (now Burlington St. E.) between Stipes' and Lottridge's Inlets, in the "hub of our greatest manufacturing district." Note the filled in tip of Sherman Inlet (middle, far right), along with the hardened shore of the bay at Oliver Chilled Plow (below Sherman). International Harvester lies immediately above the inlet. Stelco is the complex with billowing smokestacks on the point reaching out (top left) into the bay. Source: McCarthy Aeron Service Fonds, C285-1-0-0-277; Courtesy of Archives of Ontario.

in 1910.[18] Hamilton's local business practice and culture of courting industry through inducements, such as city-sponsored cash bonuses and waterfront sites for industry, no doubt led Flatt to consider his land investment in the recently annexed industrial district to be a good one. In January 1910, he purchased land for his Brightside Survey from Mary Lottridge, near the Huckleberry Point tract of land that his father's company, timber merchants Bradley & Flatt, had cleared back in 1878.[19] By May, he registered his plan of land surveyed into uniformly neat twenty-five-foot-wide rectangular parcels, and he opened the place for business, appointing H.H. Davis to manage the operation. Its development offered reasonably priced lots in the midst of a developing industrial district, promoted as a "site for Workingmen's Homes."[20] This fits with Hamilton historian Craig Heron's observation

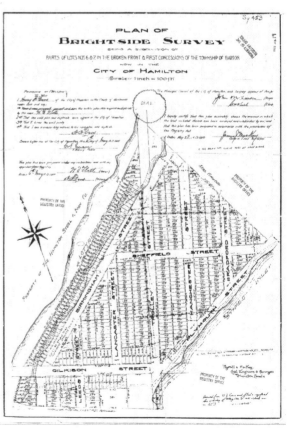

Figure 3: Plan 453, Brightside Survey, May 1910. W.D. Flatt's plan for the Brightside Survey, as registered by the City of Hamilton. Source: Plan 453. Brightside Survey. Lots 6 & 7 in the Broken Front of the Township of Barton. Registered 5 May 1910. 1:100 ft. Tyrrell & MacKay, Civil Engineers & Surveyors, Hamilton, Canada; Courtesy of Ontario Ministry of Government & Consumer Services, Land Registry Offices.

about workers' housing: "In theory workers could set up their house-holds wherever they chose, but in practice their choices were limited by many economic, environmental, and cultural constraints."[21]

Flatt's plan, situated in the midst of an industrial factory district, may not have been an ideal place from a variety of vantage points (for people's health, for example), but it did provide Hamilton workers and their families opportunities for home ownership; something that many of them took up. In creating his planned development, Flatt aimed to provide a Hamilton neighbourhood well within the means of a working-class family in the face of the city's shortage of good, clean housing.[22] By the early 1910s, local social observers and reformers had turned their attention to the city's growing social problems, especially with working-class housing.[23] "Many places are injurious to health and morals," proclaimed one *Herald* newspaper headline in 1912.[24]

Alluding to a slogan that the city used to promote itself back during the era of the World's Columbian Exposition (1893 Chicago World's Fair), Flatt assured people that Hamilton "has made good to her claim, as being the Birmingham of Canada."[25] His Brightside survey plan capitalized on this cultural connection to England's great industrial cities through street names, such as Sheffield, Leeds, Manchester and Birmingham. For his new neighbourhood, he aimed to attract "a desirable class of workingman."[26] His properties advertised low prices – from $150 to $250 a lot – with easy terms of payment.[27] One advertisement for Brightside stipulated that a five-dollar deposit and monthly payments of five dollars, gave prospective buyers the opportunity to build their home within walking distance of work in the "hub of our greatest manufacturing district." Potential buyers received assurances of good value for their money – the land was not as marshy as nearby areas, and homes built there would enjoy the bay's bracing winds. While factory life was never easy, its dangers might also help sell houses to a worker who had "the ambition to OWN his home and thereby leave his wife secure should he be suddenly taken away."[28]

Figure 4: Ad for Brightside Development, 1911. Advertisement for the industrial district. As Michael Doucet and John Weaver point out in *Housing the North American City*, printed advertisements often highlighted inducements, such as "Easy Terms," for new developments. Source: *Hamilton Times*, March 4, 1911.

In Brightside, a man could protect his family financially while saving both time and money: "He would be home five minutes after the whistle blows and be able to put the time at home that he would otherwise spend on a long walk or car ride."[29]

The social characteristics of Brightside's earliest inhabitants confirm the initial success of Flatt's designs for the neighbourhood as a place for workers. He aimed for "desirable," or the right sort of, immigrants: ambitious and respectable family men of Anglo-Saxon descent – like the characters in his books – who would work not in the Empire's timber yards but rather in the manufacturing industries of Hamilton's busy waterfront. When, in 1911, the federal census taker trekked from house to house through the neighbourhood to document its population for the Canada census, he encountered this new place in a growing city. By then, Hamilton's population had increased by 55.7 per cent over the previous decade to 81,969 inhabitants.[30] Admittedly, Brightside was just a tiny part of that city growth, lying amid factories and empty fields on the outskirts of town, which, within a few years of its founding, had three small grocery stores catering to neighbourhood needs.[31] There, according to the 1911 census, some eighty-six relatively young people started a life in a new neighbourhood. Two-thirds of them were between twenty and thirty-nine years old, with a fifth of the neighbourhood being kids under the age of nine years.[32] These earliest Brightsiders lived in some nineteen households, a handful of which took in one or two boarders to help pay the bills.[33] Most of them had recently arrived in Canada; of the sixty-two people whose census information includes their immigration date, almost a third had arrived in 1911, with most of the rest arriving less than five years earlier. Two out of every three people enumerated in the Brightside census were either British- or Ontario-born, and a handful of Italian- and Russian-born immigrants – some twenty-six people – numbered among them.[34] Everyone's job listed a manual occupation, making Flatt's design for a neighbourhood of workingmen a reality.[35]

Just a decade later, when the census taker again trekked through Brightside, this time to take the 1921 census, the small industrial neighbourhood had grown and changed considerably. This happened as Hamilton's population rose to 114,151 people, a decade-long increase of 39.3 per cent. Roughly 48 per cent of Hamiltonians with jobs worked in some form of manufacturing.[36] The neighbourhood's population had also increased, by about nine and a half times, from eighty-nine people to 846. It had proportionately more skilled and semi-skilled workers than could be found in the rest of the city – of 110 Brightsiders listed as having an occupation, some 88.2 per cent held skilled, semi-skilled or manual labour jobs.[37]

Brightside still housed workingmen and their families, however, its social composition had shifted markedly. In the decade between the two censuses, *Vernon's Directory for the City of Hamilton*, published annually, hints at changes in the social characteristics of Flatt's planned neighbourhood.[38] Judging by people's names as listed in the directories, the place was becoming far more ethnically diverse than before, as newcomers from places other than Britain arrived. The 1921 census confirmed this, in its detailed accounting of Brightside's population. By then, inhabitants with backgrounds recorded as Russian, Austrian and Italian far outnumbered those who were British born.[39] The new neighbourhood also became a place full of families with kids; the number of children under the age of nine (38.9 per cent) doubled, as did the proportion of people aged thirty to thirty-nine.[40] The records of "racial origin" of 922 Brightside inhabitants reveal that people of Russian and Austrian origin accounted for roughly half of its inhabitants, in equal measure, while people of British and Canadian origin accounted for roughly 22 per cent, also in equal measure. People of Italian origin made up almost one-fifth of the population.[41] By this time, Brightside emerged as a neighbourhood of predominantly Catholic people, with some 85 per cent of its inhabitants being (mostly) either Roman or Greek Catholic, with the rest belonging to various Protestant denominations.[42]

In those first ten years of its existence, Brightside became a going concern for Hamilton's new immigrant population; a small place nestled in the midst of a growing industrial district, with its "increasingly noisy, soot-filled, foul smelling and toxic air."[43] It provided housing that some European immigrants drawn to work in Hamilton's waterfront factories might reasonably afford. With homes so close to industry and so far from the city's centre, the neighbourhood had limited connections to Hamilton's downtown. People could walk there, if they were hardy enough, or take the electric street rail at a time when many working-class families considered things like cars and telephones to be luxuries, not essentials.

In Brightside, people's money might have been tight, but workingmen and their families could make a very good life there, and, over the next five decades, they did just that.[44] Easy access to work sites was just one feature of their neighbourhood. Its location also provided a measure of freedom for kids growing up there, since well into the 1950s they were living more or less out in the country, even though their homes stood amidst the city's booming factories. "Playgrounds were where you made them," claimed one chronicler of the neighbourhood.[45] Each generation of Brightside kids played in and explored vacant fields, trash dumps and industrial sites, all of which offered a world of adventure. Sometimes they scavenged through the copper pipes, tins, wires and other industrial detritus that lay alongside railway boxcars; this stuff they could sell back to the scrap man for the small sums that would get them to the movies. Families had informal playing fields for baseball, soccer and bocce, and formal playgrounds nearby at International Harvester (which had a mini-putt golf course in the 1920s), area schools and the football field by Procter & Gamble. If kids trekked southward past Barton Street, or westward down Burlington Street, they could play or hang out at Hamilton's Frost or Eastwood Playgrounds. There, under the watchful eye of playground supervisors, they could meet and hang out with kids from other neighbourhoods, some of whom would be classmates in area elementary schools like Robert Land, Prince of Wales, King George, Holy Rosary and St. Ann's.[46]

Yet, mostly Brightside neighbourhood kids were unsupervised, able to do what they wanted: fish in what inlets remained along the bayfront, swim at the mud flats at Burlington and Wentworth or sneak in for a furtive dip in the hydro station fountain. They built forts and "bunks" for hiding places, using railway ties for their roofs, and constructed rafts from the cedar ties used by streetcar tracks, exploring rail and sewer lines that took them out of their neighbourhood. If they could get their hands on a dinghy, they could explore the inlets and sewer outlets more fully. Sometimes they happily flung "turds" that floated by at each other, or, better, they brought back a handful of excrement from the nearby sewage treatment plant in penalty for losing a game of truth or dare. In the winter, they skated and played hockey on the frozen pond by the Laidlaw Bale-Tie Company, just south of Burlington Street.

Brightsiders had many resources available to them. While the neighbourhood had few professionals living there, it did have many owners of small businesses – such as grocery stores, restaurants and barbershops – located in and amongst the places where people lived. Most houses reportedly had a vegetable garden to help feed families. In the days of horse and wagon deliveries, some people enriched their soil with droppings scooped up from the street. Sometimes they had chickens and rabbits in their yard, or had traps devised out of door frames to catch birds for delicacies like blackbird or starling game pie. Nearby, people could hunt deer, pheasant and coyotes down by the Hilton Works, along the bay's shore. Some people made homemade wine from grapes delivered to their homes, while neighbourhood kids gleefully pilfered that delicious fruit from unattended grape trucks on delivery. During prohibition, trucks also took booze away, stuff made by bootleggers in stills hidden behind basement walls and under trap doors. People in the neighbourhood traded and bartered goods amongst themselves, and they attended nearby churches and got involved in parish life. For locals, the Martini family's Brightside Hotel, established in 1934 at the northwest corner of Burlington at Birmingham Street, provided a neighbourhood social hub until 1968; one that had separate doors for men and "ladies" and their "escorts." There, "three and four generations of the same family would come in at the same time," Brightsider Frank Bartolini once recalled.[47]

There were drawbacks to living there, too. To get to school, generations of Brightside kids had to dodge traffic as they crossed an increasingly busy Burlington Street. Then there was their neighbourhood's close proximity to a new sewage disposal plant and its outlets, along with the stuff emitting from industrial smokestacks, which drifted over and settled in the midst of people's homes and yards. As early as 1911, property owners responded to problems in their local environment, banding together to sue the city over the sewage that plagued areas of the neighbourhood. Living near a city incinerator, a dump and a hydro substation made the life of people in the neighbourhood interesting, but also a constant challenge. In decisions about making it a safer place to live and about cleaning up the environment, however, Hamilton's civic leaders consistently overlooked neighbourhoods such as Brightside.

People did push back, however, such as one son of the place, Dr. Victor Cecilioni. As "the man who chose to spend his life within the shadow of Hamilton's steel mills," Cecilioni spent a distinguished career of medical service – some fifty-seven years as a family physician – working to better the lives of steelworkers and their families.[48] His epidemiological research on high cancer and respiratory ailment rates in the industrial district stemmed from the patients that he saw in his east-end office.[49] His efforts identified and responded to environmental changes associated with Hamilton's growth as a manufacturing city with its busy port devoted to heavy industry. Many people could not help but see industrial growth as a good thing, since it fuelled the economy and provided Hamiltonians with opportunities to work.

But was it? Between the opening of the fourth Welland Canal in 1932 and the creation of the St. Lawrence Seaway in 1959, Hamilton's steel industry and related enterprises grew and colonized much more of the city's eastern waterfront. As we show in our book, *The People and the Bay*, few did anything to counteract the environmental damage of this growth, especially in the postwar period, beyond ensuring that Hamilton's waterworks produced water that was reasonably healthy for its residents and useful for its industry. For a time, people seemed to accept environmental deterioration as the price of prosperity, with pollution seen as an unavoidable reality of modern city life. This is something that Hamilton's Medical Officer of Health complained about in his 1946 *Board of Health Report*. In it, he warned that "unless more active measures are taken to prevent further pollution and to remedy so far as possible what has already taken place, future generations will rise up to condemn us for the way in which we have mishandled this natural heritage."[50]

Yet for other reasons, in that same period just after World War II, members of Hamilton City Council and those who managed Stelco focused their attention on the small neighbourhood beside the steel factory. In 1946, Brightside became another type of battleground, when the United Steelworkers of America, Local 1005, stood locked in a bitter and acrimonious eighty-one-day strike against Stelco.[51] The strike came on the heels of the war effort, after years of tremendous industrial activity, happening as wartime gains were becoming increasingly fragile.[52] In it, workers pressed for a forty-hour workweek, higher wages and recognition of their union, wanting its dues automatically deducted from paycheques.[53] With Stelco's Manchester gate actually located in the Brightside neighbourhood, and with the strike headquarters at its Wilcox gate just a block or so away down Burlington Street, the neighbourhood became a flashpoint for the strike. This placed it at the epicentre of a key battle in the history of Canadian industrial unionism; it became an important site for – and part of – what some labour historians have identified as a broader Canadian working-class revolt.[54] It seems right to see Brightside as part of this movement, since the neighbourhood and the steel company had more or less grown up together since 1910, and since so many Stelco workers lived there.

As strikebreakers camped inside the factory, Brightside became a place of support for picketers, one where offerings of baloney sandwiches, spaghetti and coffee to help nourish them could be found. The neighbourhood also provided spaces for entertainment, with music, bocce matches, professional wrestlers, dances and games of checkers to help entertain strikers, as well as free haircuts as aid to workingmen in those financially hard times. Most of all, those people sympathetic to the union and its workers could give what Brightsiders gave best in times of trouble: a sympathetic ear and a shoulder to lean on. Newspaper reports of the time, and later reminiscences of those involved, document the myriad ways in which Brightsiders gave in support of the strike.[55] Rob Kristofferson and Simon Orpana's history of the '46 strike, *Showdown!: Making Modern Unions*, documents these efforts in a richly textured and detailed graphic history that places the strike in the context of broader developments in Canadian labour history. They also focus on the role that the neighbourhood played in the strike, identifying some of its community members, like retired Stelco blacksmith Lino "Trigger" Trigatti, and the important roles that such men played in the strike and its legacy.[56] Yet not everyone in Brightside supported – or, perhaps more accurately, thought that they could afford to support – the strike. The fear of retaliation against workers

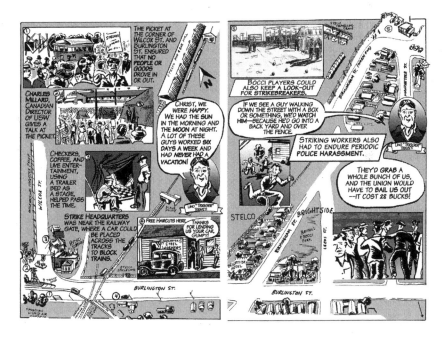

Figure 5: Brightside as Depicted in Kristofferson and Orpana's *Showdown!: Making Modern Unions*, 2016. This incredibly detailed graphic story of the 1946 Stelco Strike provides a richly engaging treatment of the role that the Brightside neighbourhood and its community members played in the effort. Source: Rob Kristofferson and Simon Orpana, *Showdown!: Making Modern Unions* (Toronto: Between the Lines, 2016), 88–89. Courtesy of Between the Lines.

was ever-present; we have heard anecdotally that some Brightsiders believed that the razing of the neighbourhood happened in retaliation for its support of the workers in the strike – an understandable claim given what transpired. In those hard times, people still had to pay their bills. Some men from the neighbourhood chose to stay in the factory and work, while others chose to stand on the picket line. This tough situation, Trigatti would recall to *Spectator* reporter Paul Wilson some fifty-five years after the fact, tore apart some families: "In some houses the strike set brother against brother, father against son and the wounds never healed."[57] Some people thought of these as "black days" better left behind.[58]

At the same time that union leaders and company managers at Stelco renegotiated the relationship between worker and employer, Hamilton's Town Planning Committee was turning its sights upon re-establishing other relationships – those between the city and its neighbourhoods. The city wanted a master plan that would inform its postwar development – something that did not bode well for Brightside's future in the years that followed. With the promise of funding under a new National Housing Act, Hamilton's city council appointed a firm, Town Planning Consultants led by Eugenio G. Faludi, to do the work.[59] Applying criteria to assess and determine the overall condition of physical structures throughout the city, he recommended, among other things, insulating Hamilton's homes from its industry.[60] Unfortunately, many residences already existed close to factories, including all of the neighbourhoods near the harbour's industrial shore and newly filled inlets, all of which Faludi's report deemed *blighted*.[61] However, Faludi did not even include Brightside in his assessment, since, due to its close proximity to industry, he did not consider it a "real" neighbourhood. This fact would have surprised W.D. Flatt, whose survey decades earlier had so thoughtfully planned such a place. And it flew in the face of those people who for decades had called the place home; people who had a rich history of living in a *real* neighbourhood, one "that seemed to feed on adversity, where immigrants learned the ropes while ducking language problems, two wars and a depression. After each bout, the community emerged with just a little more strength of character."[62]

Unfortunately, this strength of character could do little to assuage the damaging effect that Hamilton's harsh new zoning regulations had on Brightside. As informed by Faludi's report, the city's new zones designated the entire area north of the Canadian National Railway (CNR) tracks and east of Wellington Street to be reserved for light and heavy industry. Over time, this reduced the value of people's homes there, and made financial lenders unlikely to provide loans for home improvements and maintenance. Some anxious homeowners chose to cut their losses, resigned to having their properties bought up, one way or another, so they could begin life again, perhaps "moving out to the city," hopefully to a place where their home investment promised them a more secure future.[63] This out-migration came in the face of other important and interconnected developments, such as the physical growth of Stelco on the one hand, and the creation of broader infrastructure improvements on the other, both of which also deeply affected Brightside.

In the years that followed the end of the war, the fates of the neighbourhood and Stelco become more and more intertwined; the steel factory grew in size while the neighbourhood shrank. Change to Brightside sometimes happened by fits and starts, at other times it happened by stealth, as properties were quietly bought up, one at a time. This slow but steady process began while Stelco's operations reoriented and expanded in the face of broader improvements in transportation infrastructure. It started small, with Stelco's acquisition of 38.8 hectares of water lots from the harbour commission, which, through infill, created new land for development, like its new shipping docks, new coke ovens, two new blast furnaces, four 250-ton open-hearth furnaces and a wire and nail mill. By the late 1950s, its steel-making output had tripled.[64] A few years later the company continued its program of infill, after pioneering a new method that simplified its process and used a by-product, slag, to make a base for new land along the shore. On its newly created land, Stelco built further operations, such as furnaces, coke ovens and new storage areas for the iron ore and coal supplies needed to keep its operations running when the winter season interrupted Great Lakes shipping.[65] Much of this expansion had begun in anticipation of the 1959 opening of the St. Lawrence Seaway, which enabled ocean-going vessels to reach Hamilton, including shipments with new supplies of iron ore from eastern Canada.[66] At the same time, the federal government and harbour commissioners improved the harbour, which benefitted Stelco and other companies, while the provincial and municipal governments funded the building of the massive Burlington Skyway Bridge over the Beach Strip and Burlington Canal. Port and highway traffic could now flow easily and unimpeded.[67]

As Stelco expanded, prospects for the future of Brightside shrank. Faludi had noted ominously some years earlier that "individual property owners are by themselves helpless to arrest the blight of whole residential neighbourhoods."[68] Although he had not declared its properties blighted, since he had ignored the neighbourhood altogether, Brightsiders suffered a similar fate owing to their "industrial" zoning – a fact that individual property owners could do little to change. So far we have uncovered no evidence of the sorts of resistance seen in the actions of Hamilton's North Enders who battled the Urban Renewal plan that decimated their neighbourhood around the same time, such as writing letters to the editor and members of city council, holding community meetings and rallies, and petitioning the Ontario Municipal Board.[69] Industrial encroachment happened incrementally, in a tide seemingly impossible for Brightside residents to stem. While automobiles and trucks had been a novelty in the earliest days of the neighbourhood's development, they became a problem for the community in its final years. The tremendous growth of Stelco's operations had created a parking problem for the company and traffic congestion plagued its Wilcox gate during shift changes. Both became significant factors in the demise of Brightside.[70] A neighbourhood of people living in the "wrong place" could not stop pressure for road improvement amidst one of the city's most heavily used industrial traffic corridors.[71]

Journalist Paul Palango once characterized Brightside's slow demise as the steel company "gradually biting off mouthfuls of the neighborhood."[72] The paper trail left in land registry records shows that Brightside's transition from a family neighbourhood to a source of land for arterial road development and Stelco happened in two big mouthfuls, so to speak. But there were also little, almost imperceptible nibbles occurring over a number of years as property owners sold their land to the company, its agents or investors who aimed to profit from the situation; they, in turn, rented the houses out until the city and Stelco's grander designs needed the land. The first big bite began in 1956, when, by August of that year, a trust company, which had over the years bought up one hundred properties above Sheffield Street on Gage Avenue North, Manchester and Bradford Streets, granted them to Stelco for a nominal sum of one dollar each.[73] The steel company then razed the houses to open up space for rail lines into its property and much-needed parking space adjacent the long, rectangular, steel-framed buildings used for its mills, shipping offices and storage. Hamilton's Fire Insurance Map of 1961 neatly records the outcome of this transformation.[74] In effect, Stelco had bitten off almost half of the neighbourhood at its north end. Houses below Sheffield Street, like John Michaluk's family home on Lancaster Street, remained, but not for long.

The second big bite, which culminated in Stelco finally swallowing the rest of the neighbourhood, started in 1961, after the City of Hamilton hired an engineering consulting firm, C.C. Parker & Parsons,

Brinckerhoff, Ltd., to conduct a comprehensive transportation study of the city and its surrounding areas. It spent two years collecting and analyzing data, such as the relationship between travel patterns and land use. It then created a massive transportation plan that recommended a network of freeways, expressways and highways to facilitate travel in, through and around the city. It also outlined arterial street improvements for areas both above and below the escarpment, including proposed changes to Burlington Street in the industrial district. There, engineers aimed to enhance railway and automobile traffic flow in an increasingly busy part of the city, particularly at Wilcox Street, where every day Stelco shift changes caused traffic disruptions.[75]

By 1966, Hamilton's Urban Renewal Department conducted a preliminary study of the industrial district located north of the CNR main line in preparation for the city's Burlington Street Industrial Area Project. It noted approvingly that the "industrial" zoning of the area had already worked to get many homes out of industry's way.[76] Of the pockets of residential properties that remained in the area, it stated that "the past rapid process of attrition of the remaining residential lands by industry will continue . . . there is some evidence that industry holds title to some of the residential properties."[77] By design, industries would subsume the remaining residential properties there.[78] As before, a trust company acquired the homes that remained – some through expropriation by the city – and, in turn, it turned each property over to Stelco for a nominal sum of one dollar.

Those hearty souls, described by one former resident as being "mostly old-timers," who had remained after Stelco took its first big bite of their neighbourhood a decade earlier, now left the place for good as they awaited its destruction and final street closures. Nowadays, by *Spectator* reporter Paul Wilson's count, some twenty-three places remain inhabited.[79] Six houses can be found on Birmingham Street between Burlington Street and Beach Road, and ten more stand on the south side of Burlington Street between Birmingham and Gage

Avenue North. Two Brightside businesses also remain. One is Burlington Street's Venetian Meat and Salami Company, situated on its
north side. It sprang up in 1954 on the site of an old general store
and has remained there over sixty-five years. The other is the Homer
& Wilson manufacturing company, which has been firmly rooted at
its 1 Lancaster Street address for over a century. It has specialized in
metal stamping since in 1913.

These places survived the road building that constructed Industrial Drive on the land where the neighbourhood of Brightside once
stood, designed to "keep the industrial lifeline in operation" for trucks
shipping material and goods to and from Stelco. While the road builders worked, they encountered problems with what reporter Gordon
Hampson called, "Some of the worst possible terrain in the city."[80]
The road's path, he complained, "moves through virtual swampland
on the fringes of harbor inlets." As workers dutifully filled those inlets,
they destroyed what had once been nature's paradise, something enjoyed by generations of Brightside kids, with places where they played,
hunted and explored. By contrast, the new road helped workers more
easily "get to their jobs."[81]

As the local press chronicled road-building developments in the
area, however, few articles focused on the razed neighbourhood, or
stories about the people who stoically faced the death of a place that
they knew and loved. But after the dust settled, stories emerged, not so
much about the actual clearance, rather about people's recollections of
their old neighbourhood, as people's identities as Brightsiders persist-
ed intact despite their move to new places.[82] Most would remember
Brightside as a "good neighbourhood," where people helped each other and got along despite their differences – "Italians, French, Polish,
Ukrainians, and English, all living together like one big family."[83]

Yet it seems that so much more than the shared experience of hard
circumstances bound Brightsiders together. Could it be the way that
they shared those experiences that made the place so special? Perhaps.

Consider the Brightside Hotel. This iconic neighbourhood building was among those properties expropriated and destroyed.[84] In the decades that followed Ontario's 1934 legalization of public drinking, it had been the neighbourhood's "watering hole" – a site for both story making and storytelling. "This hotel is next to the Steel Co. of Canada," noted a Liquor Control Board of Ontario (LCBO) inspector in 1943, "the patrons are very hard to manage at times, [and] there is very little call for food at this hotel." Even so, he commended it for being well run: "The beverage rooms are clean and there is as good order as can be."[85]

Few could argue that the hotel served people in the neighbourhood and Stelco workers well, as generations – mostly men – went there at the end of a hard day's work to relax, refresh themselves and enjoy each other's company with a post-shift beer and a plate of peanuts in the shell. There they could cash their paycheque on a Thursday night, if their wife didn't intercept them on the way there, buy a round and catch up on local happenings.[86] It was a place to talk about the sports of the day, like the results of its bar league baseball team, one's favourite pro team or the exploits of Brightside's many sporting heroes who had made it to the big leagues.[87] There, in the hotel's final days, a gang of friends ruminating over their neighbourhood's fate gave birth to a new sports tradition – Brightside's 10 Pin Bowling League, which, in the words of Paul Palango, was formed "almost as a defense mechanism to keep Brightsiders together because things were changing fast."[88] They competed in the Hamilton City 10-Pin league at the Skyway Lanes for over sixty years, memorializing their old neighbourhood in what was reputed to be one of the longest-lived such leagues on the continent. But the Skyway Lanes closed in 2019.[89] Until then, a shared sense of loss had helped the league's creators carry on the name of Brightside over the decades through their sport.

It seems that for many people, the physical disappearance of their old neighbourhood only strengthened their connection to Brightside. In 1975, the *Spectator* published a page-long tribute to the neighbourhood written by staff reporter Paul Palango after he attended a reunion held for the old-timers of the area. "I had never lived in Brightside," he admitted, "but I was considered one of their kind because my family had lived there through the hard times."[90] He went on to assert, "Just because Brightside couldn't be seen, didn't mean it was dead."[91] These words seem to be confirmed in the years to come, as Brightside reunions followed in 1977 and 1983, organized by a Brightside Reunion Committee.[92]

The committee's 1983 Reunion, dubbed by Michael Quigley of Hamilton's *Cue Magazine* as a "monster bash for their old friends from the old neighbourhood," took much time, effort and planning.[93] It would be a decided success as roughly nine hundred people attended its formal banquet held on a Friday evening in May.[94] It was a fun and busy night with people getting together and reminiscing, with music, speeches, good food and entertainment, all overseen by the evening's master of ceremonies, John Michaluk. Attendees received a smart and beautifully crafted booklet created by the committee, *Brightside Reunion 1983: "Brightside Was When,"* a treasured thirty-six-page keepsake for people from the neighbourhood, filled with stories, cartoons, trivia questions, a map of the place and some 126 pictures of familiar faces and places. It listed scores of people's names and nicknames from the past. It also helped create new traditions, with its inclusion of the words to "Brightside Was When," a song sung at the close of the reunion night's events, done to the tune of "Auf Wiedersehn."[95] Deposited into Hamilton libraries, the booklet aimed to "add to the history of the city."[96] In creating it, the committee made an inspired move, strategically placing the now-lost working-class neighbourhood squarely on the historical record. "Who made it big from Brightside?" asked the booklet's last trivia quiz question. The answer was both unequivocal and a characteristically Brightside response – "Everybody."[97]

≡

Remembering a Hamilton neighbourhood that today is literally not on the map has its challenges. Perhaps this is why that handful of Brightsiders eagerly approached us to chat after we mentioned their old stomping grounds in *The People and the Bay*. Yet it seems that a half-century after their neighbourhood's final destruction, and more than four decades after the Brightside Reunion Committee's first big reunion of 1977, the memory of their old neighbourhood is alive, well and actually *growing*. With bowling leagues, reunions, an ongoing Facebook page and a neighbourhood memory mapping project involving art and museum installations, so many more Brightside memories have been – and are being – created.

Take, for example, the presence of Brightside in the virtual space of the World Wide Web. When former Stelco worker Stephen Lechniak created his wonderful Stelco Rod and Bar Facebook site to keep memories and photographs of its past alive, little did he know that he would touch a nerve with Brightsiders, who flocked to it, since so many of them had such deep connections to Stelco.[98] In a move both brilliant and generous, Lechniak created another page, Brightside Memories, to provide a forum for people to reminisce and share stories and photos about their old neighbourhood.[99] It's full of pictures of proud families posing on a doorstep, or of other treasures, like homemade jiggers (scooters) made out of an orange crate and wheels from a roller skate. There you can find shots of Brightside's streets, houses, athletes, school classes, landmarks and news clippings that are keepsakes from a past gone by. This is a virtual space where people connect and reminisce about a shared past – itself a living entity.

There is also the great work being done by the Brightside Neighbourhood Project to help keep the place alive.[100] After conducting interviews with former residents in 2016, Hamilton-based researchers and artists Matt McInnes and Simon Orpana, along with historians Rob Kristofferson and Nancy Bouchier, have spent much time with Brightsiders, meeting with them at the Action Research Commons

Hamilton (ARCH) in the Perkins Centre on Main Street East and the Workers Arts and Heritage Centre (WAHC) on Stuart Street. This work has been done in partnership with the WAHC with funding from McMaster University's Centre for Community Engaged Narrative Arts (CCENA).[101] The project aims to celebrate and document Brightside "through art, research, and storytelling."[102] Through interviews and meetings, we have been working with people from the neighbourhood to create a community archive and a Profane Map of Brightside – "a messy, collaborative and necessarily unfinished form" – which was exhibited at WAHC from October 2019 to February 2020.[103] In future, Brightside will be added to Hamilton's existing Workers' City walking tours, so people can learn about the place through an interactive digital phone application to convey key points in the history of Hamilton workers' culture and industry.[104] Stories and experiences of Brightsiders as recorded will also be made available. The map, oral recordings

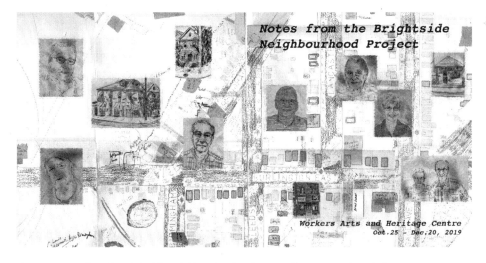

Figure 6: *Notes from the Brightside Neighbourhood Project* (Hamilton: Impressive Printing, 2019). This pamphlet's cover highlights a section of the Profane Map of Brightside created by former residents who recalled people, places and things about their childhood neighbourhood in collaboration with artist Matt McInnes and researcher and facilitator Simon Orpana. The WAHC exhibit grew as others included their own photographs and stories. Courtesy of Matt McInnes and Simon Orpana.

and related podcasts will all relay Brightside stories to inform a contemporary audience's understandings of issues surrounding urban fabrics, neighbourhoods, histories of immigration and development. By literally "putting Brightside on the map" through art, storytelling and digital media, such projects will, of course, continue our remembering of Brightside.

If the story of Brightside provides a cautionary tale about the price of unbridled "progress" in our city, it also provides a glimpse into the resiliency of Hamiltonians, and how they can and have used the past to help understand the present, and express an informed vision for Hamilton's future. For those of us who never knew or experienced the place, we would all do well to look on Brightside; we have much to learn from the place and its people.

Thanks to Matt McInnes, recipient of the 2020 City of Hamilton Visual Arts Award, Simon Orpana, Rob Kristofferson and those members of the Brightside neighbourhood who have been so generous in sharing both their time and memories. And thanks especially to John Michaluk for getting us on to this project. A portion of this research has been funded by the Social Sciences and Humanities Research Council of Canada.

Endnotes

1   Nancy B. Bouchier and Ken Cruikshank, *The People and the Bay: A Social and Environmental History of Hamilton Harbour* (Toronto: UBC Press, 2016).

2   We continue the tradition of using both terms, Burlington Bay and Hamilton Harbour, to refer to this body of water despite it technically being renamed Hamilton Harbour in 1919, since that is what many Hamiltonians have done, especially when referring to its social, cultural or environmental dimensions (as in the Bay Area Restoration Council).

3   Tyrrell & MacKay, Civil Engineers & Surveyors, Plan 453, Brightside Survey, Lots 6 & 7 in the Broken Front of the Township of Barton, Hamilton, May 5, 1910. The streets were originally laid out in a diamond fashion with some going: diagonally north-south parallel to Lottridge's and Stipes' Inlets respectively (Birmingham and Plymouth); north-south vertically (Leeds, Lancaster, Trolley [later Gage North], Manchester and Bradford); and east-west (Gilkison [later Burlington Street East] and Sheffield Streets).

4   The earliest building for this dies and metal stampings firm can be seen in the 1914 update of the 1911 insurance plan for the area, with its listing as a "Machine Shop." *Insurance Plan of the City of Hamilton, Sheet 110, March 1914*, 32 x 27 cm., Lloyd Reeds Map Collection, McMaster University, Hamilton, http://digitalarchive.mcmaster.ca/islandora/object/macrepo%3A34284/-/collection.

5   "Brightside Neighbourhood Project," email correspondence to Nancy Bouchier, August 4, 2017.

6   Paul Palango, "Brightside: Old survey levelled, but it still won't die," *Hamilton Spectator* (hereafter cited as *Spectator*), July 12, 1975, 21.

7   Palango, "With Nowhere to run, John Michaluk fights back," *Biz Magazine*, Winter 1995. Investigative reporter and award-winning author Paul Palango is a former sometime writer for the *Spectator* and *Globe and Mail*, and the son of Brightsider Arnold Palango.

8   Most recently, it was U.S. Steel Canada, however it has returned to use the Stelco moniker that had been associated with the company since around 1915 with the Steel Company of Canada. See "Bedrock Industries Completes Acquisition of Stelco," Stelco, June 30, 2017, https://www.stelcocanada.com/news/bedrock-completes-acquisition.

9   See, for example, the work currently being done by the Bay Area Restoration Council about events and issues related to Hamilton Harbour/Burlington Bay, www.hamiltonharbour.ca/index.php; Clean Air Hamilton, www.cleanairhamilton.ca; and Conserver Society of Hamilton and District, http://conserversociety.ca/.

10 Recently visionaries held a panel discussion about applying Jane Jacobs's philosophies to Hamilton's development. Emma Reilly, "Urban legend: Seeing wisdom from Citizen Jane," *Spectator*, October 15, 2017. Regarding poverty and affordable housing, see Greg Tedesco, "We must act now to build affordable housing," *Spectator*, November 9, 2015; "We must act now to build affordable housing," Opinion, *Spectator*, November 8, 2015; C. Crosbie, "The Poverty Project: 10 years later," *Spectator*, October 30, 2015; Leanne Siracusa, "Recall Code Red: Ask the tough questions," *Spectator*, April 28, 2011; and Terry Cooke, "We need courage to confront our mistakes; Code Red – Where You Live Affects Your Health; Day 7: What's next? Finding Answers," *Spectator*, April 17, 2010.

11 See Howard Elliott, ed., "Code Red: Call to Action," *Spectator*, April 10, 2010; Steve Buist, "Spec Report Finds Health, Wealth Worlds Apart in Hamilton," *Spectator*, April 10, 2010; and "About the Series," *Spectator*, April 8, 2010. The research has continued: "About the Code Red series," *Spectator*, February 27, 2019, A6; Steve Buist, "Code Red data shows stunning disparities in effects of opioid crisis across Hamilton," *Spectator*, August 6, 2019; Steve Buist, "Key highlights from Code Red: 10 Years Later," *Spectator*, September 10, 2019; and Paul Berton, "What lies behind the Born and Code Red projects? A reminder that a just society should be caring, prosperous," *Spectator*, December 3, 2011, A2.

12 John Weaver, *Hamilton: An Illustrated History* (Toronto: James Lorimer, 1982), 196, table I.

13 For overviews, see Weaver, *Hamilton*; Craig Heron, *Lunch-Bucket Lives: Remaking the Workers' City* (Toronto: Between the Lines Press, 2015); M.J. Dear, J.J. Drake, and L.G. Reeds, eds., *Steel City: Hamilton and Region* (Toronto: University of Toronto Press, 1987); Bryan D. Palmer, *A Culture in Conflict: Skilled Workers and Industrial Capitalism in Hamilton, Ontario, 1860–1914* (Montreal and Kingston: McGill-Queen's University Press, 1979); and Bill Freeman, *Hamilton: A People's History* (Toronto: James Lorimer, 2001).

14 For an extended discussion, see Bouchier and Cruikshank, "Boosting Nature: The Contradictions of Industrial Promotion, 1892–1932," chap. 3 in *People and the Bay*, 55–85.

15 These things are argued in booster publications of the day, for example, *Hamilton, Canada: The City of 400 Varied Industries* (Hamilton: Commissioner of Industries, 1912, 1914), 9.

16 According to the author, his *Trail of Love* was written "as a labor of love and has been undertaken with a view to preserving a love and veneration for the sturdily-true things of the pioneer days in Canada rather than with any thought of making it serve the commercial purpose which usually pertains to books." W.D. Flatt, *The Trail of Love: An Appreciation of Canadian Pioneers and Pioneer Life* (Toronto: William Briggs, 1916), 5.

17 T.M. Bailey, "W.D. Flatt," in *Dictionary of Hamilton Biography*, vol.3 (Hamilton, 1981), 57–58; "Community Suffers Loss in Death of W.D. Flatt," nd, ca. 1936, http://images.halinet.on.ca/70404/data; and Claire Emery Machan, *From Pathway to Skyway Revisited: The Story of Burlington*, rev. ed. (Burlington: Burlington Historical Society), 301–4. Flatt's *The Trail of Love*, published a few years after his founding of Brightside, offers visual glimpses into his family's well-heeled connections. In it, one group photograph captures the men of Hamilton's Board of Control, Board of Trade and Parks Board Society gathered on the steps of Flatt's impressive Lakehurst Villa (258). Another captures the men and women belonging to Hamilton's Horticultural Society (262) at a gathering at the villa's sumptuous gardens. Also see his *The Making of a Man* (Toronto: William Briggs, 1918), a tome about his boyhood that he dedicates to his Sunday school class (11).

18 Created in June 1910 through the merger of five waterfront companies. "Huckleberry Point Once Worthless Land! Can't Say Same Now," *Hamilton Review*, December 30, 1953, Stelco Scrapbooks, vol. 1, 171–73, Local History and Archives, Hamilton Public Library (hereafter cited as LH&A, HPL). On Stelco, see William Kilbourn, *The Elements Combined: A History of the Steel Company of Canada* (Toronto: Clarke, Irwin, 1960), 44–50, 63–78.

19 This area had become a popular swimming and picnic spot for Hamiltonians. "Huckleberry Point," *Spectator*, March 11, 1878. This involved W.D. Flatt's father's company; two years later W.D. would form a partnership with his elder brother. The area would become the home of the blast furnace that became home to Stelco.

20 Plan 453. Brightside Survey. The sale of the various lots through time is recorded in *Hamilton Wentworth Land Registry*, book H.38, microfilm E 062-092, Wentworth Land Registry, Ellen Fairclough Building, Hamilton.

21 See his masterful treatment of Hamilton workers in that day for the social, cultural and political contexts of their lives, Heron, *Lunch-Bucket Lives*, 51ff.

22 "W.D. Flatt. He has Abundant Faith" and "Real Estate Experts have Great Faith in Hamilton's Future," *Hamilton Times* (hereafter cited as *Times*), 1912, Scrapbooks, RO.2, LH&A, HPL; and Michael Doucet and John Weaver, *Housing the North American City* (Montreal and Kingston: McGill-Queen's University Press, 1991).

23 Bryce Stewart, *Report of a Preliminary and General Social Survey of Hamilton* (Hamilton: Department of Temperance and Moral Reform of the Methodist Church and the Board of Social Service and Evangelism of the Presbyterian Church, 1913); "Say Slum Conditions Exist in Hamilton," *Spectator*, May 20, 1913; "Sounds Death-Knell of the Slum Districts," *Spectator*, July 23, 1913; and "Social Survey of Hamilton in 1913," *Herald*, January 6, 1914.

24 "The Housing of the Masses in a Big City: One of the Hardest Problems Which Have Come with the Unbounded Prosperity Enjoyed by this City," *Herald*, December 21, 1912, *Times* Scrapbook, LH&A, HPL; and "Should Abate Slum Conditions: Many Places are Injurious to Health and Morals," *Herald*, June 6, 1913, 69, *Herald* Scrapbook, LH&A, HPL. The housing problem demanded more attention following the Great War: "War's Influence on House Building," *Mail and Empire*; "Veterans Want Better Housing" and "Council Will be Asked to take Action," *Spectator*, July 13, 1918; and "Workingmen Should have Good Homes," *Herald*, March 31, 1919, Clipping File, Hamilton Real Estate Board, box 1480, William Ready Division of Archives and Research Collections, McMaster University.

25 "W.D. Flatt. He has Abundant Faith," *Hamilton: The Birmingham of Canada* (Hamilton: Times Printing, 1892). On Hamilton's claims of civic and industrial greatness, see Bouchier and Cruikshank, *The People and the Bay*, 55–56, and more generally, chapter 3, "Boosting Nature: The Contradictions of Industrial Promotion," 55–83.

26 "Brightside Survey. Lots for Sale by W.D. Flatt on May 24th," advertisement. The year "1905" is penned by hand on the copy of the ad that we've seen, which may or may not be correct, since Flatt did not acquire and survey the land until 1910. This remains a bit of a mystery since, apart from the work of later writers who

had referred to this ad with its hand-written date, this is the only primary source document that we have seen that refers specifically to 1905.

27 Ibid. On home ownership, Hamilton workers and housing development in that period, see Heron, *Lunch-Bucket Lives*, 42–55; and Doucet and Weaver, *Housing the North American City*, 77–126.

28 In the industrial district. Brightside, advertisement, *Hamilton Times*, March 4, 1911, *Times* Scrapbook, LH&A, HPL.

29 Ibid.

30 Weaver, "Population Change and the Rank of Hamilton in the Canadian Urban System, 1834–1931," *Hamilton*, 196, table I.

31 According to the 1914 insurance plan for the area, the groceries were located at the northeast corner of Burlington at Leeds; the east side of Lancaster, midway up the street; and the northwest corner of Gage at Burlington. *Insurance Plan of the City of Hamilton*, March 1914.

32 Regarding age breakdown in years: over 50 years n=3 (3.4%); 40–49 n=3 (3.4%); 30–39 n=18 (21%); 20–29 n=35 (40.7%); 10–19 n=5 (5.8%) and under 9 n=22 (25.6%). Many thanks to Eric Sager, University of Victoria, for providing us with access to the digitized versions of the Hamilton 1911 Canada census.

33 See Heron, *Lunch-Bucket Lives*, 42ff, for an extended discussion of the role of boarders in working-class household strategies. Regarding Brightside boarders listed in the 1911 manuscript census, most of them lived with families in various homes; only one place, 6 Gilkison Street, was filled with boarders. It had thirteen Italian single men, mostly in their twenties and early thirties, who worked in the steel plant or foundry.

34 Born in Czarist Russia, they would include Ukrainians, Belarussians, Lithuanians and Poles. The place of birth of these eighty-six enumerated people (fifty-four males and thirty-one females) included those born in: United Kingdom n=30 (34.9%); Ontario n=24 (28%); Italy n=15 (11%); Russia n=11 (12.7%) and the United States n=6 (7%).

35 Of which thirty-seven were simply listed as labourers of undesignated types, with seven listed as semi-skilled in nature.

36 Weaver, "The Labour Force of Hamilton by Occupational Category, 1851–1941," in *Hamilton*, 197, table V. Of 40,283 people listed with occupations, 19,229 worked in manufacturing.

37 These numbers based on the 1921 manuscript census are relatively in line with those recorded in table I of *The People and the Bay* (81) and are based upon information in Vernon's Directories and published aggregate census of Canada data. Aggregate city data compared to Brightside numbers are: Proprietors – city 31%, Brightside 11.8%; Skilled and Semi-Skilled workers – city 40%, Brightside 79.1%; Labourers – city 29%, Brightside 9.1%. Dominion Bureau of Statistics,

Sixth Census of Canada, 1921, manuscript census, Ontario District No. 87 Sub District No 65. Hamilton, 27–30; and Sub District No 66. Hamilton, 2–19, available online through Ancestry.ca.

38 *Vernon's City of Hamilton Annual Street, Alphabetical, General, Miscellaneous and Classified Business Directory*, vol. 39–41 (Hamilton: Henry Vernon & Son, 1912–1914), Lloyd Reeds Map Library, McMaster University, microfilm.

39 Yet the numbers of Ontario-born dominated. Of 920 people whose birthplace is recorded: Ontario n=360 (39.1%); Russia n=148 (16%); Austria n=145 (15.7%); Italy n=103 (11.4%); UK n=67 (7.3%); other Canadian provinces n=55 (5.9%); Western Europe n=16 (1.6%); US n=14 (1.5%); Poland n=8 (0.8%); Eastern Europe n=3 (0.3%) and other 1 (0.1%). On the immigration of various peoples to Canada, see Ninette Kelley and M.J. Trebilcock, *The Making of the Mosaic: A History of Canadian Immigration Policy* (Toronto: University of Toronto Press, 1998); D.H. Avery & J.K. Fedorowicz, *The Poles in Canada* (Ottawa: Canadian Historical Association, 1982); Carmela Patrias, *Hungarians in Canada* (Ottawa: Canadian Historical Association, 1999); Bruno Ramirez, *The Italians in Canada* (Ottawa: Canadian Historical Association, 1989); and O.W. Gerus & J.E. Rea, *The Ukrainians in Canada* (Ottawa: Canadian Historical Association, 1985).

40 Age 0–9 years n=360 (38.9%); 10–19 n=120 (12.9%); 20–29 n=135 (14.6%); 30–39 n=188 (20.3%); 40–49 n=82 (8.9%); over 50 n=41 (4.4%).

41 *Racial origin* is the term used on the census form. Brightside's breakdown is: Austria n=228 (24.8%); Russia n=227 (24.6%); Italy n=180 (19.5%); Canada n=101 (10.9%); UK n=101 (10.9%); Poland n=43 (4.6%); other Western European n=23 (2.4%); other Eastern European n=16 (1.7%) and US n=2 (0.2%).

42 Regarding religious affiliation: Roman Catholic n=718 (76.7%); Greek Orthodox n=70 (7.4%); Methodist n=57 (6%); Anglican n=53 (53%); Presbyterian n=26 (2.7%); Baptist n=9 (0.9%) and Congregationalist n=2 (0.2%). This reversed the trend for Catholic/Protestant distribution for the rest of the city, according to Weaver's calculations for the 1911 and 1931 censuses, *Hamilton*, 199, table VIII.

43 Heron, *Lunch-Bucket Lives*, 48. As Paul Palango put it, "The immigrants had come to Canada looking for a heaven and instead were shuttled into the Brightside and Cabbagetowns, areas which established Canadians didn't want. They made the best of it." See his "Brightside."

44 The montage below draws from a number of sources, including the Brightside Neighbourhood Project's profane mapping done to reveal "the layered, complex and surprising textures" of that social space as it is depicted by the stories told by former residents during collaborative mapping sessions. See Matt McInnes and Simon Orpana, *Notes from the Brightside Neighbourhood Project* (Hamilton: Impressive Printing, 2019); Brightside Reunion Committee, *Brightside Reunion, 1983* (Hamilton: self-pub., 1983); Paul Palango, "Some Neighbourhood!," in

Brightside Reunion, 1983, 2–5; Palango, "Brightside"; Brightside Memories Facebook page, https://www.facebook.com/SteveStelco; and Michael Quigley, "Flying High," *Hamilton Cue Magazine*, July 1983. Also see the various fire insurance plans that meticulously document it: Charles E. Goad, *Key Plan of Hamilton, Ontario (January 1898)*; Goad, *Insurance Plan of Hamilton Ontario, Vols. 1–3 (January 1898) (Revised to March 1911 up to c. 1916)*; *Insurance Plan of the City of Hamilton, Ont.* (Toronto: Underwriters' Survey Bureau, 1947, 1948), sheet 211, HPL LH&A; and *Insurance plan of the city of Hamilton, Ontario, 1961* (Toronto: Underwriters' Survey Bureau, 1960–64, 1961), sheet 209, Lloyd Reeds Map Collection, McMaster University.

45 Palango, "Some Neighbourhood!," 3.

46 Many Brightside kids reportedly went straight into the factories, but if fortunate enough to go to high school, they typically went to Central High, or Cathedral boys or girls schools.

47 Palango, "Brightside." The Brightside Hotel changed through the years as its ownership changed hands in 1940 and again in 1947, including its layout, the types of rooms that it rented to lodgers and slight changes to its name (e.g., Brightside Public House). While always moving along with the times, regular Liquor Control Board Inspector's Reports through the years typically characterize the place as "clean," "well conducted" and "under good management." Brightside Public House, RG 36-8, B335033, Liquor Licence Board of Ontario files, Archives of Ontario (AO); on the Brightside Hotel Property, see Lots 359–60, *Wentworth Land Registry*, 359–60, 393–94, 418. Thus far we haven't uncovered the dates of the building's construction or demolition.

48 Ross Longbottom, "MD fought for Steelworkers," *Spectator*, May 30, 1992; "Dr. Victor Cecilioni Award: Stories Behind Local Place Names," *Spectator*, January 25, 2013; "Il caro dottore Cecilioni," *Spectator*, May 18, 1996; Carolyn Gleeson, "Hamilton's Clean Air Pioneer Immortalized in Steel Sculpture," *Spectator*, May 17, 1996; Kate Barlow, "Community aims to honor north-end doctor's life of devotion," *Spectator*, July 10, 1992; and "In honor of Dr. Victor Cecilioni," Editorial, *Spectator*, June 10, 1992.

49 His battles against the Workers' Compensation Board on behalf of families, along with his activist work with environmental watchdog groups like Clear Hamilton of Pollution, helped the fight for environmental justice in Hamilton. On Cecilioni's publications, see "Lung-Cancer in a Steel City – a Personal Historical-Perspective," *Fluoride* 23, no. 3 (July 1990): 101–3; "Occupational Lung-Cancer and Smoking," *CMAJ* 122, no. 5 (1980): 513; "Lung Cancer and Fluoride Are Linked by Ontario Family Physician," *Canadian Family Physician* 22, no. 376 (1976): 34; and "Lung Cancer in Hamilton," *Canadian Family Physician* 16, no. 2 (1970): 73.

50 *Annual Report of the Board of Health* (Hamilton: City of Hamilton, 1946), 18.

51 Rob Kristofferson and Simon Orpana, *Showdown!: Making Modern Unions* (Toronto: Between the Lines, 2017); Heron, *Lunch-Bucket Lives*; Robert Storey, "Workers, Unions and Steel: The Shaping of the Hamilton Working Class, 1935–1948," (Ph.D. diss., University of Toronto, 1981); Freeman, *Hamilton*, 142–51; Wayne Roberts, ed., *Baptism of a Union: Stelco Strike of 1946* (Hamilton: McMaster University, Labour Studies Programme, 1981); and Local 1005, *It Started with a Whisper: A History of the 1946 Strike* (Hamilton: Local 1005, 1996).

52 Lee Prokaska, "Labour's love never lost," *Spectator*, June 8, 1996.

53 Steve Arnold, "1005: Glorious past, fear for future," *Spectator*, July 23, 2011; Mark McNeil, "The Hamilton Memory Project 1946: The year a city lost its innocence," *Spectator*, February 28, 2006; Craig Heron, *The Canadian Labour Movement: A Short History* (Toronto: James Lorimer, 2012); Kristofferson and Orpana, *Showdown!*; Storey, "Workers Unions and Steel"; and Kilbourn, *The Elements Combined*.

54 See Bill Freeman, *1005: Political Life in a Union Local* (Toronto: Lorimer, 1982).

55 See United Steelworkers of America, Local 1005, Hamilton, Ont., Thomas McClure RC0300 Subfonds 1928–1976, Box 3 Materials related to strike of 1946, F.4 Photocopies of articles in the *Hamilton Spectator* during 1946 strike (many of which are reproduced in graphic novel art form in Kristofferson and Orpana, *Showdown!*, 77–86); F9 Photograph Album, William Ready Division of Archives and Research Collections, McMaster University; and Steel Company of Canada Strike, 1946 Scrapbook (R331.892872 STE), LH&A, HPL.

56 See Paul Wilson, "Recalling the bitter Strike of '46: Retired Stelco worker says families were torn apart forever by labour dispute," *Spectator*, October 2, 2001, A03.

57 The strike is memorialized in Bill Freeman's play *Glory Days: A Play and History of the '46 Stelco Strike*, produced in 1988 and reproduced in 2006 by Hamilton's Theatre Aquarius, http://billfreeman.ca/glory-days-play-history-stelco-strike.html; Wilson, "Recalling the bitter Strike of '46"; Peter Van Harten, "Strike at Stelco divided families: Bitter 81-day battle ended 60 years ago today," *Spectator*, October 4, 2006, A11; and Prokaska, "Labour's love never lost."

58 Palango, "Some Neighbourhood!," 5. Hamilton's liquor inspector noted the effect of tensions stemming from the strike on the area hotels frequented by workingmen (the Jockey Club, Queens, Piccadilly, Gage, Sherman, Brightside, British Empire, Picton, Bayview, International and Turbinia) in a letter copied to the Brightside Hotel. "It was remarkable that nothing serious happened," he observed. Letter, 5 October 1946, Brightside Public House, RG 36-8, Liquor Licence Board of Ontario.

59 Faludi had recently created Toronto's master plan. "Administrative History/Biographical Sketch," MG 30 B16. Finding Aid No. 1276, Eugenio Giacomo Faludi fonds, Archives Canada, http://data2.archives.ca/pdf/pdf001/p000002614.pdf.

60 *Report on Existing Conditions Prepared as Base Material for Planning, City of Hamilton* (Hamilton: Hamilton Planning Committee and Town Planning Consultants Limited, 1945).

61 Based on his data Faludi declared a quarter of Hamilton's neighbourhoods to be sound, almost half as declining and the remaining quarter blighted. E.G. Faludi, *A Master Plan for the Development of the City of Hamilton* (Hamilton: City Planning Committee, 1947), 54–60; see also Mark Osbaldeston, *Unbuilt Hamilton* (Hamilton: Dundurn, 2016), 40–47.

62 Palango, "Some Neighbourhood," 2.

63 As recalled by John Michaluk and recorded by Palango in "Brightside."

64 "Stelco begins extension near Strathearne Docks," *Spectator*, April 26, 1955; "Mark of a City's Growth: Steel," *Spectator*, November 12, 1960; "Steeltown: A Century of Steel," *Spectator*, February 11, 2012; "Stelco Timeline," *Spectator*, August 27, 2007, A10. On technological changes in this period, see Kilbourn, "Change at Mid-Century: Revolution in the Steel Industry," *The Elements Combined*, 207–42.

65 "Stelco Develops New Processes," *Spectator*, November 12, 1960; "'Waste' Wins New Role Building Roads, Docks," *Spectator*, November 12, 1960; and Paul Wilson, "SlagWorld – a cinder-ella story?," *Spectator*, September 30, 1993.

66 *Hamilton Harbour Commission Annual Reports*, 1955, 1958; Mark Sproule-Jones, *Governments at Work: Canadian Parliamentary Federalism and Its Public Policy Effects* (Toronto: University of Toronto Press, 1993), 146–50.

67 *The People and the Bay,* 145ff; on the seaway see "Hamilton Harbour Scheme given Tentative Approval," *Spectator*, September 1956; and "Port of Hamilton," *Spectator*, May 27–29, 1957. The Skyway Bridge would be renamed Burlington Bay James N. Allan Skyway.

68 Faludi, *A Master Plan for the Development of the City of Hamilton*, 50.

69 See Urban Renewal Scrapbook (R307.3416 URB CESH) and Urban Renewal Scrapbook Downtown (R307.3420971352 URB CESH), LH&A HPL; Margaret T. Rockwell, "Modernism and the Functional City: Urban Renewal in Hamilton, Ontario and Buffalo, New York, 1949–1974." (PhD diss., McMaster University, 2013); and North End Residents' Organization, *The Effects of Urban Renewal on the North End People and their Environment, 1961–1977* (Hamilton: Hamilton Public Library, 1977).

70 According to Weaver, "Noncommercial Passenger-vehicle Registration Statistics for Hamilton, 1919–1968," the number of city residents per vehicle dropped from 21.7 in 1919, when registrations began to be collected, to 3.7 by 1960. *Hamilton,* 201, table XIII.

71 On road developments, see Frank Oxley, "City Access Projects Loom Large in $67,000,000 Expenditure Plans," *Spectator*, May 16, 1957; Robert J. Hanley, "Through Highway Beginning to Take," *Spectator*, June 25, 1957; "52.5 Miles of

Roadway Completed in 2 years," *Spectator*, October 24, 1959; "Mark of a City's Growth: Steel," *Spectator*, November 12, 1960; "New Access, E-W Freeway Get Top Priority," *Spectator*, September 6, 1963; and "Autos Choking City, Hamilton Mayor Says as He Seeks Solution," *Spectator*, October 4, 1963.

72 Palango, "Some Neighbourhood!," 4.

73 This involved Brightside Survey lots 72–74, 121–29, 130–47, 196–217, 218–38, 265–78, 279–86 and 295–98. Six of them had been sold directly to Stelco by 1956, while eight had been sold to the City of Hamilton and then transferred to the trust company before being granted to Stelco. None of these properties had been expropriated. Bylaws 775 (April 24, 1956) and 7821 (July 31, 1956) dealt with road closures of the affected streets, to stop them up and sell that land to the Steel Company of Canada. *Hamilton Wentworth Land Registry*, 382–424. Book H.38, microfilm E 062-092, Wentworth Land Registry, Ellen Fairclough Building, Hamilton.

74 Underwriters' Survey Bureau, *Insurance plan of the city of Hamilton, Ontario, 1961* (Toronto: Underwriters' Survey Bureau, 1960–64), vol.2, April 1962, Sheet 209, Lloyd Reeds Map Collection, McMaster University.

75 *Hamilton Area Transportation Plan* (Hamilton: City of Hamilton and C.C. Parker & Parsons, Brinckerhoff, 1963) 127, 143.

76 *Preliminary Study of the Burlington Street Industrial Area* (Hamilton: City of Hamilton, Urban Renewal Department, 1966), 28. According to the study's calculations, the population of the area in census tract 29 (between Sherman and Ottawa Streets, north of the CNR main line) where Brightside sat decreased by 28.7% between 1951 and 1961, from 4,695 to 3,349. Based on Vernon's 1965 Directory, it estimated that some 2,799 people remained in the area overall (31).

77 *Preliminary Study of the Burlington Street Industrial Area*, 8.

78 It noted that the mean value of residential properties to be acquired for the Burlington Street project were slightly higher in value than those being expropriated in the North End urban renewal project ($10,000–$11,000 rather than the average $9,000 being paid in the North End), *Preliminary Study of the Burlington Street Industrial Area*, 27.

79 Paul Wilson, "Brightsiders – the factory zone was home," *Spectator*, December 10, 2019, G1. That is not counting the recently demolished "plywood shack" that was home to one woman in the area. See Matthew Van Dongen, "Connie lived under a bridge – until they took her home away," *Spectator*, January 23, 2020, A1-2.

80 Gordon Hampson, "Road to Give Industry Insight," *Spectator*, November 2, 1968. The four-lane highway is now called Nikola Tesla Boulevard from the Queen Elizabeth Way to between Kenilworth Avenue North and Ottawa Street, at which

point it becomes the four-lane Industrial Drive that bifurcates near where Leeds had once been into Industrial Avenue and the Burlington Street Overpass.

81 Ibid.

82 Recent newspaper articles with Brightside connections include: Paul Wilson, "The golden days of the dairy farm," *Spectator*, September 8, 2015; Jon Wells, "Michael's Song," *Spectator*, May 1, 2015; Paul Wilson, "Wheels still turn at Springy's; But after 50 years, it's time someone else grabbed the handlebars," *Spectator*, January 17, 2007, G02; Rob Faulkner, "Typicalville, then and now," *Spectator*, October 4, 2003, F01; and Paul Morley, "Searching for a missing Dam Buster; What happened to Lancaster AJ-B that flew a secret mission over Germany 60 years ago today? What happened to Hamilton pilot Frank Garbas?," *Spectator*, May 17, 2003, M12.

83 According to Art Corso, who grew up on Gage Avenue North, as reported in Mike Hanley, "Art recalls Depression picnics at Red Hill," *Spectator*, November 27, 1996.

84 Its location became part of the new Burlington Street Overpass and Industrial Drive, where the three-lane eastbound roadway came down from its northern loop. "Burlington St. Plan Endorsed" and "New route" [photo];" *Hamilton City Council Minutes* (hereafter *HCCM*), 1968, p.765, 860, Lots 359 and 360, August 28, 1968 (reg. September 6, 1968). The city expropriated a handful of properties this time, for example, BL 68-83, 64 Lancaster Street, Lot 76, a family home on the path of Industrial Avenue, on March 12, 1968 (reg. March 20, 1968), then granted November 5, 1970 (reg. December 4, 1970) by the Royal Trust Co. to the Steel Company of Canada, Ltd., for one dollar; BL No. 68-153, 567 Gage Avenue North, Lots 118–20, *HCCM* (May 14, 1968), this property had been vacant for some time, as indicated by the 1948 Insurance Map; BL 68-303, 917 Burlington Street East, Lot 40, *HCCM* (October 8, 1968), Vernon's 1965 Directory lists this property as a machine shop and it appears on the 1948 Insurance Map as well; and BL 68-247, 139 Birmingham Street, Lot 357, which also appears on the 1948 Insurance Map.

85 "Authority Holder's Monthly Conduct Report," May 18, 1943, Brightside Public House files, LCBO, AO.

86 Apparently, this practice commonly happened in Hamilton's hotels and clubs, and the LCBO had sent out a circular that aimed to stop the practice as early as April 1940. 14 August 1942, Brightside Public House files, LCBO, AO.

87 For example, Brightsider Frank Gallo, who trained with Hamilton north ender and Olympian Jackie Callura in the 1930s; the North End Hotel (a.k.a. Beer) League consisting of teams from Picton House, Brightside, Hanrahan's and Murphy's; Glen Nott, "Back-street battler won world boxing crown," *Spectator*, November 6, 1993; Ted Wilcox, "Reflection 1946: A day in the life: Things finally

back to normal," Sesquicentennial Feature 1846–1995, *Spectator*, June 8, 1996, S45; and Ted Wilcox, "I no longer ump but I still remember those insults," *Spectator*, January 11, 1999, A9. More generally see the extensive treatment of men's and women's sports in "Sports," *Brightside Reunion, 1983*, 10–13.

88 Palango, "Some Neighbourhood!," 5.

89 In 1983 Nello Giavedoni recalled its birth, "I guess the idea of keeping the name Brightside alive came 24 years ago when a bunch of us were sitting in the Brightside Hotel, which was a kind of meeting place, drinking a few beers . . . We had seen bits and pieces of the properties being eaten away and formed the Brightside Bowling League. Next year is our 25th anniversary." As reported in Denis LeBlanc, "Up to 800 Expected at second Brightside Reunion," *Spectator*, May 5, 1983, A7. Some sixteen teams played in the 1960–61 season with eighty-five men involved. On January 19, 2009, the Canadian Tenpin Federation, Inc., recognized the league's fiftieth anniversary. The Skyway Lanes, built in 1957, closed in April 2019. Jeff Mahoney, "Farewell, Skyway Lanes – a throwback to when bowling was king in Hamilton," *Spectator*, April 27, 2019.

90 Palango, "Brightside."

91 Ibid. The event reportedly sold four hundred tickets and involved fifty old-timers being treated to a home cooked meal and the opportunity to share memories. Its organizers donated $500 in profit to Big Brothers.

92 Attendance numbers vary depending on the source, with reportedly 800–950 attending the 1977 reunion, which happened a decade after Stelco's second big bite, and 800–1100 reportedly attending in 1983. Nine names of Reunion Committee members are listed on the back cover of *Brightside Reunion, 1983*, consisting of ardent and capable Brightside advocates and supporters: John Fioravanti (chairman), Stan Kane (treasurer), Gerry Andreatta, Jake Croni, Nello Giavedoni, Arnold Palango, Dave Palango, Vince Palango and John Michaluk (publicity and reunion MC). Some seventy-seven different companies helped sponsor the effort, with their advertisements peppered throughout the reunion publication.

93 Quigley, "Flying High," 12. Of this particular reunion *Spectator* reporter Denis LeBlanc claimed, "While the architecture of Brightside has been torn down, the spirit of the community has never been razed." See "Up to 800 Expected at second Brightside Reunion."

94 Brightside Reunion Agenda, 6 May 1983. Many thanks to reunion master of ceremonies, John Michaluk, for access to this and other related documents.

95 "Brightside was when / We were with our friends / And the times were rough and tough / Brightside is no more / But there's memories galore / Let's not forget our past // We're much older now, / Most have moved away / But we're here

to-day to say / Welcome everyone to your hour of fun / Because Brightside is here to stay." *Brightside Reunion 1983*, back cover.

96 LeBlanc, "Up to 800 Expected at second Brightside Reunion."

97 Ibid., 26, 32.

98 Stephen Lechniak, Stelco Rod and Bar, Facebook, which has 1,564 followers as of January 2020, https://www.facebook.com/pg/stelcosteve.

99 Stephen Lechniak, Brightside Memories, which has 480 followers as of January 2020, https://www.facebook.com/SteveStelco.

100 *Brightside Neighbourhood Project* description, August 2017. Its core members include Rob Kristofferson, Simon Orpana and Matt McInnes.

101 Ibid. ARCH is a place for community-based research and engagement, with space available at no cost for interviews, focus groups and other meetings at 1429 Main Street East (near the northeast corner of Kenilworth Avenue); WAHC, located in Hamilton's historical Custom House at 51 Stuart Street in the North End, aims to "preserve, honour, and promote the culture & history of all working people," http://wahc-museum.ca/; and CCENA "seeks to support and sustain art-based community listening, remembering, and story-making," http://ccena.ca/about-ccena/.

102 *Brightside Neighbourhood Project* description.

103 A term inspired by the writing of philosopher Giorgio Agamben, described in *Notes from the Brightside Neighbourhood Project* as "a document celebrating its own interpersonal process of production, this mapping helps us remember that it is the quality of our relationships to the land and each other that crucially shapes our neighbourhoods, cities, and world."

104 The Workers' City series offers a collection of tours, interviews, maps, photographs and other resources, which are now available online as well as through a downloadable app for mobile devices: http://workerscity.ca.

City of Immigration: Inclusion and Exclusion

Sarah V. Wayland

H amilton is a city of contrasts. Known as the Steel City, it is a sprawling place that contains bountiful green space and waterfalls, and in terms of land area is mostly rural and agricultural. It boasts a world-class university, yet its populace lags behind the province in terms of university education. It has an incredibly active citizenry and high rates of volunteerism, yet many citizens are remarkably disengaged and cynical. Finally, Hamilton is a city whose population is almost exclusively rooted in past or present immigration, yet in recent years it has had among the highest incidences of hate crimes in the country and has seen regular anti-immigration protests at city hall.[1]

Over its history, Hamilton has become home to tens of thousands of displaced persons, refugees and other newcomers. Today's Hamilton is rooted in their city-building efforts. During its manufacturing heyday, immigrant labourers flocked to Hamilton to work in the steel mills where they could earn a decent living and raise families. Among Hamilton's three most recent mayors, two are immigrants, and a third is the son of immigrants. Each of them speaks often of their immigrant roots – in Croatia, Italy and the Netherlands – and the opportunities they themselves found in Hamilton.

Yet today there are many immigrants who struggle in the labour market, experience discrimination in their housing searches and who simply do not feel welcomed. This tension between inclusion and exclusion has been present since Hamilton's founding days.

CITY OF REFUGE, FOR SOME

The area's immigration story predates the name *Hamilton*. A long-standing meeting place at the Head of the Lake for Indigenous Peoples, the first group of outside settlers to the area were refugees fleeing the aftermath of the American Revolutionary War. These included the tribes of the Iroquois Confederacy, who were uprooted from the United States for being loyal to the British. Pursued by American troops across New York state, those who survived the long trek settled in what is now the Six Nations reserve south of Hamilton, while the British Loyalists settled around what would become the city. The Head of the Lake became a gathering spot for British soldiers during and after the War of 1812 as well as others, so much so that late nineteenth century writers optimistically referred to the area as a City of Refuge.[2] On Main Street today, across from the courthouse on land once deeded to the city by its founder George Hamilton, a statue depicts the immigration of the United Empire Loyalists who fled north into Canada more than two centuries ago.

In the late 1820s, a canal was cut through the Burlington Beach, a thin strip of sand left across Hamilton Harbour by the last ice age. This created a port, which spurred trade and growth in the new Hamilton, and the city's fortunes grew, attracting large-scale migration from the United Kingdom during the 1830s. The presence of a port also put Hamilton on the front lines of two cholera epidemics, in 1832 and 1854. Cholera was often carried on ships where it spread among passengers subject to overcrowded, filthy conditions. In Hamilton's case, immigrants leaving behind famine and hardship in hopes of a better future were often the very ones devastated by the disease, with hundreds unfortunate enough never to start life in a new land.

Fear of disease was such that reports exist of angry mobs wielding pitchforks and clubs to prevent ships from docking in 1832.[3] As a precaution, newcomers were often held in isolation in quarantine camps where they were subject to the same overcrowded and unsanitary conditions experienced at sea. The first two persons to succumb to cholera were German immigrants, and it is believed that most deaths were among immigrants from Germany, Scotland, England and Ireland.[4]

Irish immigrants were an exceptionally stigmatized group, and the poor in general were blamed for spreading disease. Indeed, the largest number of deaths occurred in the areas they inhabited, namely the outlying districts near the bay and Corktown.[5] With the exception of members of the newly arrived Sisters of St. Joseph, people were largely fearful of helping the cholera victims, and many of the sick, dying and dead were simply abandoned. Close to four hundred persons, most of them believed to be newly arrived immigrants, were buried in Burlington Heights just west of Hamilton's iconic high-level bridge, their mass graves today memorialized by a Cholera Stone along York Boulevard.

Hamilton was officially designated a city in 1846. By the time of the 1851 census, only 9 per cent of Hamilton's population was born in Canada. For the most part, residents were born in England, Scotland, Ireland and, to a lesser extent, in the United States. The population was growing rapidly, increasing 150 per cent between 1846 and 1850. According to historian Michael B. Katz in his book *The People of Hamilton, Canada West: Family and Class in a Mid-Nineteenth-Century City*: "They came for various reasons: poverty-stricken Irish people fleeing the potato famine and a depressed, exploited society; young Scottish merchants seeking their fortune; English artisans in search of opportunity and independence; fugitive slaves seeking freedom. As they sorted themselves out in their new setting, they created a complex and stratified society."[6]

At this time, according to Katz, perhaps because Hamilton's people were nearly all immigrants, racial prejudice was not as apparent as in some other cities, and Hamilton was home to a prosperous Black community. Hamilton was an important stop on the Underground Railroad in the mid-1800s. Hundreds of Black people escaping slavery in the United States settled in Hamilton, including a thriving "Little Africa" community on Concession Street.[7]

Within this context of immigration being predominantly from the British Isles, divisions within the community were more easily seen between Protestants and Roman Catholics than by nationality or race. The English and Anglicans were not disproportionately wealthy and were widely distributed across socio-economic status. Katz also notes "there was more intermixing of classes and ethnicities in Hamilton's first decades than might be imagined."[8] According to Katz, "Its social hierarchy relied less on birth than achievement, with a growing entrepreneurial class that was largely immigrant, though excluded Irish Catholics."[9] Across the board, Irish and Catholics were the poorest.[10]

Immigration is characterized by movement. Immigrants uproot themselves in search of opportunities, and today they are more mobile than the Canadian-born population, more willing to move again and again in search of employment, investment and opportunity. This held true in Hamilton's early days as well. Between 1851 and 1861, only 35 per cent of Hamilton's population remained within the city. Not surprisingly, across classes, homeowners were less transient. Among the transients, some were entrepreneurs and skilled workers – including clerks, merchants, shoemakers, tailors and lawyers – and some were labourers.[11]

Many immigrants were bound for the United States. From the 1850s up to the 1920s, economic prospects were viewed as being better south of the border. Hamilton historian John C. Weaver wrote that

Hamilton was "an expedient station on the immigration trail that led to America."[12]

In terms of neighbourhoods, there was some ethnic clustering but no immigrant ghettos. For example, Corktown became mostly but not exclusively Irish in the 1850s, but most of Hamilton's Irish did not live in Corktown.[13] Housing was relatively scarce at that time and people may have taken whatever accommodation they could get. Or perhaps workers selected housing based on proximity to their workplace. Walking was the principal form of transportation for most residents, with only the very wealthy able to afford horses or carriages.

From 1871 to the end of the century, Hamilton's population doubled from 26,880 to 52,634, and approximately 90 per cent of immigrants originated from the British Isles. Canada was after all a Dominion of Britain, and Canadian immigration authorities encouraged migration from the United Kingdom, United States and western Europe. Labour from further afield was vital to economic growth but prompted nativist sentiments, manifesting in policies such as the "head tax" on Chinese immigrants and the "continuous journey" clause of the 1910 Immigration Act, which in effect prevented immigration from India and Japan. The burning issue in Canada at the turn of the century was how to fill labour shortages while absorbing and making loyal citizens from "hordes of strangers." Across this young country, hostility to foreigners was evident in immigration policies, exclusionary politics and public opinion – yet immigration proceeded apace.[14]

The beginnings of heavy industry in Hamilton at the turn of the century acted as a magnet for labour migration. Economic development fundamentally changed the ethnic nature of the city's population growth, attracting non-English speakers from continental Europe, many of whom were unskilled labourers seeking employment in iron and steel plants. By 1910, immigrants from Italy numbered about 1,500, including a significant number from the town of Racalmuto in Sicily. As many as one-third of today's Italian-Hamiltonians have roots in Racalmuto.

New arrivals faced plenty of discrimination. City directories at the time often listed Italian immigrants not by name but literally as "an Italian," and some employers just referred to employees by number or assigned them a name rather than learn a worker's actual name.[15] The *Hamilton Spectator* on June 27, 1907, reported a citizen request to the Mayor of Hamilton to petition the Dominion Government to stop the "dumping of broken immigrants" into the city. Immigration did not stop, and indeed a local shelter was created for immigrants in 1913.

THE WAR YEARS

Immigration and labour have always been related. Employers sometimes hired new immigrants as a challenge to their ranks of skilled labourers, and they were occasionally used as strikebreakers as well. It was widely thought that immigrants worked for low pay and did not stir up trouble. This may have been largely true, yet immigrants were behind some of Hamilton's labour disruptions. At Dominion Steel Foundry, for example, a strike by fifty-five "foreigners" in 1916 prompted the firm to ask for permission from the Immigration Department to bring in one hundred Black labourers from the southern United States.[16]

Immigration to Canada peaked just before the beginning of the First World War, tapered off during the 1920s and dropped sharply during the Depression of the 1930s and wartime years of the 1940s. It began to pick up again after the end of World War II when the economy began to grow quickly and required new labour. Throughout this period, driven by the affordability, proximity to employment and existing ethnic populations, immigrants concentrated in the Barton Street East neighbourhoods of Hamilton.

At the time of World War I, Germans were the second largest ethnic group in Hamilton, behind the English. Some of these individuals were not actual immigrants but descendants of immigrants who had arrived as early as 1790. By the twentieth century, the local Germania

Club had hundreds of members, including many non-Germans. In the face of anti-German sentiment that arose during World War I and World War II, the Germania Club voluntarily shuttered its doors, re-opening in 1946.[17] During World War II, Germans were fingerprinted and had to check in regularly with the RCMP.[18]

Similarly, with the rise of Mussolini to power in Italy, security concerns related to Fascism spilled over into Hamilton. On June 11, 1940, city council passed a unanimous resolution to create civilian Home Guard units "to restrain subversive activities." Within a week, 1,500 persons had volunteered, but no saboteurs or spies were ever found. The subsequent entry of Canada into war and the enactment of Defence of Canada Regulations across the country were devastating to local Italians. By the spring of 1941, eighty local men and one woman had been arrested and detained, and most were interned at Camp Petawawa, hundreds of kilometres from Hamilton. Many had no political connections to Fascism. Some were criminals and this was a convenient way to remove them from Hamilton. Hundreds of other Italians were laid off or lost their jobs.

"Enemy alien" status remained on the books until 1947 when it was repealed in the face Canada's postwar labour market needs. A bilateral agreement with Italy allowed for sponsorship of family members. Many took advantage, leaving a devastated Europe for Canada, and in 1958–59 more Italians came to Canada than did Britons. More than two hundred thousand Italians arrived in Canada in the 1950s, with nearly twelve thousand of them settling in Hamilton. The vast majority of this immigration was permanent, family-based migration.[19]

Hamilton's postwar economic expansion was aided by the arrival of displaced persons or DPs (today referred to as refugees) to fill some local labour shortages. A few articles in the *Hamilton Spectator* provide details of this new immigration. By early 1948, the arrival of forty Hungarians, Romanians, Yugoslavians and Ukrainians marked the third cohort of DPs coming to work as housekeepers in private homes and institutions.[20] Later that year, the Hamilton Cotton Company sought to remedy a labour gap in the textile industry by bringing forty young women from camps in Germany, with forty single men to follow. They were mostly from the Baltic countries, and most had some textile experience.[21] The federal government continued to admit persons from DP camps in Europe through the 1950s. Because of its facilities, one hundred persons suffering from tuberculosis were sent to Hamilton to receive treatment. Often arriving in family units, these DPs were Yugoslavians, Polish, Czechoslovakians and citizens of other "Iron Curtain" countries.[22]

Accounts indicate that these newcomers were diligent in learning English: in 1949, 258 diplomas in basic English and Canadian citizenship were awarded by the FR Close Technical Institute to DP students who represented many European nationalities.[23] By 1952, Central School was offering language courses to three thousand persons from thirty-two countries!

Politicians began to create relationships and to curry favour with immigrant communities. Mayor Lloyd Jackson invited eight representatives from the city's ethnic groups to attend the 1950 inaugural meeting of Hamilton Council. Victor Copps also reached out to ethnic leaders, and he even visited Gagliano Aterno, a town in Italy that was the birthplace or ancestral home of about five thousand Hamiltonians.[24] In 1962, Copps parlayed this broad-based support to become the first Roman Catholic mayor of Hamilton.

Despite the growth of immigration from continental Europe, immigration from the United Kingdom continued to be important to Hamilton. In 1957, an Anglican Immigration Centre opened to provide assistance for Britons. In the basement of an Anglican church at Ottawa and Barton, the centre assisted newcomers in finding employment and accommodation, reportedly helping to find jobs for 150 immigrants in short order. A chaplain for immigrants was named, himself an immigrant who had arrived in 1946.[25]

IMMIGRATION HEYDAY IN THE POSTWAR YEARS

Canada's postwar expansionist approach to immigration meant more continental Europeans arriving in Hamilton. By the time of the 1961 census, they surpassed those born in the UK. Soviet-occupied countries became a source of immigration, with persons arriving from the Baltics, Poland, Serbia and Croatia. In response, new ethnic churches, recreation halls, newspapers and political organizations were created.[26] Hamilton's Ukrainian community dedicated *Migration*, another bronze statue featuring a multi-generational group of larger-than-life immigrants to commemorate these journeys. Today, this statue can be found in the plaza just west of city hall.

For decades, the Dutch primarily arrived as expert farm labourers and were in great demand. Many of them were sponsored through the Dutch Reformed Church and lived on farms in Hamilton's outlying areas such as Jarvis, Winona and Hannon.[27] The *Spectator* reported two hundred to three hundred Dutch farm workers and their families arriving in June 1947 alone. The Dutch doubled their numbers in Hamilton between 1951 and 1961. In connection with the Christian Reformed Church, the Dutch community opened several primary schools, followed by Hamilton District Christian High School, opening in 1956, and eventually Redeemer College in 1982, institutions that have now grown beyond their Dutch roots.[28]

Most notable for Hamilton was the arrival of more Italians, spurred by the lifting of restrictions on immigration in 1947. Hamilton's Italian population grew from six thousand in 1951 to 17,500 by 1961. During the 1960s, more southern Europeans arrived, with Italians accompanied by Portuguese and Greek immigrants.

The arrival of more continental Europeans brought to the fore many restrictions against ethnic groups. For example, covenants in the Westdale neighbourhood forbade home sales to "Negroes, Asiatics, Bulgarians, Austrians, Russians, Serbs, Rumanians, Turks, Armenians . . . or foreign born Italians, Greeks or Jews."[29] These covenants did not stand the test of time, and legal segregation by nationality and religion was struck down by the courts in the 1940s and 1950s.

The 1971 census found 30 per cent of Hamilton's population to be foreign born, with three-quarters of them having arrived since 1945. More people owned cars, and housing opportunities were expanding. Working immigrant families from the Barton Street East area were moving up the Mountain and to suburbs, leaving behind ethnic stores, churches and restaurants.

IMMIGRANT DIVERSIFICATION

Immigration from other parts of the world grew, and refugees continued to form a significant portion of newcomers. In 1972, about one hundred Asians expelled from Uganda arrived in Hamilton. Some of them were highly skilled but found it challenging to find work without "Canadian experience," a term that would haunt many skilled immigrants in the decades to come. Hamilton was one of eleven Canadian cities to accept Ugandan refugees, and a local committee was created to assist them.[30]

Canada's Immigration Act of 1976 contained a unique provision that allowed for the private sponsorship of refugees, a practice that would grow in subsequent decades and for which Canada would become an example to the world. The terms of private sponsorship allowed organizations and even informal groups to sponsor refugees by agreeing to be financially responsible for them for up to one year and assisting with their settlement needs. In response to the Vietnamese boat people crisis, City of Hamilton alderman John Smith established The Mountain Fund to Save the Boat People in 1979. Along with a few friends, Smith set out to resettle to Hamilton as many Vietnamese refugees from camps in Southeast Asia as funds would allow. The Mountain Fund exceeded everyone's expectations. By the time it closed down in 1994, it had assisted more than three thousand refugees.[31]

The original fundraising goal of the Mountain Fund was ten thousand dollars, but that goal was far surpassed. Its work did not proceed without some local backlash from residents who voiced their concern that Hamilton would be importing communists. Many of these refugees initially settled in the Queen Street North area, where there continues to be some concentration of population as well as a presence of Vietnamese grocery stores and restaurants.

By the early 1980s, local businesses were hard hit by recession and Hamilton had lost its pull relative to other parts of the province. In particular, Hamilton experienced a dramatic fall in arrivals from Italy and the United States. The well-established Italian ethnic area in the city's North End was beginning to break up, with many people moving to suburbs and Stoney Creek.[32]

Hamilton ranked behind only Toronto and Vancouver in terms of its percentage of immigrants. By 1995, 24 per cent of Hamilton's population was foreign born. Yet this immigrant population was aging, reflecting earlier waves of European immigration rather than newer arrivals from Asia and Africa. In order of ethnic affiliation, Hamiltonians were English, followed by Italian, Polish, German, Dutch, French and Portuguese. Despite its diversity and history of immigration, discrimination had been ingrained in many residents, along with a fear of the unknown.[33]

CONTEMPORARY IMMIGRATION TO HAMILTON

Since the 1990s, immigration levels to Canada have remained fairly steady at just under 1 per cent of the population. Hamilton has seen annual arrivals in the two thousand to four thousand range, with a low of 2,066 in 1998 and a high of just over 4,600 in 2005. Immigration has continued to diversify in terms of countries of origin. Refugee arrivals in particular reflect various crises around the world. In recent decades, Hamilton has received refugees from Somalia and the former Yugoslavia, along with the Karen people from Myanmar. Colombians, Iraqis and Iranians also comprised many of the city's refugees in the 2000s.

The most recent wave, and one of the largest, has been from Syria. Facilitated by federal government policies, more than 1,400 Syrians moved to Hamilton in late 2015 and 2016, most of them arriving within only a few short months of each other. The collective local response to their arrival was huge, with many volunteers and service providers working overtime to find them housing and assist with settlement needs. At the same time, lively public debates occurred between refugee supporters and others who felt that we should be helping "our own" before helping others.

One of the biggest impacts will be felt in the long run as more than half of the Syrians were under the age of fifteen at their time of arrival. As such, they will largely be educated in Canada, speak fluent English and most likely make this country their home. Their ongoing integration is another significant chapter in Hamilton's long history of incorporating ethnic communities into its civic fabric.

SETTLEMENT SERVICES

Whether from their own communities, faith-based organizations, non-profits or government, immigrants have often relied on specialized services to facilitate their settlement in Canada. Many of these organizations formed in the wake of refugee inflows. For example, at the height of the arrivals of Southeast Asian refugees, in 1980 the Circle of Friends for Newcomers (Hamilton) was founded as a coordinating committee of various agencies to respond to the settlement needs of government-sponsored refugees. The coordinating committee put in place a "Circle of Friends" host program with a coordinator and trained volunteers to provide friendship and practical support to government-sponsored refugee families and single individuals. Other early initiatives included a clothing closet; drop-in centre; English classes for women, with a nursery for babies and toddlers; and job-search classes for men.

Also in the 1980s the Inter-Church Committee for Refugees formed to assist refugees arriving from Central America. In a high-rise building at John and Burlington Streets, volunteers welcomed seventy-six women and their families immigrating to Hamilton. The informal network of volunteers assisted with immediate needs including temporary shelter and provisions, orientation to the community and search for employment. With financial support from the Sisters of St. Joseph, in 1988 the St. Joseph Immigrant Women's Centre was born. It was renamed the Immigrants Working Centre in 2015, and today the IWC operates from four locations around Hamilton and helps thousands of newcomers each year from over thirty nationalities.

Around the same time, Hamilton's long-standing voice of immigration and diversity faced its own crisis. In debt and experiencing a loss of government funding, the Hamilton and District Multicultural Council closed its doors in December 1991. In its stead, Wesley Urban Ministries was awarded a government contract to provide interim immigrant settlement services.

On the heels of this closure, and in the context of multiple new organizations springing up around the city, in 1992 the Social Planning and Research Council released a report recommending the creation of a single immigrant settlement and integration service organization. This "one-stop shop" would serve immigrants as well as refugees.[34] In 1993 Settlement and Integration Services Organization or SISO opened its doors, serving nearly two thousand clients its first year.[35]

Over the next fifteen years, SISO would become the largest settlement agency in Hamilton and a powerful voice for immigrant concerns, securing the ears of ministers in the provincial and federal governments. SISO grew to more than 150 staff members, and it provided support for thousands of newcomers while receiving millions of dollars in government grants. It became so well known that sometimes immigrants arriving at Pearson Airport in Toronto would simply tell their cab drivers to take them to SISO.

A CHANGING CONVERSATION AND MUNICIPAL ACTION

In the immediate aftermath of the September 11, 2001, terrorist attacks in the United States, three local men set fire to Hamilton's Hindu Samaj Temple, believing it was a mosque. In response, people from various organizations, businesses, political sectors and the like came together with the goal of creating a civic resource centre and finding strategies to make Hamilton a more inclusive and peaceful place for everyone. Originally named Strengthening Hamilton Community's Initiative, in 2006 it was renamed the Hamilton Centre for Civic Inclusion (HCCI).[36]

The local conversation around immigration started to change. The *Hamilton Spectator* began drawing attention to immigration as important for Hamilton's future population and labour market growth. Local advocates pushed the City of Hamilton to take advantage of newly available federal funding to create a local immigration partnership and web portal for immigrants. A July 16, 2007, editorial in the *Hamilton Spectator* entitled "Immigration Policy Blues" argued that Hamilton was "losing its edge" on immigration attraction and retention and called for the municipality to act.

In 2009 the City of Hamilton received federal funding to create the Hamilton Immigration Partnership Council (HIPC), a community-based roundtable to address settlement and inclusion beyond the usual settlement service providers. Members were from settlement services, health care, education, business and government. HIPC created an immigration strategy, and community leaders began to speak of Hamilton as being in competition with other cities for skilled newcomers.[37]

The advent of HIPC was timely in that the need for communication and coordination around immigration issues was suddenly more necessary as the local settlement landscape was about to change drastically. Financial irregularities within SISO came to light in 2010, and the organization suddenly closed early in 2011, resulting in a redistribution of programs to Immigrant Women's Centre (now Immigrants Working Centre), YMCA and Wesley Urban Ministries.

Immigration has long been Hamilton's lifeblood, with newcomers taking employment across the continuum from menial labour to high-skilled positions, and immigrants have strong rates of business ownership. In Hamilton, the economic contributions of immigrants had gotten lost amidst the focus on settlement service organizations and the need to improve inclusion. Recognizing that Hamilton faced economic consequences from losing its mantle as an economic magnet, leadership within the City of Hamilton made a modest but proactive move to work on economic development–focused immigrant attraction and retention. The Global Hamilton initiative was launched in 2014 and resides with the city's Economic Development division, focusing on business start-up, support for small business owners and retention of international students. That same year, Hamilton's city council unanimously approved a motion permitting undocumented migrants access to municipal services, becoming the second city in Canada (after Toronto) with such a policy, commonly known as a "sanctuary city."

IMMIGRATION AND THE CITY: ATTRACTION AND RESISTANCE

The question of municipal action around immigration is interesting and increasingly timely. Cities are on the front lines in terms of receiving immigrants, and so much of newcomers' early experiences in Canada are connected to their experiences in specific cities, including their housing, neighbourhoods, transit, access to education and employment. And immigrants are very likely to live in urban areas, especially large urban areas. Yet municipalities have no jurisdiction over immigration and have little power when it comes to so many of the federal and provincial policy areas that directly impact the lived experiences of newcomers.

It is estimated that within two decades, approximately one in every three people in the Canadian labour force will be foreign born.[38] Hamilton will continue to receive newcomers in all immigration categories, but our population is not being replenished: more than half of Hamilton's foreign-born population arrived here before 1980. Since 1995, Hamilton's foreign-born population has held steady around 24 per cent, but the percentage of Hamilton's population made up of recent immigrants (arriving within the past five years) has declined to 2.5 per cent.[39]

These newcomers continue to expand the linguistic and cultural spectrum of Hamilton, with the top three languages of recent immigrants spoken at home being Arabic, Tagalog/Filipino and Spanish.[40] Within the Hamilton region, the most common mother tongues aside from English and French are, in descending order, Italian, Spanish, Arabic, Chinese languages, Polish, Punjabi, Serbian and Tagalog. If Hamilton wishes to grow and prosper in the coming decades, it needs to be more proactive around immigration.

Yet immigration is not universally embraced by residents of Hamilton, almost all of whom are descendants of immigrants themselves. Recently, xenophobia, Islamophobia, anti-Semitism, racism and other expressions of exclusion have been on display in various forms, including graffiti, name-calling and hate crimes. Most visible have been the regular demonstrations by anti-immigrant Yellow Vests in front of Hamilton City Hall and in other locations around the city, sometimes joined by Proud Boys, Sons or Soldiers of Odin, and other extreme-right and neo-Nazi adherents. In response, larger groups of Hamiltonians have felt compelled to counter-protest with pro-diversity signs, chants and even songs.

This recent manifestation of anti-immigrant sentiment is not unique to Hamilton: it is part of the "Trump effect" and spillover of American politics into Canada as well as the rise of populism worldwide. That it has been met with considerable local resistance by ordinary citizens of

Hamilton is a positive sign, as is the city's attempt to ban hate-related activity from public property.

In short, Hamilton needs immigrants, yet the tensions of inclusion and exclusion continue as they have throughout Hamilton's history, and with most of the costs falling upon newcomers and other marginalized groups. These tensions show no signs of abating.

BACK TO THE FUTURE

Monuments around the city tell their own stories of immigration to Hamilton. From the 1928 United Empire Loyalists statue where a family of four walks northward on their journey to a new land, the father clutching in his hand the deed granting him land on this side of the Niagara River, to Immigrant Square in front of LiUNA Station on James Street North, Hamilton features poignant memorials to real people. Immigrant Square recognizes the thousands of Hamiltonians who entered the city at this former CN train station, now a national historic site, and then made their lives here.

All of these monuments depict a mythical family or group to represent a particular cohort of immigrants who came to this city at different points in history: Loyalists, economic immigrants and refugees. However, to my mind, the simple cholera stone that stands all but forgotten along York Boulevard is the most poignant of all, commemorating the many lives lost, lives of unknown immigrants and forgotten dreams never to come to fruition.

There are thousands of heart-wrenching and moving stories of immigration to Hamilton, most of them untold and many unremembered into future generations. Though these stories refer to specific points of departure and reasons for emigrating, they are also universal. People came here seeking better lives for themselves and for their children, sometimes making great sacrifices in the process, often facing various forms of exclusion, and, very occasionally, meeting with success beyond their wildest dreams.

References

Buist, Steve. "Finding Home in Canada." *Hamilton Spectator*, May 24, 2017. (Article three of three in the series A New Life in Hamilton.)

Cumbo, Enrico Carlson. *The Italian Presence in Hamilton: A Social History: 1870–2000*. Toronto: printed by the author, 2000.

Dam, Huyen. "Becoming Vietnamese-Canadian: The Story of the Vietnamese Boat People in Hamilton." Master's thesis, McMaster University, 2009.

Davey, Ian, and Michael Doucet. "The Social Geography of a Commercial City, ca. 1853." In *The People of Hamilton, Canada West: Family and Class in a Mid-Nineteenth-Century City*, by Michael B. Katz, 319–42. Cambridge, MA: Harvard University Press, 1975.

Den Boggende, Gijsbert Gerrit Jacob. *Dutch Calvinist Immigrants in Hamilton and the Hamilton Christian School 1937–1960*. Master's thesis, University of Toronto, 1991.

Hamilton Spectator, various.

Hawkins, Freda. *Canada and Immigration: Public Policy and Public Concern*, 2nd ed. Kingston and Montreal: McGill-Queen's University Press, 1988.

Johns, Brianna K. "Changing Waves: The Epidemics of 1832 and 1854." In *Ch2olera: Hamilton's Forgotten Epidemics*, edited by D. Ann Herring and Heather T. Battles, 42–51. Hamilton: McMaster University Department of Anthropology, 2012.

Katz, Michael B. *The People of Hamilton, Canada West: Family and Class in a Mid-Nineteenth-Century City*. Cambridge, MA: Harvard University Press, 1975.

Knowles, Valerie. *Strangers at Our Gates*. Toronto: Dundurn Press, 1992.

Nolan, Mary K. "Immigrants not always welcomed." *Hamilton Spectator*, August 18, 1999.

Terpstra, John. *Falling into Place*. Kentville, NS: Gaspereau, 2002.

Turner, Andrew. "The Blame Game." In *Ch2olera: Hamilton's Forgotten Epidemics*, edited by D. Ann Herring and Heather T. Battles, 72–79. Hamilton: McMaster University Department of Anthropology, 2012.

Weaver, John C. *Hamilton: An Illustrated History*. Toronto: James Lorimer and National Museum of Man, 1982.

Endnotes

1   Twenty-one per cent of Hamilton's population has a university certificate, diploma or degree, compared to 27 per cent of the population of Ontario and 25 per cent of Ontario's population outside of the Greater Toronto Area (Statistics Canada, National Household Survey, 2011). On volunteering, see Hamilton Community Foundation's *Vital Signs* report, https://www.hamiltoncommunityfoundation .ca/vital-signs-2015/belonging-and-leadership-2015/. On hate crimes, see Nicole O'Reilly, "Hamilton ranks second highest for hate crimes in Canada – again,"

Hamilton Spectator, June 14, 2017, and Meagan Deuling, "Hamilton has the highest rate of hate crimes in Canada: report," *CBC News*, July 23, 2019, https://www.cbc .ca/news/canada/hamilton/hate-crime-statistics-canada-hamilton-1.5221663.

2   John Terpstra, *Falling into Place* (Kentville, NS: Gaspereau, 2002), 275.

3   Mary K. Nolan, "Immigrants not always welcomed," *Hamilton Spectator*, August 18, 1999.

4   Brianna K. Johns, "Changing Waves: The Epidemics of 1832 and 1854," in *Ch2olera: Hamilton's Forgotten Epidemics*, ed. D. Ann Herring and Heather T. Battles (Hamilton: McMaster University Department of Anthropology, 2012), 43.

5   Andrew Turner, "The Blame Game," in *Ch2olera: Hamilton's Forgotten Epidemics*, ed. D. Ann Herring and Heather T. Battles (Hamilton: McMaster University Department of Anthropology, 2012), 76–77.

6   Michael B. Katz, *The People of Hamilton, Canada West: Family and Class in a Mid-Nineteenth-Century City* (Cambridge, MA: Harvard University Press, 1975), 2–3.

7   Steve Buist, "Finding Home in Canada," *Hamilton Spectator*, May 24, 2017, A8.

8   Katz, *The People of Hamilton*, 187.

9   Katz, *The People of Hamilton*, 187.

10   Katz, *The People of Hamilton*, 25–26.

11   Katz, *The People of Hamilton*, 20–21.

12   John C. Weaver, *Hamilton: An Illustrated History* (Toronto: James Lorimer and National Museum of Man, 1982), 140.

13   Ian Davey and Michael Doucet, "The Social Geography of a Commercial City, ca. 1853," in *The People of Hamilton*, Michael B. Katz, 339.

14   Valerie Knowles, *Strangers at Our Gates* (Toronto: Dundurn Press, 1992); Freda Hawkins, *Canada and Immigration: Public Policy and Public Concern*, 2nd ed. (Kingston and Montreal: McGill-Queen's University Press, 1988).

15   Mary K. Nolan, "Immigrants not always welcomed," *Hamilton Spectator*, August 18, 1999.

16   Weaver, *Hamilton: An Illustrated History*, 112.

17   *Hamilton Spectator*, March 2, 1888; May 11, 1915; and May 22, 1940.

18   *Hamilton Spectator*, September 8, 1989.

19   Enrico Carlson Cumbo, *The Italian Presence in Hamilton: A Social History: 1870–2000* (Toronto: printed by the author, 2000).

20   *Hamilton Spectator*, January 23, 1948.

21   *Hamilton Spectator*, July 30, 1948.

22   *Hamilton Spectator*, December 8, 1959.

23   *Hamilton Spectator*, April 30, 1949.

24   Weaver, *Hamilton*, 191.

25   *Hamilton Spectator*, June 18, 1957; July 26, 1957; and September 24, 1957.

26   Weaver, *Hamilton*, 169–72.

27 *Hamilton Spectator*, April 16, 1927; June 6, 1947; July 23, 1951; and April 22, 1954.

28 Gijsbert Gerrit Jacob Den Boggende, "Dutch Calvinist Immigrants in Hamilton and the Hamilton Christian School 1937–1960" (master's thesis, University of Toronto, 1991), ii. The author notes that the school was founded by Dutch immigrants yet Dutch was never taught in the school, nor was it intended to be only for Dutch students. Yet the population of the school remained exclusively of Dutch origin for its first three decades.

29 Cited in Weaver, *Hamilton*, 103.

30 *Hamilton Spectator*, November 2, 1972, and September 28, 1975.

31 Huyen Dam, "Becoming Vietnamese-Canadian: The Story of the Vietnamese Boat People in Hamilton" (master's thesis, McMaster University, 2009), 5–6.

32 *Hamilton Spectator*, July 4, 1983.

33 *Hamilton Spectator*, April 27, 1995.

34 The SPRC proposal was not a new idea: it had proposed as early as 1970 to create a central information and services and a network of neighbourhood centres for all people in Hamilton. It was to be a general information centre for all residents, plus special services for immigrants (*Hamilton Spectator*, July 30, 1970).

35 *Hamilton Spectator*, July 30, 1994.

36 *Hamilton Spectator*, March 16, 2002.

37 *Hamilton Spectator*, March 20, 2009.

38 Laurent Martel et al., "Projected trends to 2031 for the Canadian labour force," Statistics Canada, August 2011, http://www.statcan.gc.ca/pub/11-010-x/2011008/part-partie3-eng.htm.

39 2016 Census of Population, Government of Canada, 2017.

40 2016 Census of Population, Government of Canada, 2017.

The Red Hill Expressway, One-Way Streets and Hamilton's Car Culture

Paul Weinberg

The epic martial sounds of Richard Wagner's "Ride of the Valkyries" come to mind (crediting Raise the Hammer for the apt metaphor) whenever I bravely or more accurately foolishly steer my bike, while wearing a helmet, onto the fast lanes of the one-way thoroughfare Main Street, heading east in the lower older city of Hamilton. To avoid traffic, I hug the side of Main not knowing what will force me off eventually – the cars and transport trailers jostling for space or the Hamilton city bus. The retail stretch passing by me is made up of derelict or boarded up storefronts, as well as a line of older houses where residents cope daily with the cacophony. (Hamilton's revival is nowhere to be seen.) We are still living under the lockdown regime of COVID-19 but that has not diminished the cavalcade going who knows where from the downtown; while a similar rush of metal is heading west along a parallel one-way thoroughfare, on King Street. People behind the wheel typically ramp up their speeds on one-way streets – with the momentum assisted by the synchronized traffic lighting that allows drivers to reach a destination in the lower city in roughly twenty minutes. Meanwhile, the stress is just too much for even a regular cyclist like myself and so I scurry for safe ground over the curb onto the narrow sidewalks that line Main. With not a pedestrian in sight and many blocks between traffic lights I end up walking my bike. Somebody cycles by me, pushing me to get out of the way.

This is just a sample of how unfriendly Hamilton streets remain for cyclists, pedestrians and even prudent drivers as I write this in the spring of 2020. In the wake of the COVID-19 pandemic and social isolation, the City of Hamilton showed a willingness to allow eating and drinking establishments to expand their patios into the sidewalks and yet it flatly turned down petitions by local people to go the route of other North American cities and open up roads to pedestrians and bicycles, reports Lynda Lukasik, executive director of Environment Hamilton. This later proposal appeared to hit a sensitive nerve in the bureaucracy and among elected city councillors. Plus, there is also no appetite at Hamilton City Hall to expand the network of bike lanes across all of Hamilton, including separated bike lanes beyond what few exist now. The notoriously car-centric Toronto is gingerly going that route and putting the Hammer to shame. Biking in Hamilton is still viewed primarily as a recreational activity, rather than a viable means to travel to and from work, visit people or go shopping. Plus, says Lukasik, an avid cyclist herself, there is the credible perception that it is unsafe to bicycle in Hamilton, which has deterred sufficient women from cycling here. That may be changing with the municipal SoBi bike-sharing program, which almost got shut down by the city council, but has since been given a reprieve because of a private donation. Half of the twenty-six thousand SoBi subscribers happen to be women, Lukasik adds. "When you start to look at the socio-economics of who the riders are, my understanding is that Hamilton is sort of a stellar standout example of inclusivity in a bike share program."

Car culture is a ubiquitous reality across North America and the world at large but here in Hamilton it is especially resistant to change. Hamilton is dominated politically by cars and developers, to paraphrase a letter written to the *Hamilton Spectator*. Add to that the chronic underfunding of the Hamilton public transit system and the intractable debate about a proposed east-west LRT to reinvigorate a depressed lower city of Hamilton, including the downtown. Residents living in denser and older neighbourhoods tend to be bigger users of public transit while bus service is sporadic or non-existent in the suburban sprawl communities.

"Why should we spend money that only benefits that one portion of city?" is a common refrain heard from some local politicians in the suburbs on top of the Niagara Escarpment or the towns that were forced to amalgamate with Hamilton in 2001 by a previous provincial government. Indeed, investments in public transportation can benefit the entire city of Hamilton, says urban consultant Paul Shaker at Civicplan. He also notes that Hamilton's financial success lies in a robust downtown that has suffered neglect since the 1970s following a ruinous urban renewal process. "The downtown area is the single largest employment cluster in the city. There are more jobs spread through the rest of the city, but as an employment node, downtown is the largest."

To understand the polarization in Hamilton I am looking at two controversies that have shaped Hamilton's car culture in the past fifty years: the building of the expressway in the north-south Red Hill Valley (even after it was designated as parkland) from the QEW along Lake Ontario south to the Lincoln Alexander Parkway and the creation of a maze of one-way streets that have played a role in the hollowing out of Hamilton's downtown core. And two powerful male civic leaders in Hamilton have represented competing visions for how people will view the city: early twentieth-century parks promoter and influential lawyer/politician Thomas B. McQuesten and largely forgotten Hamilton city bureaucrat Ray Desjardins.

RAY DESJARDINS AND THE TWENTY-MINUTE CITY

By all accounts Ray Desjardins ran Hamilton's traffic department with an iron determination between 1966 and 1983. The larger-than-life city bureaucrat played a major role in some of the significant and contentious traffic decisions in Hamilton at a time when cars were king. These included the establishment of one-way streets, synchronized traffic lights, the banning of on-street parking downtown and the Red Hill Valley Parkway.

Marty Hazell, who today is the director of strategic initiatives for the City of Hamilton, started out as a student on his eighteenth birthday in the mid-1970s working for its traffic department. He describes Desjardins as a domineering personality with more clout than many elected politicians. His boss was not shy when it came to expressing a point of view on any subject. "[Ray] had arguments with politicians and he would never back down; I remember shouting matches within his office ... If it wasn't going his way, he got louder," Hazell recalls.

Hazell believes that if Desjardins was still alive today in the twenty-first century, he certainly would have faced a personal challenge handling civic engagement from the general public. "I don't know how Ray would have dealt with stakeholder consultation."

Desjardins functioned when cars and trucks were the most important forms of transportation on the road and there was no thought of sharing it with cyclists or pedestrians. His philosophy was simply this – nothing should impede the smooth flow of traffic through the city. He was in tune with the times. Traffic engineering came of age in the 1950s with the massive adoption of the automobile, expansion in highways and the growth of cities and suburbs. The internal combustion engine represented progress and the wave of the future. This was decades before scientists were publicly sounding the alarm of fossil fuel emissions heating up the atmosphere and the planet.

On issues related to development in the downtown, Desjardins made no bones about his disagreement with city planners. Hazell still can hear his former boss emphasizing that you have got to be strong with the planners and argue with them.

A *Hamilton Spectator* article on Desjardins's retirement in 1983 reported how Desjardins became furious with the planners' suggestion to narrow King Street in order to create pedestrian malls. "When I came here, King was jammed up, people were mad at each other. It stunk of fumes. If you think that's better, you are wrong," Desjardins told the newspaper.

One city official who did tangle with Desjardins was Victor Abraham, who started working in Hamilton's planning department in 1968 and later gravitated to the city planning director's position. He emphasized that the conversations with the traffic manager were always amicable and civil. "Ray had a mandate to move the traffic and we had a mandate to make the city livable."

One of Desjardins's measures was to establish synchronized traffic lights on the one-way streets in the lower city to speed up the traffic. Abraham was opposed as he preferred to make Hamilton more like Toronto in terms of the number of traffic lights in the downtown. But Desjardins refused to budge. "We were more interested in the people, particularly downtown. We felt that downtown shouldn't be dominated by one-way streets. And the [traffic] lighting systems should be such that people would go a couple of lights and stop . . . Ray wanted the traffic to move," says Abraham.

CONVERSION OF DOWNTOWN HAMILTON THOROUGHFARES TO ONE-WAY STREETS

One of Desjardins's priorities upon his own arrival in Hamilton to head its traffic department in 1966 was to complete a plan conceived a decade earlier by US traffic engineer Wilbur Smith to convert about twenty-seven miles (or 43.45 kilometres) of two-way streets in the older city into a maze of one-ways for the downtown. A number of mid-sized North American cities had made the same move because their narrow streets in the core had been designed to fit horse-and-buggy traffic, not the mass use of cars by the 1950s. Toronto was a notable exception in not pursuing this strategy.

Smith's plan involved the twinning of one-way streets such as Main and King – one eastbound and the other westbound – in order to facilitate speed of traffic flow. It seemed to make sense for Hamilton at the time. Manufacturing was a major employer and thousands of factory workers were arriving at and leaving from industrial plants in the vicinity of Hamilton Harbour at specific shifts during the day and night. The one-way streets were also ideal for trucks carrying materials and supplies for the manufacturers.

Main, King, James, John, York and King William were the first streets to be converted this way in October 1956. These were the busiest arterial roads in terms of carrying traffic across the central business district. "Business Owners Attack One-Way Streets: Roads Become Race Tracks Traffic Committee Told" was the headline and subhead the *Hamilton Spectator* chose for its article on a committee hearing where downtown business people were reporting on the negative impact of the one-way conversion:

> Members of the transportation and traffic committee, sitting last night in a committee room packed with businessmen from areas affected by one-way streets heard requests for major changes in the system.
>
> Decreasing business returns, the refusal of old customers to visit the stores, large numbers of heavy trucks passing through the downtown area, the alleged conversion of King Street into a highway – all these and many subjects were hurled at the committee by protesting businessmen from King Street East and West, James Street North and York Street.

Further conversions of downtown streets were delayed until Desjardins came along to finish the job. "They really expanded the one-way streets [under Desjardins]," says Hazell.

In addition, no parking was permitted "on 90 per cent" of the major arteries in Hamilton including Ottawa, Kenilworth, Main and King Streets, his former employee states. Downtown businesses were invariably affected by the city policy, as it appeared to discourage people from leaving their parked vehicles close to a front door. After Desjardins's retirement on-street parking swept back in the late 1980s and early 1990s.

Desjardins and other traffic managers often touted the safe road conditions of the one-way streets. However, six months after Hamilton introduced its first batch of one-way streets in October 1956 an additional ninety motor vehicle accidents had occurred at thirteen intersections, revealed Wilbur Smith and Associates in a follow-up report. Among the causes, the consultancy revealed, were "excessive cross-weaving because of limited lane delineation and multi-lane operations; limited signal visibility at certain locations; improper driver positioning prior to making turns and general unfamiliarity with one-way streets."

Smith observed from studies of peak traffic before and after his single-directional street plan was introduced that one-way streets "considerably improved driving speeds in central Hamilton and that the one-way streets performed effectively. Route speeds increased as much 65 per cent." From the perspective of both Smith and Desjardins fast-moving traffic on one-way streets across Hamilton's core represented efficiency. In more recent years there has been a greater recognition that vehicles travelling at high speeds on highways, major arterial roads or residential streets will lead to collisions, injuries and death for pedestrians, motorists and cyclists.

Historically, one-way streets have also contributed to the decline of neighbourhoods and retail strips in Hamilton's lower city, says Montreal-born David Cohen, a former elected city councillor in the old town of Dundas and retired communications specialist. He and his family moved to Hamilton from Toronto when Desjardins was still running the traffic department. Cohen is a long-time critic of the one-way street, complaining that it has made Hamilton the kind of city where drivers speed through without bothering to stop and visit the shops, restaurants or local art gallery. In 1996, he spelled this out in an article headlined "Traffic passes by in 'hello-good bye' city" for the *Spectator*.

When I encountered Cohen, the man was wearing his characteristic beret and still keen to discuss traffic. Little has changed, he said and cites the example of the major eastbound one-way/multi-lane thoroughfare Main Street, which is dominated by intimidating fast-moving cars and trucks. We stood where Main Street represents an effective dividing line between the plaza that fronts Hamilton's city hall on the south side and the incongruous back side of the Art Gallery of Hamilton and the Hamilton Convention Centre on the other side. Few people are visible on the opposing sidewalks here (beyond the hardy folks waiting and shivering for the rare bus at the transit stop in the wintery evenings), even though this should be in theory the lively centre of Hamilton. Instead, this is a sterile and indifferent setting. David Cohen explains, "Traffic should converge on the city centre, not flow through it."

Since Desjardins's departure from the scene (he died shortly after his retirement) city planners have been carefully chipping away at the legacy of the master traffic engineer. The good news is that parking is now allowed on downtown streets in Hamilton. But the pace of converting streets from one-way to two-way is incremental and highly political due to the popularity of one-way streets among local drivers who like the convenience of zipping from one end of the lower city to the other. The one-way conversion of Queen Street is the latest to experience this political tension.

As late as 2013 more than one hundred one-way streets existed in Hamilton, according to former city councillor and urban planner Brian McHattie. How many exist today is not something even the city seems to know, I discovered after making some phone inquiries at Hamilton City Hall. Among the successful conversions from one- to two-way streets in Hamilton is the one that occurred on James Street North, which is now a vital, albeit gentrified, strip of independent stores, art galleries, music venues, coffee shops and restaurants.

Then Hamilton city traffic manager Martin White, whom I contacted a few years ago, was frank about the challenge to win support for new conversions to two-way at the local city council. "You need the buy-in of people here who work for the city and you need the drivers to buy it. You need the city culture to change to have that buy-in."

Maybe one day it will happen, but right now Hamiltonians are in no mood to give up the two major one-way east-west thoroughfares in the lower city, Main and King.

Currently, the inefficiencies of the one-way streets are becoming too glaring to ignore. There are more lanes on the lower city streets than there is traffic to fill them, says Ryan McGreal, the editor of the urbanist website Raise the Hammer. "Total traffic volumes have been falling steadily since 2000. Most lower city streets are characterized by free-flowing traffic at or above the speed limit even during rush hour. That is insanity. If we repurpose some automobile lanes to serve as continuous, protected bike lanes, wider sidewalks and so on, we will be making more effective use of scarce and expensive public infrastructure."

THOMAS McQUESTEN AND THE CITY BEAUTIFUL MOVEMENT

Ray Desjardins is virtually unknown today. In contrast, Thomas McQuesten is an historically influential and multi-faceted figure who emerged in Hamilton in the second decade of the twentieth century and is the subject of two biographies by local historians. McQuesten was the complete opposite to Desjardins's bullying personality, preferring instead a low-key "stealthy" (his word) approach to furthering his agenda of promoting nature, green space, conservation, heritage and design.

Raised by a strict teetotalling mother and missionary, Mary McQuesten, following the death of her husband, Isaac (an alcoholic and melancholic businessman who had squandered the family fortune through bad investments and died bankrupt), it could be argued that Mary's disciplinary regime served to teach Thomas McQuesten the value of contributing to the community.

In order to put the McQuesten family on a firmer financial footing, the earnings generated from teaching by Thomas's sister Ruby were invested to help finance the young Thomas's education. This set him on a successful path to become a lawyer and Ontario Liberal politician, as well as lift up the family from genteel poverty. Today, on Jackson Street West stands the historic Whitehern house where three generations of the McQuesten family lived from 1852 to 1968 and is now maintained as a historical site and city museum. There are no family heirs or descendants because the highly judgmental Mary McQuesten vetoed the prospective life partners that Thomas and his siblings had individually considered for marriage.

McQuesten was an elected alderman on Hamilton City Council from 1913 to 1920 at a time when Hamilton was the largest industrial centre in Canada (the two major steel companies, Stelco and Dofasco, were still headquartered here). Industrial activity was already polluting the Hamilton Harbour lands. Furthermore, the sensitive and untouched Cootes Paradise wetlands were facing serious development pressure.

Concerns about its future led to the founding in 1920 of the Hamilton Bird Protection Society, the precursor to today's Hamilton Naturalists' Club. Membership was largely made up of the city's most prominent people (including members of the McQuesten family) such as merchants, doctors, lawyers, teachers and accountants. The new organization reached into the education system where nine thousand schoolchildren were involved in the building of birdhouses and essay writing on conservation, say Nancy Bouchier and Ken Cruikshank in their book, *The People and the Bay: A Social and Environmental History of the Hamilton Harbour.*

If Ray Desjardins was upfront about his views about traffic, McQuesten represented the complete opposite as an influential behind-the-scenes mover and shaker in the Hamilton Board of Parks Management. He was never its chair, leaving that job to a colleague. Separate from city council and made up of unelected business people, the Parks board relied on its own source of revenue derived from one mill in the property tax levied (i.e., the amount per $1,000 on a property's assessed value). This helped to finance McQuesten's purchase and assembly of open green spaces for the sole purpose of creating parks, including parcels in the Red Hill Valley. In 1927 the Parks board managed fortuitously to rescue 161 hectares in the Cootes Paradise wetlands that were in the hands of a land developer in tax arrears. McQuesten had this and surrounding space transformed into a protected 2,450-acre space of the Royal Botanical Gardens (RBG). Reflecting an elitist view that nobody should be allowed to live in a protected park or green space, especially the most marginalized of people, McQuesten and the Parks board also successfully pushed for eviction of the impoverished families living in shacks or boathouses in the vicinity. In a mitigating move former residents were given relief work on the Rock Garden, which became the basis for the RBG. Today the RBG is the largest nature preserve of its kind in Canada and involved in the continued restoration of the wetlands.

In 1934 McQuesten was elected as representative from a Hamilton constituency into the Ontario legislature and subsequently joined the cabinet as the minister of highways in Mitch Hepburn's Liberal government. But that post did not put an end to his park building and heritage promoting activities. Throughout his career in and out of government McQuesten surrounded himself with talented gardeners, urban planners and architects whom he recruited for various projects in Hamilton and elsewhere in Ontario, such as the Niagara

Parks system, the Queen Elizabeth Way (Canada's first major high-way), restored 1812 fortifications, a reforested Niagara Escarpment (in Hamilton at least) and the province's first landscaping school. He represented the tail end of a City Beautiful movement that had its genesis in the mid-nineteenth century with the creation of major North American urban green spaces like New York City's Central Park under the direction of US landscape designer Frederick Olmsted.

Simply put, McQuesten believed that beauty, aesthetics and nature were essential ingredients for achieving a moral society, says Mary Anderson, author of *Tragedy & Triumph: Ruby & Thomas B. McQuesten*. This was applied in his planning of the Queen Elizabeth Way, which opened in 1939 between Toronto, the Niagara Peninsula and Buffalo. Anderson describes how McQuesten hired professional landscapers to selectively plant pine and spruce along the roadside to evoke scenic orchard land or mixed woodlots for the drivers passing, as well as monuments at the entrances. A combination of a forty-foot-high column of classical beaux arts design, courtesy of William Somerville, and an imperial British stone lion by sculptor Frances Loring graced the Toronto entrance until the mid-1970s when highway widening resulted in their removal to the nearby Sir Casimir Gzowski Park on the east side of the Humber River.

As the key arterial road for the Golden Horseshoe, today the QEW is a great economic success from the perspective of commerce and tourism. But it is hard to take seriously claims by McQuesten that he was producing an aesthetic experience for the driver of a motor vehicle. He did find it difficult to keep his city beautification ideals intact in the face of cost-conscious and utilitarian-minded city representatives and institutions. In retrospect, the park promoter's move to have the RBG protected by provincial Ontario legislation was an intelligent one because of the volatility in his own municipal backyard. But he did not quite reckon with new manifestations of harm coming decades later, such as the recent sewage spill from the city or global climate change. It would require more than the blessing of the Queen and her representative in Canada to keep a nature preserve intact.

Not all of McQuesten's commissioned projects – such as an ambitious grandiose entrance for Hamilton – were implemented. And sadly, the gorgeous Sunken Gardens on the McMaster University campus were unceremoniously discarded long after his death to make way for a medical complex that opened in 1972.

THE SHIFT TO HIGHWAYS AND EXPRESSWAYS

The tension between the twin legacies of McQuesten and Desjardins in Hamilton was best reflected in the debate surrounding the building of the Red Hill Valley Parkway.

A highway through the Red Hill Valley – in northeast Hamilton – was first conceived of as early as 1950 in the city planning document *Major Street System for the City of Hamilton* (also known as the *Wilson Bunnell* report). It was still a pristine natural presence, says McMaster University geography professor Walter Peace, flowing seventeen kilometres from its source near Ryckman's Corners on the Mountain (the local name for Hamilton's portion of the Niagara Escarpment) to its mouth at the eastern end of Hamilton Harbour. But pressures of city expansion would start to appear. In the post–World War II period of prosperity – nurtured by greater unionization and federal mortgage insurance that made home ownership affordable – young families were leaving the lower city for larger lots in suburban communities above the escarpment. At some point the city had physically reached the western side of the Red Hill Creek valley while farms were still active on the eastern side. Simultaneously, population pressures in the 1950s and 1960s below the escarpment had resulted in an expanded access to the largely rural top of the escarpment with new city services such as roads, water and sewage.

However, the proposed highway came into conflict with Hamilton's 1947 official plan that sought to make the Red Hill Valley part of a protected greenbelt. In the words of its author, chief planner and modernist E.G. Faludi, it would serve "as a natural barrier between densely built up areas and future developments." This followed the intentions of Thomas McQuesten, who had arranged the purchase in 1929 of 645 acres of the Red Hill Valley as part of a network of city parks, notes Walter Peace. Other open areas included the Chedoke Creek valley, the Beach Strip and the escarpment itself. McQuesten had made clear in a 1929 newspaper interview that the purchase of these Red Hill Valley creek lands in particular would "preserve for all time one of the outstanding spectacular areas in the County of Wentworth."

Despite McQuesten's and Faludi's plans for the Red Hill Valley, nothing further happened and so this area languished into the 1960s, as the last farms disappeared and the city bought up the remaining parcels. A truck sewage line was installed along the city's length of the creek and some of its grounds became a site for garbage dumping. As one activist in the Friends of Red Hill Valley who led hikes in the valley recalled, "There were old cars and shopping carts, mattresses and all kinds of junk that had been thrown in there and nobody had cleaned it up."

THE RED HILL GETS A HIGHWAY

By the early 1970s the pro–Red Hill expressway forces were mobilizing. Among the most aggressive was the Hamilton Automobile Club, which was founded in 1903 as a sporting and hobby organization for wealthy men, but by the early 1970s it was a policy-driven body focused on the needs of the car driver. The Automobile Club collaborated with the Hamilton Chamber of Commerce in 1973 to produce a report for city politicians and planning staff. Predictably, the two lobby organizations called for a highway between escarpment suburbs and the industrial waterfront, along with the enticement of companies to the new industrial parks on the Mountain. But they also warned against investments in new public transit because of a clash with "the needs and aspirations of the people." The proof lay, it was claimed, in the growth of automobile registrations, which demonstrated "a prefer- ence for personal mobility provided by the car."

Another more powerful player on the pro-expressway side was the Ontario government and its Ministry of Transportation and Commu- nications. A technical advisory committee of non-elected municipal and provincial planners and engineers was formed and it partnered with Hamilton traffic chief Ray Desjardins to "exert pressure" on Hamilton City Council to drop its opposition to a north-south trans- portation corridor through the Red Hill Valley, reports Richard Oddie, the author of a 2008 Ph.D. thesis that is the most exhaustive account of the Red Hill expressway saga.

Marty Hazell had just started as a co-op student at Hamilton City Hall in 1975 and has a vivid memory of his boss's passionate engage- ment with this issue. "Ray was involved in the initial talk about the Red Hill freeway . . . I know myself and another fellow were doing all of the displays for him to take to meetings, to talk about the principles of the freeway, way before it was even conceived."

Desjardins's views dovetailed with those of former city controller Jack MacDonald who was elected in 1976 as mayor of Hamilton on a pro-development/expressway "ambitious city" platform. By the end of the following year both Hamilton City Council and the new regional council of Hamilton-Wentworth had dropped the long-standing policy to leave the Red Hill Valley alone by endorsing, for the first time, an expressway along its snakelike path. "The exact reasons for this abrupt change in position remain unclear to this day," wrote lawyer Michael Jeffrey in his 1982 account of events surrounding the Red Hill in Hamilton.

One explanation, reported Jeffrey, was an ultimatum from the Ontario transportation and communications ministry that Hamilton either seriously examine the Red Hill Creek as a possible route for the north-south expressway crossing the escarpment or lose subsidies for property acquisition work on the planned path for an east-west highway, the future Lincoln Alexander Parkway, on the Mountain.

A detailed account for what transpired next comes from Richard Oddie. The city and region's pro-expressway decisions were challenged by environmental groups, which resulted during the early 1980s in the province setting up joint board hearings involving two representatives of the Ontario Municipal Board (an adjudicator on development decisions by a municipal council, the majority of which were met with approval) and one representative of the Environmental Assessment Board. One challenge for those seeking to preserve the Red Hill Valley was that the Ontario Environmental Assessment Act, which was passed in 1975, excluded municipal projects from having to undergo an environmental assessment.

Joint board hearings were held to deal with policy matters covered by different provincial planning acts. Oddie suggests they represented a political strategy by the province to placate public concerns about what remained wild and natural in the Red Hill Valley within urban Hamilton but not go off the rails. That explains the exclusion from the joint board hearings of two other legislated bodies with a history of concern about the use of the Red Hill and a regulatory say in its natural makeup – the Hamilton and Region Conservation Authority and the Niagara Escarpment Commission. In the end the joint panel in 1985 ruled in favour of the expressway on the Red Hill. Michael Jeffrey, as chair of the Environmental Assessment Board, stated in a lengthy dissent that the expressway proponents had failed to provide traffic demand data to prove that the project was necessary. He was also concerned that the project would "inhibit the preservation of this area as a continuous natural environment and is in fact incompatible with that natural environment."

WHAT IF THE HAMILTON CONSERVATION AUTHORITY HAD GOTTEN ITS WAY?

As early as the 1970s some Hamilton politicians were quietly biding their time, waiting for the right moment to approve a highway on the Red Hill despite the city's official position of maintaining the status quo in the valley. This may explain the city's inaction with regards to opening up the last remaining slice of wilderness within urban Hamilton on the part of the Parks board. Ben Vanderbrug, who still speaks in a soft Dutch accent, had just started what was to be a successful thirty-three-year career as general manager of the Hamilton Conservation Authority.

He and Hamilton parks manager Ernie Seager took the initiative to negotiate a draft agreement whereby 250 acres of Albion Falls (a beautiful, heavily wooded, southerly portion of the valley) would be transferred from the City of Hamilton, the owner of the entire Red Hill Valley, to the conservation authority for a symbolic dollar. This move was in the spirit of a 1968 document, entitled the *Hamilton Region Conservation Report*, from the Ontario government's department of energy and resources management, which directed the conservation authority to do the following: "That the Authority in conjunction with the city of Hamilton maintain the valley of Redhill Creek between Albion Falls and Greenhill Avenue in as natural a state as possible, catering only to such passive recreation activities as nature study, walking for pleasure, winter snow-shoeing or trail skiing, horseback riding and controlled picnicking."

Vanderbrug and Seager had agreed that the conservation authority had the expertise not only to protect Albion Falls but make this area more accessible for the general public with the building of a trail and other services for visitors. To implement their plan the conservation authority would invest $300,000 into this portion of the Red Hill Valley with half coming from provincial coffers. But the Parks board (by then a committee of Hamilton City Council with some non-elected representation) flatly rejected the idea.

Vanderbrug says he personally discovered that it was Jack MacDonald, a powerful member of the Parks board and future mayor (he was not on city council at this point), who put the "kibosh" to the transfer of ownership of Albion Falls to the conservation authority. Apparently, MacDonald had privately raised the price of the 250 acres to $1 million from the symbolic dollar. The new amount was never presented on paper as a formal proposal from the city to the conservation authority, according to Vanderbrug. Instead, it appears the members of the Parks board brought up some technicalities that put the proposed transfer into limbo. "Suddenly, the whole idea of the authority taking over the 250 acres had become a non-issue. We didn't have the money and we stepped away from it," says Vanderbrug.

The background to all of this is that the Hamilton Conservation Authority and its counterparts across Ontario are provincially mandated by the Ontario government through legislation to manage and preserve sensitive local watershed areas. In Hamilton, the local public agency had started out at its inception in 1966 as the Hamilton Region Conservation Authority (before dropping *Region* from the name). Under its first chair, the Honourable Thomas Beckett (then a litigation lawyer and later a judge), there was an aggressive strategy of buying up privately owned vacant lands, particularly in the Dundas Valley, and converting them into protected natural areas. When I interviewed Beckett, now in his nineties, he said it never occurred to him that he was following a tradition set by Thomas McQuesten.

Beckett was also opposed to the province's 1967 proposal to have a four-lane highway "rip through the heart" of the Dundas Valley between Peters Corners (the intersection of Highways 5, 8 and 52) and where Mohawk Road and Highway 403 meet. The project was subsequently killed in face of a fury of opposition from local Ancaster and Dundas residents.

A different outcome awaited the Red Hill Valley. MacDonald is long gone, as are other members of the Parks board, and his side of the story is lost in the mist of history. But Beckett backs up Vanderbrug's account about Albion Falls. "If Ben and Ernie had made their arrangements and MacDonald hadn't interfered the Red Hill Creek Valley would have been in the hands of the conservation authority, or most of it."

As mentioned, there is nothing in the Parks board 1970/71 minutes on the proposed takeover of Albion Falls about what MacDonald wanted to charge and the rejection of what Vanderbrug and Seager had negotiated. Instead, there appeared to be a delay of any decision due to an unresolved property tax dispute between the conservation authority and the Parks board. Vanderbrug says he has no recollection of this and maintains strongly that the minutes do not contain the full story of the negotiated agreement in 1970 with Ernie Seager. He speculates that the conservation authority may have requested a reduction of the property tax for the acquired Albion Falls. "Conservation authority pays taxes on land it holds, it can be substantial, a huge proportion of our budget."

AFTER THE RED HILL VALLEY PARKWAY WINS APPROVAL

The 1985 joint decision by the Ontario Municipal Board (OMB) and the Environmental Appeal Board (EAB) did not end matters for the expressway on the Red Hill. But it emboldened the pro-expressway leadership in Hamilton.

More appeals and further lobbying were undertaken by the environmentalists, delaying construction for two decades. By the 1990s patience was running out at the regional government of Hamilton-Wentworth (governing Hamilton and surrounding municipalities before the 2001 amalgamation). A small minority was creating roadblocks for an expressway that the majority of Hamiltonians wanted, argued Terry Cooke, regional chair of Hamilton-Wentworth. Currently, the head of the Hamilton Community Foundation, the former politician echoed his earlier statement. "There was also a sense of the democratic voice of the community, had manifested itself around this issue and a plan . . . municipal councillors felt a very strong imperative in the electorate to complete what they had started."

This no-nonsense position may also explain Hamilton-Wentworth's decision to boycott the 1999 federal government environmental assessment process. Local politicians like Cooke saw the hand of Sheila Copps (a popular east-end Hamilton MP and deputy PM in the Jean Chrétien Liberal government) as the puppet master behind a scheme to kill the road. "She was involved in a clandestine campaign to scuttle or at the very least delay construction of the project," Cooke told the *Spectator*. But environmentalists were lobbying for the assessment, says Don McLean, then head of the Friends of Red Hill Valley. He also mentions that Ottawa had a legal obligation to investigate whether the proposed Red Hill expressway met the legal requirements of the federal Fisheries Act, since the creek was teeming with a variety of species of fish including salmon.

The federal environmental assessment came to an end in April 2001 after the newly amalgamated City of Hamilton managed to stop the process in its tracks, courtesy of a favourable decision by a Federal Court of Canada judge. But with victory in sight the city was not in a forgiving mood. The city – led by Larry Di Ianni, the newly elected mayor, following the November 10, 2003, municipal election – embarked a year later upon an eleven-year quixotic $75-million lawsuit to punish the federal government scientists at Canada Centre for Inland Waters whose homes were for a period in jeopardy and certain Liberal cabinet ministers including Copps. In the end the city spent a little over $3 million in legal bills. What Hamilton received in the 2015 settlement was a federal harbour property (currently the Discovery Centre) that at least one city councillor, Sam Merulla, says Ottawa was already keen on relinquishing.

"I think the save the valley movement deeply frightened the powerbrokers and they may have been looking for revenge," says McLean.

"And don't underestimate the stupidity of councillors who thought they could shake down the federal government for money or the persuasiveness of the [city lawyer] who had just 'saved' the expressway with his successful legal battle to stop the federal environment assessment."

HAMILTON AS URBAN TRANSPORTATION HUB

The original rationale for the highway on the Red Hill was that a north-south route would serve as a conveyor belt for factory workers between their homes on the upper escarpment and their jobs in the factories in the vicinity of Hamilton Harbour. But circumstances had changed. Between 1981 and 1996 close to half of local manufacturing jobs were lost as industrial companies reduced their workforces and further automated their operations in face of foreign competition. By the end of the twentieth century, the majority of jobs were in the services sector, particularly in health care. As well the loss of its status as a major industrial centre made Hamilton more of an extension of the Greater Toronto Area.

The lower and older city was in decline and so Hamilton City Hall developed the new argument that the Red Hill expressway would serve as the economic engine for new industrial, commercial and residential development on the upper escarpment. In this scenario people would move to suburban developments and possibly be employed in one of the companies enticed to the new industrial parks. Added to the mix was an east-west complementary highway, the future Lincoln Alexander Parkway and the John C. Munro Hamilton International Airport. The airport was always struggling in the shadow of the much larger Pearson International Airport in the Greater Toronto Area.

Hamilton's business and political leaders were now positioning their city as a transportation hub for trade in services and products back and forth across the Canada-US border under free trade with the US and Mexico, says Richard Oddie. What David Cohen would later mock as the "hello-goodbye" city of Hamilton was now a serious official policy.

THE SUMMER OF 2003

Four decades of lobbying, public education campaigns and articles in the Opinion section of the local daily newspaper came to naught for the Friends of Red Hill Valley. Following the abrupt end to the federal environmental assessment there were no more legal hurdles for the city's expressway project. The last item was the upcoming November 2003 municipal election where the future of the Red Hill would emerge as the main issue but the city already had the legal right ahead of the vote to deploy the road construction crews.

Local activist Ken Stone, a veteran of 1960s' protests, anticipated this situation. He had previously warned local politicians that people such as himself were prepared to occupy the valley to prevent the road from being built. The valley preservationists wanted to turn the Red Hill Valley into a large urban park. And so, preparation for non-violent civil disobedience began by a group that came to be known as the "Showstoppers." The name was coined by Larry Di Ianni, the Stoney Creek–based city councillor heading Hamilton's expressway implementation committee before he was elected mayor

At first the prospects were promising. An August 4, 2003, rally against the expressway in the valley attracted hundreds of people. But as the month progressed smaller numbers were showing up to confront the road-building crew from Dufferin Construction, the company contracted by the city to begin work on a bridge at the end of Greenhill Avenue off Mount Albion. Few Hamiltonians were prepared to risk arrest and jail in face of the permanent court injunction issued in September 2003 that banned efforts by the protesters to interfere with the construction of the expressway. One former *Spectator* reporter I interviewed years later says that the opponents of the expressway were essentially ahead of their time. They were making their case before there was an understanding of the threat of climate change – a term that was not widely used in 2003. It is possible that in our age of social media, there would have been a greater ability to communicate and mobilize protest.

On the positive side the Red Hill issue made substantial difference in the lives of those who chose to be engaged at whatever level, according to Hamilton lawyer Jane Mulkewich. "It was a transformative time. It changed people's marriages, people's careers. It changed people's thinking, it inspired new organizations such as Environment Hamilton and the CATCH [Citizens at City Hall]."

THE INDIGENOUS CLAIM TO THE VALLEY

Hamilton still faced a serious hurdle from another source. As early as August 10, 2003, Indigenous protesters living in Hamilton – some if not all were from the Six Nations of the Grand River – had set up a sacred fire and a longhouse a short distance in the valley from where the Showstoppers were facing off against the construction crew. They were backing a Haudenosaunee land claim to the Red Hill Valley that was based on the 1701 Nanfan Treaty with the British Crown and which guaranteed them hunting and fishing rights within what is now known as Southern Ontario. The treaty had received recognition in the Ontario courts and so a legal challenge mounted against the city's highway project was theoretically possible. (The Six Nations community was founded near what is now Brantford following the granting of thousands of acres of land ten kilometres deep on either side of the Grand River to the Haudenosaunee Confederacy after the American War of Independence in 1784.)

As early as mid-2001, Norm Jacobs, a Mohawk elder and a member of the Haudenosaunee Environmental Task Force, began posting signs on trees along walking trails in the Red Hill Valley stating that this was Six Nations land. He did make a temporary exception later in the summer of 2003 for the Showstoppers and supporters from other First Nations who joined the protest that was building up against the city highway project. He had previously pursued a successful campaign against the dumping of waste on Six Nations territory. Jacobs also had strong personal links with the traditional council of hereditary chiefs at the Haudenosaunee Confederacy. This council continues to meet and make decisions based on an historical collective process at Six Nations even after the federal government officially replaced it with an elected band council for the reserve in 1924. (A portion of the Six Nations community today views the elected band council as illegitimate and an imposition by Ottawa.)

Jacobs viewed the preservation of the natural world in the Red Hill Valley "as part of his personal responsibility as a Haudenosaunee," says Susan Hill, a professor of history at the University of Toronto, director of the Centre for Indigenous Studies at the University of Toronto and a Haudenosaunee herself. "One of Norm's key messages was to say 'you don't need to give everything up [in a modern technological society]. But you do need to think about what you are leaving behind because of the compromises you have made.'"

Shortly after his no trespass signs were up, he also put the City of Hamilton on notice that there was insufficient oversight of archaeological material found in the ground during the road construction and linked to a long-standing Indigenous presence in the valley. This was most notably the Neutrals, a Haudenosaunee-related Indigenous people who had inhabited the valley centuries earlier. A petition was presented by Jacobs, demanding full disclosure of city-sponsored archaeological digs, courtesy of an untendered contract with a private company.

Jacobs addressed city hall and received local media attention. Of particular concern for Hamilton politicians was a potential Indigenous disruption of their expressway plans. Then law student Jane Mulkewich was in charge of the legal fund to back a court challenge by Larry Green, who was also a Mohawk. He was one of the original Indigenous firekeepers based in the longhouse that was constructed as part of the valley protest. A few prominent lawyers with a background in Indigenous jurisprudence were assembled to fight the case.

But Jacobs's death from cancer in the late summer of 2003 created a vacuum in the Indigenous opposition to the Red Hill expressway. In the spring of 2004 Green dropped his legal claim against the city when the Haudenosaunee Confederacy reached a settlement on the Red Hill with the city. (The separate Six Nations–elected band council stayed away from these discussions.) The only financial compensation in the deal consisted of the awarding of a tree-planting contract for the valley to a Six Nations company following the construction of the expressway.

One explanation for the confederacy's move is that the Hamilton city officials were hell-bent on seeing the project built and there was nothing legally available to stop them at the end of 2003. In retrospect, Susan Hill views the result as ultimately "progressive" because this was the first time that any level of government in Canada was willing to sit down with a traditionalist Six Nations administration that had no official status. "The Confederacy got a pretty good deal considering they couldn't stop the expressway. They managed to set up a framework for the recognition of rights and maybe of the medicinal plants [in the Red Hill Valley] which is huge. There's an active effort [in Hamilton] to protect, collect, maintain, build and enrich the medicinal plants in the valley."

THE 2003 ELECTION

The contentious mayoralty race in the 2003 Hamilton municipal election helped to decide the Red Hill issue once and for all. Mayoralty candidate and former Stoney Creek councillor Larry Di Ianni successfully ran on the virtues of the project and managed to polarize the contest against his anti-expressway opponent, David Christopherson, a former city councillor and ex-NDP provincial cabinet minister. Christopherson understood what he faced and promised a compromise: a post-election city council vote that would determine once and for all if the project would go ahead. Valley preservationists had no choice but to support Christopherson but this stance did not endear him to the commuters living in working-class communities on the Mountain and in the northeast of the city. These normally labour- and NDP-leaning citizens swung over to Di Ianni to the tune of 51 per cent, leaving Christopherson with 39 per cent of the vote. Less than half of the electorate turned out to vote. "There was a huge pent-up desire to see this road built. I was just either bold enough or tough enough or strategic enough to seize the moment to say we're doing it. I wasn't timid about it," Di Ianni recalls in retrospect.

Di Ianni was also the recipient of fulsome support from Hamilton's home-building and trucking industries, both of which were to benefit from the expressway. His campaign manager told the *Hamilton Spectator* that Di Ianni had managed to raise as much as $250,000 in campaign funds, $120,000 of which was spent on TV, radio and print advertising. His backers included such powerful local figures as Terry Cooke, the former regional chair; Joe Mancinelli, vice president of Labourers' International Union of North America; Tony Battaglia, CEO of TradePort International (the company running the John C. Munro Hamilton International Airport); the De Santis developer family, owners of Multi-Area Developments; and Jeff Paikin, president of Hamilton-Halton Home Builders' Association.

Peter Graefe, a McMaster University political scientist, says an underfunded mayoral candidate backed by the valley preservationists faced a well-financed media campaign from the elite figures and companies in Hamilton backing Di Ianni. He says the pro-expressway side made questionable promises about jobs remaining in the city and local residents not having to commute a great distance if the Red Hill was constructed. At the same time the *Hamilton Spectator* was brimming with advertising from a home-building industry that would ultimately benefit if the highway was built to service new suburban and car-dependent communities. "The elite organs in the city did not actually allow for a proper debate with a clear airing of likely facts about this expressway and its impact," Graefe explained.

Echoing this concern was Joan Little, a former Burlington alderman and Halton councillor in a *Spectator* column following the election. "Both the Spec's and CHTVs pre-coverage on Hamilton's mayoralty race appeared to me to be one-sided – little exposure for David Christopherson, much on Larry Di Ianni. Then 'local' CHTV deemed the vote too trivial to pre-empt sitcoms before 10 p.m. – an insult to citizens who care about their communities." David Christopherson frankly told the *Spectator* that he lost because his campaign ran out of money and thus could not compete effectively against Di Ianni. "At the end of the day, money's still a big factor in elections."

Following Di Ianni's victory nothing stood in the way of the bulldozers and the highway construction crew except for a handful of idealistic young people. In an act of civil disobedience defying an injunction against any interference with the city project, they had positioned themselves high in the trees on plywood platforms and were supplied with food and other necessary items by supporters on the ground. Seven tree sitters lasted as long as 103 days and afterward faced civil contempt charges and court costs that were potentially "ruinous," wrote a sympathetic *Hamilton Spectator* reporter. But "common sense had prevailed," stated Bill Dunphy and the city abandoned a legal action designed primarily to punish these environmentalists. In a settlement the majority of the tree sitters individually agreed to pay fines and court costs (comprising a still hefty $15,000 per person), allow the highway project to proceed, not counsel or incite anyone to do further disruption and stay out of this section of Red Hill Valley. One held out for a court appeal and another person went AWOL.

A different kind of gathering occurred in late June 2004 at the corner of Upper Albion and Rymal, involving about three hundred celebrants.

A groundbreaking ceremony was taking place to mark the first homes to be constructed in the $1-billion Summit Park suburban residential project between Trinity Church Road, Highway 56 and Rymal on the Mountain. The *Hamilton Spectator* reporter covering the event remarked that the "reverent crowds" inside a makeshift tent reminded her of the excitement surrounding Barnum & Bailey Circus and "the Greatest Show on Earth." Newly elected Hamilton mayor Di Ianni and other elected pro-expressway councillors were on hand to congratulate Aldo De Santis, the president of Multi-Area Developments and the builder of this new suburban community.

The future of Summit Park was clearly dependent on the approval for the construction of an expressway on the Red Hill. Multi-Area Developments and the De Santis family were major backers of Larry Di Ianni and other pro-expressway candidates for council in the November 2003 municipal election, donating $25,000. Two years later in the February 5, 2005, coverage of the annual Hamilton-Halton Homebuilders' Association the *Hamilton Spectator* described the keynote speaker for "the state of the city," Mayor Di Ianni, as "a white knight on a steed" for what he had accomplished for local residential construction. More than a decade later Summit Park is still selling single-family homes for a planned ten-thousand-person community.

After all of the hoopla Di Ianni did not last more than one term as mayor. He lost the subsequent mayoralty race in 2006 because of the publicity surrounding his pleading guilty to six charges of accepting campaign donations for the 2003 contest that were greater than the legal limit set by the Ontario Municipal Elections Act. Another thirty-five charges were withdrawn. He was the first public official ever convicted under the Ontario Municipal Elections Act. Di Ianni was ordered to pay $4,500 to a charity and write an essay about his experience as a lesson learned for *Municipal World* magazine.

In retrospect, the pavers and Hamilton's large commuting population found common cause, remarks independent journalist Joey

Coleman, who normally sides with the urbanists and progressives in his city. But as a young person growing up poor in the 1980s and 1990s on Congress Crescent on the east side of the Red Hill Creek, he identified with the widely held sentiment that the expressway would take away the noisy and foul-smelling diesel trucks clogging up the north-south arteries connected to the upper escarpment such as Centennial Park Drive.

"The big selling point for the expressway on the east side was the trucks and diesel pollution would be taken quickly up to the Mountain. It wouldn't be on our streets anymore." Coleman sensed a definite antagonism between the more affluent expressway opponents in west-end neighbourhoods like Westdale and people like himself in the lower economic environs of northeast Hamilton.

But Lynda Lukasik provides another point of view as a former losing anti-expressway candidate for city council in a northeast Hamilton ward in the 2003 election. An environmentalist with a Ph.D. in planning, Lukasik disagrees with the notion that the Red Hill Valley Parkway reduced the congestion on those north-south arterial routes to and from the upper escarpment. She counters that while trucks are more likely to use the Red Hill Valley Parkway to reach their destinations, other forms of traffic have replaced them and are now crowding the north-south routes including Centennial Park Drive.

"The Red Hill may have solved the truck traffic issue on Centennial. Some of those residents had it in their mind that trucks on the expressway would reduce traffic volume. That was a little ridiculous because the municipality was quietly releasing studies during the Red Hill days where they were admitting that as soon as the expressway was built more development on the upper escarpment was going to mean traffic volumes would ultimately exceed pre-expressway volumes," says Lukasik. She adds that had the Red Hill not proceeded, the city might have been forced to approach land use and development in a more "creative" manner.

REPERCUSSIONS:
AFTER THE RED HILL VALLEY PARKWAY GETS BUILT

The Red Hill Valley Parkway was finally open to traffic in 2007. The name was adopted to reflect "early modernist visions of a carefully engineer[ed] road seamlessly integrated with the surrounding landscape," observes Richard Oddie. Hamiltonians themselves simply use the name "Red Hill" to refer to the expressway. And that makes sense because, notwithstanding efforts by the city engineers to restore the original natural path of the Red Hill Creek, it remains a seriously diminished presence. People do not visit the creek anymore to escape the noise and stress of the city. "I'm almost afraid to go back because I'm afraid of what I might see there," says Walter Peace, the editor of *From Mountain to Lake: The Red Hill Creek Valley*, the definitive text on the valley.

His childhood memory starts with a relatively untouched strip of fields and trees running along the Red Hill Creek from the mouth of Lake Ontario to Albion Falls on top of the Niagara Escarpment. Peace grew up as a child on Cochrane Road in working-class east Hamilton and played on occasion in the valley near his home. There was a baseball diamond nearby. He also attended classes up to grade six at Red Hill Public School. Distant relatives farmed for generations right up to the 1960s in the southerly portion of the Red Hill Valley. The Peace farmhouse still stands as a preserved heritage site today.

The professor is a walking repository of basic knowledge and lore about the valley. *From Mountain to Lake*, a collected volume that Peace both edited and contributed to, covers the valley's geological past, its long-standing Indigenous presence and the clear-cutting of forests and wetlands by early nineteenth-century European settlers. Peace's book was published in 1998 at a time when the valley's fate was already "shrouded in uncertainty and controversy" (his words in the preface). A Conservative government in Ontario had proceeded after its 1995 election victory to restore funding for the proposed Red Hill expressway after it had been withdrawn by the previous NDP administration led by Bob Rae. Peace and others in Hamilton, including the local conservation authority, saw a need to document the history and environment in the Red Hill Valley ahead of the impending road construction.

"So that's how we got started on the book project," the professor recalls. As a young person he was not fully acquainted with the valley's history until it became the basis in the later 1970s for his M.A. thesis. "There's an awful lot of stuff that I learned that I didn't know. I spent much of my life to that point in that area. So, it was really important. And it just furthered my resolve that I was against the project – perhaps just too personal for me."

The challenge for the valley preservationists was that many Hamiltonians had little awareness of a natural area tucked away in the post–World War II industrial northeast suburb. The Friends of Red Hill Valley sought to remedy this in the 1990s by leading hikes in the valley. Their purpose was to counter a widely held perception that the Red Hill Valley was an eyesore after years of degradation. Sewage was present in the creek, and garbage and industrial wastes had been dumped or were buried in the valley (especially in the vicinity of Hamilton Harbour).

A different picture of the valley was made available earlier in 1995 by the Hamilton Region Conservation Authority and the Hamilton Naturalists' Club in a joint research project. Among the findings was that there were close to six hundred different plants, twenty-four types of mammals, forty-five varieties of butterflies, 136 types of moths, eighteen species of fish, fifteen species of amphibians and reptiles, and seventy-eight different kinds of birds bred in the Red Hill Valley. Since traffic began going up and down the Red Hill Valley Parkway no credible independent study has been conducted to update the biological state of the valley. Questions remain such as what is happening to the migratory birds or even the air quality, McMaster University professor of biology James Quinn explains.

"There was a wildlife corridor connecting the escarpment to Lake Ontario, it was a heavily used wildlife corridor. [The highway] totally destroyed that corridor. It is a matter of the inability of species to use that corridor. It is no longer a corridor; there are species that have to remain under cover, when they are moving along in the forested landscape and all of a sudden, the forest ends. That's the end of the road."

Fellow biologist and Friends of Red Hill Valley activist Dr. Joseph Minor estimated that at the height of the debate the city had cut down forty-seven thousand trees in the Red Hill Valley during the road construction. However, the city maintained that a lower number of eleven thousand trees were removed. "Either way, there is no denying the fact that the valley was heavily wooded and a huge amount of vegetation was removed for the expressway. This would have a number of negative effects on the environment," he says.

"But the overall environmental effects are far worse than simple land clearance. The cleared land was sealed with asphalt, which further negatively affects the environment. If the pavement was allowed to sit idle, then the damage would stop there, but it doesn't. It gets worse. Thousands of vehicles travel up and down the valley spewing pollution."

Deteriorating air quality is occurring in the immediate vicinity of the Red Hill Valley Parkway according to a published 2009 academic study by the School of Geography and Earth Sciences at McMaster University, reported in the article "An Exploration of Issues Related to the Study of Generated Traffic and Other Impacts Arising from Highway Improvements." This stems from the increase in the emissions of carbon monoxide, hydrocarbons and nitrogen oxide from the increase in cars and trucks on the road.

In addition, Cancer Care Ontario in its 2016 *Prevention System Quality Index* reported that downtown Hamilton had the worst municipal air quality in Ontario.

THE DEAL WITH THE HAUDENOSAUNEE

One feature of the 2004 deal reached between the city and the Haudenosaunee Confederacy was the establishment of a stewardship board for the Red Hill Valley. This body has joint municipal and Six Nations representation and carries a budget of $150,000 from the city. It has been delegated to develop a master plan for valley ecological restoration. After years of discussion and reports there is an impasse between the two sides, says Sheri Longboat, a Haudenosaunee Mohawk and band member of the Six Nations of the Grand River who currently teaches environmental design at the University of Guelph.

"A formal master plan was not announced," she explains. Longboat says the differences of opinions between city and Haudenosaunee representatives on the joint stewardship board arose from the "different worldviews and hence approaches to planning" that typically arise in any "cross-cultural collaboration." As a start the city has negotiated a deal with the Haudenosaunee for four contemplative areas along the Red Hill Valley trail. The Turtle, Eel, Bear and Nest are all marked in the form of rocks and plants.

The objectives of the joint steward board of the Red Hill Valley include a commitment to "acknowledge and honour ancestral experiences," along with the establishment of an environmental interpretive centre and ecological restoration. However, progress still appears to be slow and largely invisible on the education front. An unknown number of Indigenous artifacts found in the valley during the construction phase and dating back eleven thousand years in some cases still sit in storage in Toronto rather than on permanent display in Hamilton in a public facility. Ward 5 city councillor Chad Collins, explains that finding a suitable location within the escarpment overlooking the Red Hill Valley is expensive and challenging.

"It falls within the Niagara Escarpment Commission lands which are very strict in terms of what can be hooked in or around the escarpment. There are servicing challenges. It is quite a way away from water and sewage services. But for us, just looking at the site, in a perfect world it would make an ideal location for an interpretive educational centre because of the view of the Valley. There's a connection between the Valley and the escarpment itself," he says.

All this reflects the reality that the proponents for preserving the Red Hill Valley faced an uphill battle in both Indigenous and non-Indigenous communities in Hamilton. At the same time what has inspired local environmental activists who fought and lost at Red Hill and continue with other battles is the story of the Dish with One Spoon. About a thousand years before contact with European settlers the Haudenosaunee and the Anishinaabe reached an understanding to protect and conserve what was bountiful and fertile here in southern Ontario, including Hamilton and the Niagara Peninsula. They reached an understanding to share space for agriculture, hunting and fishing. It carries special resonance for those who worry about the diminishing of nature.

THE BATTLE CONTINUES

You cannot talk about the Red Hill without mentioning Don McLean who led the opposition starting in the early 1990s to its construction through his writing, lobbying and activism. It has been commented that he successfully made the transition from a one-issue activist to a weekly commentator through his column that appears both on the Citizens at City Hall website and in *View* magazine on a whole host of messy aspects of local city hall decision making. Currently, his big subject is climate change and it is reflected in his activity with Hamilton 350.

Clearly Hamilton is a tough political nut to crack for even the most committed environmentalist around. The Red Hill Valley Parkway is here to stay. Nobody here, not even Don McLean, is talking of following the examples set in Paris and Seoul, Korea, of reducing and even dismantling highways. Indeed, we appear to be going backward in Ontario. Just when I thought such big projects were over, along comes an Ontario provincial government scheme under Doug Ford to build a new multi-billion toll-based highway across agricultural fields, forest, wetlands and a portion of the Greenbelt in neighbouring York, Peel and Halton.

Incidentally, the heavily used Red Hill Valley Parkway, which was built for about $245 million, continues to attract controversy. In 2019 a judicial inquiry was established to investigate the suppression of information by Hamilton City Hall staff. It involves a 2013 internal safety report detailing slippery conditions on the accident-prone parkway. There is currently an outstanding $250-million lawsuit by family members of parkway crash victims. Here, Don McLean offers some insight. He says that accidents are inevitable on this highway because it follows the winding path of the Red Hill Creek and is thus a potential death trap for so-called stunt drivers (a commonly discussed phenomenon in the Hamilton car culture). A March 4, 2019, article in the *Hamilton Spectator* reported that more than 40 per cent of vehicle crashes on the Red Hill Valley Parkway between 2013 and 2018 occurred in a less than four-kilometre stretch of the northbound lanes heading towards the QEW, nearly four hundred reported collisions between Mud Street West and King Street East. During that time period there were 982 crashes on the entire parkway with 249 crashes on the ramps.

WHAT WOULD McQUESTEN THINK?

McQuesten is held up as a hero by Hamilton's conservationists. Yet his first biographer, John Best, in an April 2000 letter to the *Hamilton Spectator* rightly emphasized that Thomas McQuesten was also a major road builder, responsible for the Sherman and Kenilworth Access roads to open up the Mountain, in addition to the QEW. McQuesten also had no objections to the placing of the King's Golf Course in the valley. What is undeniable is that he viewed highways as an efficient means for travel as long as the drivers were not reckless. The other biographer, Mary Anderson, emphasizes in her book that McQuesten, as the Ontario Minister of Highways in the 1930s, was uncomfortable with the speed of drivers on the QEW. He threatened to suspend driver licences and impound vehicles but his campaigns for auto safety had no impact, she writes. "Safety became a major moral issue for Tom as traffic and fatalities increased. He struggled in Parliament [i.e., the Ontario legislature], making many speeches in an attempt to establish and enforce speed limits. Many members were lobbying for removal on the grounds that the speed limit, which in 1935 was 35 miles an hour, was being ignored and was not being enforced." It appears that McQuesten understood the dangers cars posed early on.

References

Anderson, Mary. *Tragedy & Triumph: Ruby & Thomas B. McQuesten.* Dundas, ON: Tierceron Press, 2011.

Best, John. "Parks Pioneer Was Also A Road Builder." Letter to the Editor. *Hamilton Spectator,* April 3, 2000.

Bouchier, Nancy B., and Ken Cruikshank. *The People and the Bay: A Social and Environmental History of Hamilton Harbour.* Vancouver: UBC Press, 2016.

"Business Owners Attack One-Way Streets." *Hamilton Spectator.* Quoted in Leach, Jason. "Downtown Business Rail Against One-Way Streets." Raise the Hammer, June 7, 2010, https://www.raisethehammer.org/blog/1758/downtown_businesses _rail_against_one-way_streets.

Dunphy, Bill. "Red Hill Tree-Sitters Cheered Judge's Ruling." *Hamilton Spectator,* July 13, 2005.

Hill, Susan. "'Travelling Down the River of Life Together in Peace and Friendship Forever': Haudenosaunee Land Ethics and Treaty Arrangements as the Basis for Restructuring the Relationship with the British Crown." In *In Lighting the Eighth Fire: The Liberation, Resurgence and Protection of Indigenous Nations,* edited by Leanne Simpson. Winnipeg: ARP Books, 2008.

Jeffrey, Michael, A. Ball and M. Henderson. *In the Matter of an undertaking of the Regional Municipality of Hamilton-Wentworth to develop and construct the Mountain East-West and North-South Transportation Corridor to connect Highway 403 in Ancaster to the Queen Elizabeth Way in the eastern portion of the City of Hamilton; and ancillary matters related thereto.* Toronto: Office of Consolidated Hearings, 1985.

Johnston, Bill. "You Have to Sell Your Views, Says One-Way Traffic Chief." *Hamilton Spectator*, June 30, 1983.

Kang, Hejun, Darren Scott, Pavlos S. Kanaroglou and Hanna Maoh. "An Exploration of Issues Related to the Study of Generated Traffic and Other Impacts Arising from Highway Improvements." *Environment and Planning B: Planning and Design* 36, no. 1 (February 2009): 67–85.

Leach, Jason. "Downtown Business Rail Against One-Way Streets." Raise the Hammer, June 7, 2010, https://www.raisethehammer.org/blog/1758/downtown_businesses _rail_against_one-way_streets.

Maclean, Don. CATCH: Citizens at City Hall. http://hamiltoncatch.org.

Oddie, Richard. "Alternate Routes, New Pathways: Development, Democracy and the Political Ecology of Transportation in Hamilton, Ontario." Ph.D. diss., York University, 2009.

O'Reilly, Nicole. "Crash Hot Spots on the Red Hill Valley Parkway." *Hamilton Spectator*, March 4, 2019.

Peace, Walter, ed. *From Mountain to Lake: The Red Hill Valley Creek*. Hamilton: printed by the author, 1998.

Rockwell, Margaret. "Modernism and the Functional City: Urban Renewal in Hamilton, Ontario and Buffalo, New York (1949–1974)." Ph.D. diss., McMaster University, 2013.

Silverman, Caroline, Maria Chu, Alison Rothwell, Penney Kirby, Mohammad Haque, Marcia Bassier-Paltoo, Corinne Hodgson, et al. *2016 Prevention System Quality*. Toronto: Cancer Care Ontario, 2016.

Sleightholm, Sherry. "Residential Boom, Hamilton Poised for Unprecedented Growth." *Hamilton Spectator*, February 5, 2005.

———. "Unique Living New Era of Housing at Summit Park." *Hamilton Spectator*, June 26, 2004.

Smith, Wilbur. "Operational Analysis of One-Way Streets (1957)." Local History and Archives, Hamilton Public Library.

Walters, Joan. "City's powerful helped elect Di Ianni." *Hamilton Spectator*, November 12, 2003.

Whitehern Historical Museum, the multi-generation McQuesten residence. www .hamilton.ca/attractions/hamilton-civic-museums/whitehern-historic-house -garden-national-historic-site.

The Challenge of Ethical Development: Sky Dragon and Downtown Gentrification

Kevin MacKay

The Sky Dragon Community Development Co-operative was present in Hamilton's downtown long before the core began its headlong rush into the jaws of urban gentrification. In early 2000 the downtown was a textbook example of rust-belt blight, yet in a mere fifteen-year stretch the narrative has been completely inverted, and today downtown Hamilton could serve as a classic example of successful urban renewal. Like many of the small arts businesses and organizations that took root in the core in the late '90s and early 2000s, the Sky Dragon Co-op envisioned a revitalization quite different from what eventually transpired. When the co-op was founded there was a sense of common purpose downtown, and a belief that development could be ethical, not predatory; that it could build community, not displace and disperse it.

This is not to say that the changes in downtown Hamilton have all been negative. After a decade of grassroots development by a gritty homegrown arts community, an explosion of new growth has once more transformed the core. The real estate market is one of the hottest in Canada, investment is flooding in from Toronto and the downtown has once more regained its status as a cultural and business centre. Buildings are being renovated, businesses are being opened and people have returned to the core to live and work. If this is gentrification, then downtown Hamilton arguably needed *some* measure of it. And yet, each positive development has come with considerable cost. Most of the poor and working class have been either physically displaced through new development or priced out of downtown by skyrocketing rents. Many of the first creative businesses have also succumbed to the flood of big-money development – the small galleries and boutiques that drove the renaissance are now closed to make way for higher end fare. The once tight-knit downtown community has largely scattered – some finding root on Ottawa Street, some further east on Barton Street. To many that put their roots down in Hamilton's abandoned core and breathed it back to life, the change has been lightning quick. Gentrification, long dismissed as scaremongering by uncritical boosters of downtown development, is now an incontrovertible fact.

Hamilton's transformation raises questions about whether urban revitalization must always end up displacing marginal populations, destroying grassroots arts communities and exacerbating inequality. The Sky Dragon Co-operative was formed by a group of long-time Hamilton activists to promote an ethical, sustainable approach to community development. The co-op was able to realize some aspects of this alternative vision, but ultimately failed to achieve its larger goal of steering Hamilton's revitalization in a progressive direction. As Executive Director of the co-op and a long-time resident of downtown Hamilton, I have begun to reflect on what our organization's experience says about the challenges inherent in sustainable community development. It is my hope that understanding the tensions and contradictions that confronted Sky Dragon can help us tackle future problems of community development in Hamilton. More broadly, telling Sky Dragon's story might just improve the chances of success for other organizations, and other communities, struggling to control the process of development.

GROWTH AMIDST THE CRACKS

The Sky Dragon Co-operative emerged through a very organic process of engagement with the City of Hamilton and its inhabitants. I came to Hamilton in 1989 as a student in the visual art program at McMaster University. I moved from Sarnia, which in ways is a smaller version of Hamilton. For the first few years of my studies I lived in the Westdale student ghetto. First on Leland Avenue, then on Whitney, then on Merricourt. The university and student housing were my life, and the downtown was a rundown and depressing place. What I didn't realize at the time was that I was encountering Hamilton just as the city was buckling under an unprecedented wave of industrial job losses and economic hardship. In the '80s the Otis Elevator and Firestone plants had closed, and by the early '90s layoffs at Stelco and Dofasco had both factories operating at half their historical employment numbers.

The industrial job losses of the '80s and '90s impacted other local businesses, and Hamilton's once vibrant downtown began decaying to the state that I first encountered in the early '90s. Economies are interconnected systems – for better *and* for worse. If a new factory or other major employer enters a community, it brings a bump in car purchases, housing starts and new retail businesses. However, if you've lost your job, you don't eat at restaurants, buy expensive new clothing, trade up in the housing market or go to the theatre.

While I completed my undergrad at McMaster the economic situation only grew worse, and by 2001 the *Hamilton Spectator* was reporting that, "by just about any measure, Hamilton's downtown is seriously ill." Businesses were closing, storefronts were empty and buildings were falling into disrepair. "Downtown decay" and "downtown revitalization" became oft-repeated phrases in the debates at city council and in community meetings. Slowly, a sense of fatalism crept in, leading one city bureaucrat to infamously (and inaccurately) declare, "We have to understand that the businesses won't be coming back."

While the downtown imploded and working families struggled to make ends meet, one of the interesting side effects of urban blight began to unfold. As the city core became a no-go zone for many, its empty buildings, cheap rents and beautifully decaying architecture became a magnet for artists of all types. Empty storefronts slowly turned into grassroots art galleries, and the many cavernous upper floor spaces became studios where an avant-garde underground thrived. In 1994 I became one of these artists, first taking a second-floor studio at James and Rebecca Streets with a friend, then in 1996 moving to a space on the third floor of 24 King Street East – the stately Minden Building that overlooked Gore Park.

At 24 King East I first opened up the Screaming Thing Studio/ Gallery with a number of other artists. Gallery shows of local visual artists were punctuated by music and performance art events. Rent was incredibly cheap ($200 a month for approximately 1,800 square feet), especially considering that I lived in the studio space as well. The habitation was illegal, but was commonplace, with most of the artists downtown living "on the sly" in their commercial studio or gallery spaces. The elderly Minden sisters – one living in Montreal, the other in New York – had a soft spot for young artists. As long as we kept up the spaces, rent would stay cheap, and a student like me could keep myself afloat on OSAP, odd jobs and epic help-pay-the-rent art parties.

I eventually came to inhabit two floors at 24 King, and as my studies moved from art to politics and ecology, the space began taking on a more community-minded, activist character. It also became a place to pursue twin passions for martial arts and meditation, leading the Sky Dragon Zendo to be formed. The zendo had martial arts, meditation and qigong classes several days each week, with Sifu Paul Stiles (a gold sash Master of the Sunny Tang Wing Chun lineage) overseeing instruction, and myself assisting. When the gallery closed and a new community space emerged, the name Sky Dragon stuck. It referenced heaven and earth, yin and yang, and seemed like a more poetic name than the Hamilton Community Development Organization. Instead, in 2002 the Sky Dragon Community Development Co-operative was born.

A number of experiences contributed to the creation of Sky Dragon. First was my involvement in the battle to save Hamilton's Red Hill Valley from expressway development. The Red Hill fight introduced me to a community of activists, and also gave me a crash course on ecology, community organizing, economics and local political corruption. Another formative experience was attending the April 2001 Summit of the Americas protest in Quebec City. I arrived in Quebec City as a naive idealist and returned home fully radicalized. My partner was arrested at the protest and held for three days in Orsainville prison, on the outskirts of the city. We were both tear-gassed, and I was also concussion-grenaded and shot with plastic bullets.

In 2002 I travelled to Ottawa to take an internship at the North-South Institute (NSI) – at the time a prestigious research institute that focused on global trade and finance. The NSI was primarily concerned with poverty reduction, and the four months I spent there increased my understanding of how global capitalism leads to constant misery, warfare and ecological destruction for most of the world's people. It was at the institute that I made my first presentation on the Sky Dragon Community Development Co-operative. It was presented as a model of how economies in the global north could be community-centred, socially just and ecologically sustainable. The incisive feedback I received from the research team was invaluable in developing Sky

Dragon. Sadly, the NSI was later defunded during the Harper years, and the incredible group of scholars was scattered.

THE SKY DRAGON CO-OPERATIVE

The Sky Dragon Co-operative was envisioned as a way to translate a radical critique of macro-level societal dysfunction into a viable, local alternative. Industrial capitalism is predicated on a precarious workforce, growing inequality between rich and poor, unpredictable global markets that regularly destroy local economies, an oligarchic political structure and an inexorable exhaustion of ecosystems. To counter this, the co-operative intended to develop community projects based on triple-bottom-line sustainability – economic, social and ecological. There were numerous needs that we envisioned the co-op meeting – good jobs, community spaces, affordable housing, green building and political advocacy. The co-op would strive to make each project economically viable, and to return any surplus income to a development fund that would seed the next project. Community need and the vision of the co-op's members would determine new projects, and each development would be controlled by the people who ran it and used its services. At its most ambitious, the co-op was inspired by the Mondragon Cooperative – the Spanish network of worker-owned businesses that collectively employed over seventy thousand people, and which had succeeded in creating a massive system of social ownership in the midst of a hostile capitalist order. Sky Dragon wanted to be the Canadian Mondragon, and we thought of no better place to start this network of ethical development than in Hamilton.

Sky Dragon was also intended to be an organization that would create inclusive community. The founding directors had all been long-time activists in different progressive causes, and each had encountered the limitations of an "ultra-radical" politics based on small, marginal groups that prized ideological purity above organizing effectiveness. Thus, while Sky Dragon was definitely a child of the political left, it rejected sectarianism and instead sought to build common understanding and collective action among a broad spectrum of individuals, communities and organizations. To this end, our members reached out equally to labour, environmentalists, women's groups, Indigenous activists, artists and the queer community.

In 2002 the group that would become the first directors of Sky Dragon was assembled. Along with myself, the co-op included Dr. Graeme MacQueen and Dr. Don Wells, two McMaster professors with long histories of social justice activism; Dan Smith, an old friend who combined progressive working-class politics with an MBA in finance; Rashne Baetz, an environmental engineer; and Philippa Tattersall, a physician at the North Hamilton Community Health Centre. In 2004 the co-op incorporated as a non-profit worker co-operative.

Each member of the Sky Dragon board brought a passion for sustainable development and for renewing Hamilton's downtown core. To us *renewal* meant a halt to the frustrating process of "demolition by neglect," in which the city's architectural heritage was left to rot by absentee owners, and then torn down to create parking lots. We wanted to see the adaptive reuse of the core's old buildings, and their transformation into affordable housing, artistic and community spaces, and locally owned businesses. Our first step would be to create the Sky Dragon Centre – a living example of ethical development. It would be a multi-use community centre and affordable housing development located in a newly renovated heritage building. It was intended to be a concrete example of the kind of alternative politics and economics that until then had only existed as an abstraction.

Finding a property and raising the needed capital to purchase and renovate it became the immediate concerns of the co-op. To this end we did exhaustive community outreach – holding meetings, asking for letters of support, contacting our local politicians. We also reached out to the City of Hamilton – then owner of numerous abandoned properties in the downtown core – seeking a partnership.

The response to our outreach was revealing, with enthusiastic feedback and support from community organizations and local politicians and an almost complete dismissal by city bureaucrats. Managers of the city's property portfolio disdainfully told us that we were free to purchase any building "at market value." Staff from the department of Downtown Renewal routinely failed to show up to scheduled meetings and made their lack of interest in our project painfully clear when they did deign to appear. Equally revealing was the complete indifference we met from nearly every charitable foundation and public fund that we approached with our project proposal. Trillium, the Atkinson Foundation, the Laidlaw Foundation, the Hamilton Community Foundation, United Way and the Canadian Alternative Investment Co-operative were just a few that refused to even consider supporting Sky Dragon.

In the face of near-universal rejection by traditional sources of non-profit funding, the co-op realized that we would need to raise our own capital and take a creative approach to financing. What we *did* have was community support and the willingness of co-op members and volunteers to put sweat and effort into building the Sky Dragon Centre. After consultation with the Catalyst Centre, another non-profit worker co-operative based in Toronto, we decided to sell $1,000 community bonds to raise sufficient capital to purchase and renovate a building. In late 2004 we started selling bonds, and also started holding regular events at 24 King Street East. Dance and animation classes, film screenings and activist talks started building a community of supporters around the co-op. This was further enhanced in May of 2005 by beginning publication of *Mayday Magazine*, a progressive monthly newsmagazine edited by local artists Matt Jelly and Lauren Olson.

The co-op's early development was given crucial support by one outside source – the Canadian co-operative community. Through the Ontario Co-operative Association Sky Dragon was able to secure money to incorporate, while the federal Co-operatives Secretariat provided funds for us to hire two staff on limited contract to begin programming at 24 King and to found *Mayday Magazine*. The support of the co-operative community, although modest, was constant throughout Sky Dragon's development, and reflects the unique characteristics of grassroots co-operatives. Only co-operative developers were willing to help start a new organization with a radical vision and a commitment to self-sustainability.

THE SKY DRAGON CENTRE

As an organization with no capital, Sky Dragon needed a special set of circumstances to secure and renovate a building – either an owner willing to work with the co-op, or the city willing to partner on a property they owned. Through 2004 and 2005 Sky Dragon looked at several buildings, twice making detailed development proposals for specific properties. Both of these proposals failed. However, in early 2005 Jeremy Freiburger, a friend of the co-op, connected us with Margaret Ashfield, the owner of an over one-hundred-year-old, three-storey brick building on King William Street. The building was perfect – a manageable size and right in the city core. Margaret's family had owned the building for over forty years, and she was willing to sell. Luckily, she was also community-minded and was open to working with our organization on its vision of downtown renewal.

At the time Sky Dragon had no cash, but did have about $15,000 in pledged community bonds. Luckily, Sky Dragon also had Dan Smith and his knowledge of finance. Dan and the board developed a plan to sign a six-month lease-to-own agreement with Margaret Ashfield for a predetermined sale price. Then, the co-op would work furiously to renovate the property, such that at the end of the lease period, we could get the building appraised at significantly higher than the agreed-on sale price. The difference in equity would then help Sky Dragon secure a mortgage for the purchase and a line of credit to finish the renovations. The plan was risky, but the co-op went ahead regardless, taking occupancy of 27 King William in July of 2005. After two lease extensions, an intensive community bond drive and long days put in by a largely volunteer construction crew, in 2006 Sky Dragon was able to appraise the building at $300,000. This then allowed the co-op to obtain a mortgage with the Teachers Credit Union for the $204,000 purchase price and to secure a $40,000 line of credit to help finish the building renovations. Against steep odds, the Sky Dragon Centre became a reality.

Securing a property severely taxed Sky Dragon's capacity, but the co-operative would soon realize that the entire process of community development is unpredictable, challenging and stressful. Our original plan for sustaining the building was to create a learning centre on the ground floor; however, the woman intended to head up the centre suddenly secured a job running an English school in Korea. With our main source of learning centre expertise gone, the co-op quickly switched to Plan B – opening a fair trade/organic café. This had more financial risk, but ended up being an important driver of the centre's community outreach and community development work. In late 2006 the Bread and Roses Café was established by new co-op member Karen Burson and quickly became a vibrant cultural and artistic space.

Before Bread and Roses opened its doors, the renovated basement and ground floor of the centre were already hosting numerous events. Local non-profits held meetings, the Hamilton Sudanese community organized weekly cultural events and several art exhibits were staged. In 2006 the co-op hosted a Rock the Block event at the centre to raise awareness of the large heritage building on the corner of King William – the Lister Block – that was in danger of being torn down. Working with the city heritage committee, downtown politicians and local activists, Sky Dragon helped sway the city towards redeveloping Lister.

In 2007 the second floor of the centre was renovated, creating a large dance and yoga studio, a meeting room and a treatment room.

The Sky Dragon Wellness Centre was established, and the dance, meditation, martial arts and yoga classes moved from 24 King Street East to the new building. The dance studio also doubled as a movie screening room on weekends, with several community talks and screenings occurring each week. It wasn't long before the Sky Dragon Centre became a constant whirlwind of activity. On certain nights there would be five or six events happening at the same time, with every space filled by community meetings, talks and workshops. To a surprising extent, the diverse activity reflected the original co-op vision of an open, progressive space. It was used equally by several different communities and owned by none. Anarchists, communists, social democrats, liberals, environmentalists, First Nations, artists, working class, middle class, poor – all utilized the centre, organized and attended events, and contributed to the community.

FINANCIAL CRISIS

Despite this success in achieving its community development goals, throughout the centre's existence cash flow was always tight. The challenges of renovating and maintaining an old building put a constant strain on the co-op's finances, and it took several years (until 2014) until the property was fully renovated. Despite the shoestring budget, from 2006 through 2011 the café was continually improved. When Bread and Roses opened in the summer of 2006 it only had two residential coffee makers, a second-hand residential stove, a used beer fridge and a couple of microwaves. In 2008 new co-op member Marg Ann Roorda began transforming Bread and Roses into a fully functional restaurant, and when the café was handed off to Home-grown Hamilton in the summer of 2011, it had an espresso machine, a commercial dishwasher and stove, and taps for draught beer. In 2008 a coffee roaster was also installed and the Sky Dragon Roastery was launched. During this time office spaces were created in the centre basement and on the second floor, and groups like Greenpeace, the

Well: LGBTQ Community Wellness Centre, Canada World Youth, the Wiccan Church of Canada and the Canadian Centres for Teaching Peace became long-term tenants. The renovations needed to create these spaces were supported by a generous second mortgage provided by two Hamilton physicians – Gordon Guyatt and Maureen Meade.

Despite the co-op's expanding revenue-generating capacity, high debt service costs and the demands of constant renovations kept the organization running at a small, but consistent deficit. In 2010 this situation came to a head when the Teachers Credit Union announced they would pull the co-op's mortgage, and the federal and provincial governments came looking for back taxes. These immediate threats, coupled with the realization that the co-op could no longer sustain itself financially, led to a Save the Dragon campaign. At two public meetings, the second attended by over 250 people, the co-op raised additional funds from community bonds and charitable donations and began a process of restructuring.

The restructuring of Sky Dragon was not only a response to financial issues, but was also to address growing tensions within the organization itself. These tensions had grown between the co-op members and its non-member workers, as well as between the co-op and the various communities that supported and used the space. Although the goal of an open, non-sectarian space had been largely realized, it was not perfect, and in particular there were repeated conflicts with a group of youth that wanted to bring the centre further in line with their more radical politics.

To address its myriad structural issues, Sky Dragon explored the idea of changing from a worker co-op to a multi-stakeholder co-op. This would distribute decision making and create additional member classes for café workers, bondholders, community partners and tenants. In the winter of 2010 the co-op started this ambitious restructuring process with a transitional board that at one point included eighteen members, but soon shrank to around twelve consistent members.

While the transitional board met and the co-op struggled to resolve its financial and organizational challenges, fears of gentrification were growing in the core. Around the co-op, other downtown buildings were slowly being purchased and renovated to house new cafés, restaurants, galleries and small businesses. This development was starting to displace poor residents and inflate rents, and the centre's ultra-radical contingent became militantly anti-gentrification in response. Increasingly, Sky Dragon became caught between local building owners and small gallery/small business operators on one side, and the activists that opposed gentrification and community displacement on the other. The co-op could see the perspective of both sides, and saw a role for itself in creating dialogue between the various groups and bringing them together to decide how downtown development should unfold.

Despite the Save the Dragon campaign and the downtown economic recovery, within a year the co-op was forced to realize that its business operations were simply not viable. *Mayday Magazine* had already stopped publication in late 2010, and by the spring of 2011 the decision was made to close the Bread and Roses Café. In its place, Homegrown Hamilton opened up – a new café owned and operated by Sky Dragon member Mike Pattison and co-op mortgage holder Tim Lidster. Homegrown would continue and expand the café's role as a local music and art supporter, while discontinuing much of the community development work engaged by Bread and Roses.

During the time of Homegrown's operation, the co-op effectively went into hibernation. It no longer operated businesses or engaged in community work, and as a result the planned transformation into a multi-stakeholder co-operative was abandoned. Instead, Sky Dragon focused on creating more office and studio spaces, maintaining the property and finally becoming financially sustainable. From 2012 to 2016 Sky Dragon was largely a passive observer to the changing face of downtown Hamilton. When in 2015 development reached a tipping point, and investment capital from Toronto began flooding the core, the co-op's assessment of Hamilton's renewal was decidedly ambivalent. In some ways the changes were positive, but in other ways they spoke to failed opportunities and to the dissolution of community.

At the end of their lease in 2016, the co-op parted ways with Homegrown Hamilton – an organizational divorce based on "irreconcilable differences." In a somewhat ironic twist, the inflation of Hamilton's downtown real estate market allowed the co-op to refinance 27 King William, reduce debt service costs and pay out all back debt. In 2019 a five-year lease was signed with new ground-floor tenant Relay Coffee, and after fourteen years at 27 King William, the co-op was finally operating in the black.

THE CHALLENGES OF ETHICAL DEVELOPMENT

Twelve years into its community development project, the Sky Dragon Co-operative began plans to redevelop 27 King William. The renovations will add three units of housing to the building, along with expanded community space on the second floor. Most importantly, an elevator will be added, making all floors accessible. A lack of accessibility had long made Sky Dragon's office, studio and meeting spaces less usable by the community.

Against all odds, the co-op was able to survive over a decade of organizational turmoil and acute financial stress. This is an accomplishment, and yet it is also true that the organization that exists today is quite different from the one that operated the Sky Dragon Centre from 2006 through 2011. Back then the co-op ran a magazine and a café. It employed numerous community members; trained high school, college and university co-op students; engaged in extensive community organizing campaigns; and was actively involved in city political and economic debates. Today Sky Dragon does almost none of these things, and this begs the question of whether, in order to survive economically, the co-op had to ultimately abandon its more progressive economic, social and ecological goals.

The co-op wasn't created to pursue just any kind of development, but to create a model of ethical development. What made this goal so difficult to realize in practice? Similarly, what do the difficulties experienced by Sky Dragon say about the larger problems of gentrification and community displacement? In hindsight, the process of Sky Dragon's development was made difficult by a series of tensions. Each of these tensions confronted the co-op with existential threats, and each also reflects difficulties that will face any organization seeking to enact ethical, progressive development within a similar context.

Community Organizing vs. Community Economic Development
Upon reflection, Sky Dragon's life cycle has been defined by a conflict between two related, yet often antagonistic mandates – to pursue both *community organizing* and *community economic development*. These two organizational functions are most certainly connected, but are also substantially different in their goals, methods and measures of success. Community organizing (CO) involves the self-organizing of communities to redress social inequalities and create political change. Based largely on the work of Saul Alinsky in the 1950s and '60s, CO was instrumental in creating change in poor neighbourhoods, in organizing civil rights struggles and in organizing industrial workers. CO seeks to build capacity in communities that are politically marginal, such that they can effectively advocate for their own interests. CO groups may not be formally incorporated and may have short-term lifespans as communities come together around particular threats or issues and then disband when they have achieved their objective.

In contrast, Community Economic Development (CED) focuses on creating economic and social infrastructure, such as community spaces, affordable housing, ethical businesses and good community jobs. CED often involves incorporating an organization that has as part of its goal fundraising, attracting capital investment, construction, maintenance of properties and the running of businesses. Because of their focus on economic development, CED organizations have to adhere to banking regulations, building codes, city policies and procedures, corporate laws and insurance provisions that might not similarly constrain CO organizations.

Both CO and CED organizations seek positive change in the communities they operate in. However, CO often involves opposing current legal, political and economic structures; challenging and critiquing them; shaming political and business leaders; and acting in a manner that is perceived as "outside the rules" of standard legal and political frameworks. CED organizations, on the other hand, must by their very nature work within standard frameworks. The demands of development permits, professional standards, financing requirements, governing legislation and insurance stipulations can severely constrain the kind of political action that CED organizations can engage in.

Throughout its history, Sky Dragon was more than once confronted by contradictions between CO and CED priorities. The co-op had an explicit politically progressive mandate that, while helping to rally a base of supporters and fulfill organizing and educational objectives (to raise awareness about peace, social justice, LGBTQ+ and environmental issues), also alienated potential investors and clients. An example was *Mayday Magazine*, which published a series of articles by Noam Chomsky during Israel's 2008/2009 invasion of Gaza. The articles were critical of the invasion and of the state of Israel, and as a result *Mayday* lost several advertisers. As well, on a number of occasions Sky Dragon members heard from Hamilton residents directly and on social media that the residents would never support what they considered a "hippy, commie, gay, anarchist" organization. Finally, Sky Dragon's dismal track record at securing government or foundation funding could be related to the organization's overt politics. The co-op may have unintentionally exacerbated this problem by including macro-level social and political critiques in its funding applications.

At least one potential funder was frank in identifying this as a major reason why an application for support was rejected.

Sky Dragon's experience raises the question of to what extent both CO and CED functions can be productively contained in the same organization. In many ways this tension hurt Sky Dragon's financial sustainability, and thus impaired its CED goals. However, at times Sky Dragon's CO capacity proved a powerful source of sustainability, seen in the organization's ability to raise $100,000 in community bonds from ideologically affiliated community members, to raise $50,000 in additional emergency funds from its supporters in 2010 when the co-op was in danger of bankruptcy, and to prevent Teachers Credit Union from repossessing the centre before the co-op could secure a replacement mortgage. These incidents suggest that CO and CED functions, while complicated and potentially contradictory, are not necessarily incompatible.

Macro vs. Micro Levels of Social Change
Another challenge affecting Sky Dragon's development was the tension between the co-op being inspired by the need for macro-level change, yet carrying out its development activities at the micro (community) level. At the macro level, progressive politics can seem quite clear. Being pro-worker, anti-racist, feminist, anti-poverty and ecologically sustainable is both ethically defensible and easily conceptualized on an abstract level. However, "on the ground" the application of these political positions becomes muddier.

Examples of this abounded. Sky Dragon took a strong stance in support of local First Nations communities. However, the co-op was financially unable to stop serving alcohol in its café, despite this request from Native elders who, understandably, would only hold events in "dry" spaces. Sky Dragon also took a stance in support of the downtown poor and homeless, but the co-op eventually found it had to place limits on panhandling in the café, in admitting patrons who were visibly intoxicated, in preventing people from using café washrooms to take intravenous drugs and in preventing homeless youth from using the roof of 27 King William to access nearby abandoned buildings.

The tension between macro and micro levels of change also manifested in the co-op's energy being occupied by a struggle to control micro-level contexts, while macro-level goals were either postponed or abandoned. Construction ended up taking years longer than anticipated due to a chronic shortage of funds and the energy demands of organizing work and running the Bread and Roses Café. As well, 27 King William proved too small to incorporate the affordable housing aspect of Sky Dragon's mandate, leaving this key objective of the project unrealized. Sky Dragon planned on paying community bondholders back in three years, but most remained unpaid twelve years after the project's founding. Finally, the co-op was unable to continue running the two most effective community engagement aspects of the project – *Mayday Magazine* and the Bread and Roses Café. The failure of these two ethical businesses greatly undermined the organization's community organizing goals.

Part of what inspired supporters of Sky Dragon was the ambitious vision of a sustainable community development generator that would create a series of projects and meet a variety of pressing community needs. In reality, the organization struggled from day one to realize a fraction of its goals, and spent most of its time fighting to keep its one development project from bankruptcy.

To be fair, the tension between macro and micro change was not all Sky Dragon's fault. When one considers those aspects of the project that the co-op had immediate control over, the organization exhibited considerable resourcefulness. Sky Dragon was able to leverage a large amount of development impact with very little money. The co-op was also able to raise project funds completely outside of traditional frameworks, and to use limited finances and volunteer energy to sustain intensive organizing activities for six years. Despite all of its challenges, the co-op was able to push close to full sustainability, and would have achieved it had any outside funding been secured.

At the same time, Sky Dragon operated at the whim of larger social processes over which we had little control. The level of economic depression downtown from 2005 through 2010 was acute, with severe negative impacts on the co-op's businesses. When the Sky Dragon Centre opened its doors there was no Art Crawl, no downtown arts district, no Supercrawl and no surge of condo and restaurant development that now drives the core's economic renaissance. Decaying infrastructure was a constant challenge, and the demolition of buildings on either side of the co-op's property led to King William Street being closed for several months, which further discouraged business. Finally, just as Sky Dragon was getting its businesses up and running, the 2008 global financial crash dealt another blow to levels of business and co-op revenues.

Hamilton's broader economic depression also meant that Sky Dragon struggled to meet an intense level of community need. The Sky Dragon Centre was established in a neighbourhood in crisis, and it opened its doors to all. However, the co-op was soon nearly overwhelmed by problems with drug use, squatters, theft, violence and its threat, mental health issues and poverty. Our organization's progressive mandate, and the politics of the individual members and supporters, encouraged us to meet these problems head-on, and to not shy away from dealing with difficult populations or difficult situations. To a certain extend the co-op was successful in this regard, as the centre became known as a safe and welcoming space to many marginal communities. However, with no government or foundation funding we had very limited capacity to deal with these issues. The co-op did its best, but its best wasn't nearly enough to deal with the level of need downtown. This resulted in severe member burnout.

Ultimately, Sky Dragon chafed against the constraints of its operating environment – the wider context of global, industrial capitalism.

The same processes that shaped Hamilton's economy over the years also played a determining role in the co-op's growth and development. In many ways these processes were hostile to the co-op's project and to its survival, and they were also forces over which the organization had little control.

The fact that macro-level structural limitations can have a determining impact on the success of local, sustainable alternatives suggests an important role for legislative and political change. As Canadian law and government policy currently exist, they tend to reinforce standard models of business, development, production and consumption. In such a hostile climate, sustainable alternatives are much less likely to survive due to their incurring costs above and beyond those incurred by conventional competitors. Even if sustainable projects do manage to survive, the need to adapt to a hostile legislative climate will tend to blunt their progressive aspects. Sky Dragon was an example of this Catch-22. The co-op could have continued to prioritize its progressive, community advocacy goals, and would surely have failed as a result. Instead, the co-op opted to change its operations, focus on community economic development and survive.

Progressive Mandate vs. Financial Sustainability
Likely the most powerful tension faced by Sky Dragon was that between the demands of economic sustainability and aspirations toward progressive organizational and political goals. Sky Dragon's struggles with financial sustainability affected every aspect of its operations and every relationship within the organization, and between the organization and the wider community.

The Bread and Roses Café was intended to run as ethically and sustainably as possible. To this end the café ordered from the Ontario Natural Food Co-op, an organization that provides locally produced organic food to restaurants and grocery stores. The café also sourced fully recyclable takeout containers; purchased fair trade and organic coffee; bought wine from Frogpond Farm, Niagara's first certified organic winery; served local micro-brew beer and sourced food from local organic farms. Bread and Roses was militant about recycling, used green bin composting before almost any other Hamilton restaurant and tried to keep its prices as low as possible.

The success of Bread and Roses at walking the ethical and sustainable food talk came at a heavy financial price. Due to the higher cost of local, organic and fair trade food, the café's cost of goods sold (COGS) was double that of standard restaurants. Due to community pressure to keep prices low, the café continually underpriced its food in relation to the cost of production. This twin trap of higher than usual cost and lower than necessary revenue was what eventually led to the café's closure.

Internally, the chronic and critical lack of funds impacted every aspect of the co-op's activities. Few of the worker members were able to be paid. Dan Smith and I were partially paid during the period of initial property renovation in 2005/2006. With no money to pay a construction crew fully, the workers during this time took part of their wages as community bonds. When principal renovations were completed in the fall of 2006, Kevin and Dan were laid off, and Mike Pattison was paid to continue construction until 2008. Apart from these instances, the only two co-op members who received a regular salary were the managers of *Mayday Magazine* and the Bread and Roses Café. These salaries were little more than minimum wage, and the ability to sustain them was always precarious.

Given the lack of resources to pay them, most of the co-op members and managers had to be employed outside Sky Dragon in order to continue to be active in the organization. This led to a situation where much of the membership were not paid employees, while the paid café staff, many of them college and university students that worked part-time, were not members.

Co-op members made major decisions that affected the entire co-op, both in their role as board members and as managers of Sky

Dragon's various businesses. Non-member workers, most of them young, felt left out of these decisions, and resented the decision-making hierarchy. What became clear over time is that many of the young workers, volunteers and activists involved in Sky Dragon understood the organization to be more of a *collective* – a non-hierarchical organization that extended equal decision-making power to all participants. This organizational form reflected the fluid nature of the grassroots community organizations that many young workers and volunteers belonged to. These groups tended to have fluctuating membership, minimal hierarchy and consensus-based decision making.

Sky Dragon's reality as an incorporated non-profit co-operative clashed with this understanding of it as a grassroots collective. In the co-op, membership entailed employment (at least theoretically), individual cash investment (members had to purchase a $1,000 bond), legal liability and responsibility – not only for a property, but also for the interests of community investors and for the livelihood of other co-op employees. The greater legal and financial requirements of membership in a co-op encourage them to limit it to those individuals who are seen as mature, trustworthy, skilled, experienced and committed enough to meet them. Differences in level of commitment, investment and interest between co-op workers and members were a constant source of tension. To co-op members, many of the young workers and volunteers didn't possess the needed characteristics for membership – often because their employment was part-time and temporary. In contrast, the youth felt marginalized from decision making and perceived the co-op membership as closed and controlling.

It should be stressed that the majority of youth employed or volunteering at the co-op were hard-working, committed and trustworthy. For most of these individuals the experience was positive, and provided opportunities for learning, input and engagement far beyond what a normal part-time job or volunteer position would allow. However, there were problems with some volunteers who were marginally committed, and with some café workers who were poor employees.

The tension between the co-op's political aspirations and its financial difficulties also manifested within organizational decision making. When Bread and Roses was in financial trouble, the co-op board was unable to make key changes that would have alleviated financial strain, as they would have also traded away certain aspects of the organization's progressive mandate. Using less expensive inputs or adequately pricing its food and drinks were politically impossible choices for a board that was ideologically driven. The difficulty in making appropriate business decisions also reflected the co-op's conflicting allegiances. Sky Dragon had an obligation to its bondholders, mortgage holders and charitable donors. These stakeholders invested money in the co-op's vision, and expected that money to be wisely managed and ultimately repaid. Sky Dragon also had an obligation to its members and employees, who shared an interest in the co-op's continued financial viability, but also had a wholly justified need to receive appropriate remuneration for their work. Meeting this financial obligation was a constant source of stress for the co-op. Finally, Sky Dragon also had an obligation to the downtown community and the broader progressive community in Hamilton. These groups were most supportive of the co-op's advocacy and activism, and were less concerned with the challenges of balancing budgets and keeping mortgage holders happy.

Upon reflection, Sky Dragon's difficulty in meeting the expectations of multiple stakeholder groups could have been alleviated through organizational change. An issue with having one board to run several different businesses and community advocacy projects was that not all board members had the same level of interest or expertise in all of the co-op's activities. If the co-op had considered compartmentalizing its business aspects from its advocacy and activism aspects, creating separate decision-making bodies and protocols for each, then it would have been more effective at dealing with the many challenges it faced.

Instrumental vs. Grassroots Activity

A final tension that Sky Dragon struggled with was between what community development researchers have termed *instrumental* vs. *grassroots* activity. Instrumental activity refers to the daily organizational tasks needed to maintain the co-op's viability. Running the businesses, managing the co-op finances and repairing and renovating the property took up much of the co-op's time, energy and resources. These things required specialized skill and were not open to just any supporters. In support of these tasks, non-members became engaged primarily through centre events (music, art shows, talks, film screenings, fundraisers) and through being consumers of the centre's products – food, coffee, etc. In Sky Dragon's experience, the demands of owning and maintaining a building and running businesses meant that instrumental activity, organized by the co-op's management, grew to dominate the organization's practice. In contrast, grassroots activity led by non-members and the community became an increasingly smaller fraction of the co-op's work.

Despite the dominance of instrumental concerns, the co-op was able to participate in some important grassroots causes. These included the final years of the Red Hill fight, the Caledonia land reclamation standoff, the campaign to save the Lister Block, the 2011 Toronto G20 protest, the 2012 Occupy movement, the United Steelworkers of America Local 1005 lockout (workers at U.S. Steel, formerly Stelco), the Halton Eco Festival, the Hamilton and District Labour Council annual Labour Day parade, the LGBTQ Queer Prom, the Trans Day of Remembrance, Hamilton Pride, Books to Bars and four consecutive Mayday Festivals (which were organized by the co-op itself). This grassroots organizing work was, for many Sky Dragon members and supporters, the lifeblood of sustainable community development. Unfortunately, the co-op always struggled to find the time and resources to participate in it.

SKY DRAGON AND DOWNTOWN GENTRIFICATION

Sky Dragon was founded in a Hamilton battered by deindustrial-ization. As industrial jobs vanished, a ripple effect tore through the downtown core. Businesses closed, moneyed citizens moved to the suburbs and buildings fell into decay. This was the situation when the Sky Dragon Centre opened in 2006, and for years after there was little development activity downtown. However, from 2008 through 2010, small galleries and businesses began opening on James Street North, and the James North Art Crawl began building interest and excitement about an arts district in the core. By 2011 and 2012, vacant downtown buildings began to be purchased and redeveloped by local residents and newcomers from Toronto. These small-scale developers opened arts-based businesses and restaurants, while some rooming houses and other low-income rental units started being converted to artist's studios, higher rent apartments and condominiums.

In 2010, *Mayday Magazine* published an article on gentrification, with the author arguing that it was happening in Hamilton's core, and that it was being driven by the arts community. In the article the author called artists "the foot soldiers of gentrification," and warned that it was only a matter of time before an influx of big money from Toronto developers would create a property conversion process that pushed out poor people and would change the character of the down-town irrevocably. The article generated an intense negative outcry from the arts community. In particular, many poor and working-class artists and gallery owners resented being implicated in a process of big-money development and of being accused of not respecting Ham-ilton's culture or history. Even though *Mayday* clearly published a wide range of opinions, and Sky Dragon officially separated the magazine's content from the co-op's official position, it started becoming the tar-get of anger from the arts community.

The co-op grew increasingly concerned about the schism in the community around gentrification and saw a danger that this division might undermine any chance at forming a diverse coalition around a progressive development vision for downtown. In an attempt to re-establish dialogue, I wrote an article saying that gentrification was happening, but that there had also been some positive aspects to the development downtown. At the time I was writing, much of the buildings and businesses were locally owned, and the new owners weren't just sitting on empty buildings, but were fixing them up and making them live again. Finally, there was more support (financial and in terms of city assistance) for the city's artists and musicians. Unfortunately, my *Mayday* article did little to change the growing polarization in the gentrification debate. A few weeks after it came out, anti-gentrification activists went out late at night and stuck "fat cat" stickers on all of the windows of downtown gallery owners.

In a subsequent *Mayday* article I decided to invite all downtown stakeholders to come to a meeting at Sky Dragon to talk about the issues around gentrification and about what we could do to address them as a community. At first some of the anti-gentrification activists participated in the organizing committee for this community meeting, but then they demanded that the location of the talk change. There were likely several reasons for this, one being that some of their community now saw the co-op as a compromised, gentrifying organization. However, as I had personally invited people to our space, and as our organization was in the middle of the debate, I said that moving the location wasn't an option. The anti-gentrification activists then pulled out of organizing and denounced the meeting ahead of time.

Despite an active campaign to get people to boycott the spring 2010 meeting at Sky Dragon, nearly everyone involved in the debate ended up attending – anti-gentrification anarchists, professors and grad students from McMaster, downtown gallery owners, co-op supporters and downtown residents. The Bread and Roses café was filled to capacity. Attendees were randomly divided into four groups, where they collectively worked through a series of questions concerning downtown development – its pros, its cons and how they would like to see it unfold. The event went well, with tense, but respectful conversation and debate at every table. Unfortunately the full-room wrap-up was taken over by screaming from both sides at the end of the night and in a matter of seconds the meeting got completely out of hand. In the interests of safety the event was shut down.

In the ensuing weeks the centre became isolated, with both sides denouncing the co-op as an agent of the opposite side. Sky Dragon's original plans to collate and publish recorded material from the community meeting and to form an association to further discuss downtown development all went out the window. The co-op was struggling with its own intense financial challenges and internal issues, and no one in the organization had the energy to continue to try to bridge the toxic divide. From that point onward, Sky Dragon was forced to focus on internal matters, and began pulling back from community engagement.

LESSONS LEARNED

The lessons to be learned from Sky Dragon's participation in downtown development are primarily lessons learned from failure. In the end, critical community concerns around rent increases, a loss of affordable housing stock, the displacement of poor and low-income residents, the criminalization of poor residents and a loss of locally owned small businesses all came to pass.

Along with the anti-gentrification activists, Sky Dragon saw these potential impacts and the organization did what it could to organize against them. However, we also saw the positive changes that members of the arts community saw – the return of a certain level of economic prosperity, and the revitalization of our built heritage. Upon reflection, the anti-gentrification camp proved ineffective at communicating with stakeholders on the other side of the debate, and, most importantly, to those who hadn't yet developed a strong opinion. There were those who saw both positive and negative sides to the development process, along with artists, business owners and building owners who were concerned about many of the same issues around redevelopment and who might have become allies.

A contingent of anti-gentrification activists included McMaster professors and graduate students who somewhat ironically came from more privileged backgrounds than many of the artists and small gallery owners they rather comically denounced as "fat-cat gentrifiers." While these university activists contributed an important analysis of gentrification and its impact on marginal populations, they seemed fatally disconnected from the lived reality of much of the arts community – most of who, when the debate was playing out, were struggling to sustain themselves. The anarchist contingent also largely refused to dialogue with downtown business or property owners, instead choosing to draw battle lines based on essentialist notions of class.

To a doctrinaire Marxist, the young gallery owner became a "petit bourgeois shopkeeper." The artist trying to make a living selling their wares at Art Crawl became "a foot-soldier of gentrification." The local resident who purchased a building downtown, renovated it and created space for artists and retail businesses became a "capitalist," a "gentrifier," a "fat-cat landlord." By painting the various players downtown with broad ideological brushes, anti-gentrification activists erased their real diversity. This led to missed opportunities to create allies, to generate collective power and to meaningfully impact the process of development. Instead, anti-gentrification activists more often turned potential allies into committed enemies, and marginalized themselves.

Had critics of gentrification instead engaged city hall, municipal councillors, local social service agencies and local media, they may very well have effected changes to municipal development and housing policy. Changes to bylaws and city planning and development practice could have significantly reduced the displacement of marginal populations, and the targeting and criminalization of youth and the poor. The net result of this failure was tragic, and it seems clear that when the anti-gentrification side disengages from institutional struggle and public debate, then big development money will win, every time.

Although unfairly stereotyped by anti-gentrification activists, the downtown business and gallery owners exhibited their own weaknesses, and proved themselves largely unable to acknowledge the obvious signs of gentrification and the looming dangers should the process run away. Instead of being able to understand the anti-gentrification perspective and empathize with marginal communities being displaced, the arts community tended to denounce both, to close ranks and to disengage from dialogue.

Part of the problem with the downtown gallery and business owners was that, engaged as they were in a difficult task – doing what they were doing out of love for their art and their city, struggling financially to sustain their business, making little to no money, with several of them failing – they tended to see themselves as wholly morally justified in their actions. The co-op also fell prey to this at times, leading us to justify actions that were ultimately morally ambiguous. Examples include confrontations with the youth who would climb up our building to access abandoned buildings on either side along with calling the police on these same youth when our tools were stolen numerous times during the renovation process; and removing and banning certain disruptive or aggressive people from the centre. In each of these instances the co-op was responding to what we perceived as direct threats to our viability. However, each instance also put us in conflict with many of the downtown's most vulnerable people. These situations were difficult for co-op members, and contributed to stress and burnout.

When reflecting on the totality of the co-op's experience, I can conclude that only serious and sustained dialogue between different perspectives could have changed the course of downtown gentrification. Sky Dragon tried to bridge the gap between two worlds – that of local entrepreneurs and developers, and that of anti-gentrification community activists. We failed, but it is possible we could have succeeded if our organization wasn't itself so depleted. It is also possible that another organization could have led the way in sustaining community dialogue. Apart from having the necessary resources and capacity to engage the development debate, the organization would also have needed to be perceived by all sides as relatively neutral. Other possibilities include social service organizations such as the Social Planning and Research Council or the YWCA, the city, community centres and faith groups. Ultimately, the lesson is that some group or coalition of groups needs to take leadership in establishing and maintaining dialogue. If camps become polarized and radicals disengage, then gentrification will proceed unchecked.

Macro-Structural Change

Over eleven years of community development work, one of the core beliefs that drove the Sky Dragon's founding was confirmed. Progressive community organizations need to capture and to build capital. Sustainable, ethical, local economies will only be realized when communities can meet organizing power with economic power, and with the social infrastructure that can build, focus and sustain movement. No one actor, development organization or community will be sufficient to do this larger scale work. As such, we need to become much more effective with building alliances and coalitions. We also need to work at municipal, provincial and federal levels to create structures that encourage ethical, sustainable development, and that discourage development that harms and displaces vulnerable communities and destroys ecosystems. Ultimately, the goal of this political work is to shift the environment from one hostile to transformative projects like Sky Dragon, to one in which such projects are actively facilitated and nurtured. Until such a macro-level transformation occurs, local alternatives will continue to struggle for survival, and the destructive

capitalist cycles of economic boom and bust, gentrification and community displacement will continue.

HOPE AMIDST THE BOOM

Despite the serious changes that Hamilton's downtown is now experiencing, and the undeniable negative effects of gentrification, there
are some signs of hope. First, the Sky Dragon Centre has managed to
survive and is now redeveloping its property at 27 King William Street.
The development will add three housing units, along with two large
community meeting and activity spaces on the second floor, and an
elevator that will make all floors of the building accessible for the first
time. The design and construction will be as sustainable as possible
and the additional spaces will see the co-op return to providing community programming and doing community outreach. Most importantly, the redevelopment will allow the co-op to pay out its remaining
creditors and will enable it to finance future affordable housing and
community-use developments throughout Hamilton.

Another good news story is that the Hamilton Community Land
Trust, formed in 2014 with the goal of securing land to build affordable housing, was finally able to secure property in 2017. Although the
property, on Wilson Street in downtown Hamilton, will only house a
single-family dwelling, it is a victory for a creative community project
that was directly attempting to address the problem of community
displacement. Finally, there has also been some success in helping
tenants organize to resist evictions and to improve housing standards
from the local anarchist community. Although the various actors
working against community displacement aren't yet coordinated, the
fact that they continue to exist, and continue to move forward, is cause
for hope. Even more promising is the idea that these isolated actors
might one day converge, and that a broad-based stakeholder group
capable of making future development both ethical and sustainable

could finally be realized. In this sense, Hamilton may yet become an example of progressive urban revitalization, and not simply another example of urban gentrification.

On the Fence: Reflecting on Four Years in Hamilton

Kerry Le Clair

S ettling into a new city is a learning process, but for me it has been a homecoming too. I was born in Hamilton in the '70s, but we moved away when I was two years old. Over the ensuing years, my trips back to Hamilton were rare and were mostly to take advantage of the great nature spots and hiking trails. I had little sense of the transformation that had taken place over the decades, taking the city from the mostly middle-class, fairly blue-collar and quite homogenous steel town it was when I was an infant to a post-industrial, arts-friendly and culturally diverse city with thriving service industries and a deeper economic divide. Or something like that. I'm still trying to figure out what Hamilton is and is not, and which of the prognosticators to listen to regarding what it *will* be. For now, I am working on finding my place in it, a journey I started when I moved back here in December 2014.

My initial inkling of what it could take to feel like I belonged here came from my first conversations with neighbours. The inevitable question when people noticed my unfamiliar face in their midst was "Where did you move here from?" My reply, "Toronto," was met with the occasional groan and eye roll followed by "Ugh, not another one," or better yet, sometimes an enthusiastic "Me too!" We Toronto transplants are the bane of some diehard Hamiltonians' existence, for reasons both well founded and completely unfounded. Each time I got the groan and eye roll response, I was reminded that plenty of people receive far more hostile indications that they might not be welcome in a new city than a mild indication of disdain, so I counted myself lucky.

During those early days of exploring my neighbourhood in the city's north Sherman Hub area, I often thought back to the dire warning of the Hamilton real estate agent who advised that "the good people live on the Mountain." Far from the rumoured glorious Mountain locales she favoured, my new digs were blocks away from the industrial core of the city. Just north of Barton Street, with its stretches of unoccupied storefronts and abandoned buildings, mine is a part of the city that can feel overlooked. Some neighbours sarcastically remark that our greatest purpose is to provide overflow parking on game days at the nearby Tim Hortons Field. Still, this is a neighbourhood as vital as any other, with busy streets and people always in motion. Yet demographic studies paint a relatively bleak picture of the north Sherman Hub, spotlighting higher exposure to air pollutants, higher cancer rates, lower incomes and low voter turnout.

I don't know how to gauge presumed goodness in people, but I know it cannot be measured by statistics or postal codes.

I spent a good deal of time getting to know my new surroundings, taking advantage of the luxury of a flexible schedule owing to my freelance career. One of the best first steps I took was to volunteer with Environment Hamilton by helping to collect information on tree health and air quality. Not only was this a chance to get to know an incredible local advocacy organization, it literally took me down just about every street and alleyway in my area. I attended community association meetings close to home and throughout the city, went to neighbourhood gatherings of every kind, took part in community workshops and activities, and sat in on city council meetings. Soon enough, when conversations in these spaces led to questions about where I lived, I had shifted from being an erstwhile Toronto person to being someone from the wrong side of the proverbial tracks – in my case, the wrong side of Barton Street. It seemed somehow perplexing to new folks that I would meet that, all things being equal, I would opt to live where I do. The confusion grew when people learned that I have a university education and a professional occupation, as if these factors should be manifest in the neighbourhood I choose to live in. My response to these reactions ranged from silent bemusement to emphatic defensiveness. Neither reaction was very productive, but those experiences set me on a course to treat my neighbourhood with more dignity and respect than some folks may think it deserves.

Back on the home front, as that first brutal winter gave way to springtime 2015, I had modest plans for the outside of my home: a little flower garden, a small front yard tree and maybe a fresh layer of Tremclad on the porch railing. Slowly, those little projects took shape and, as a happy by-product of feeling connected to my community, I began to see my house not just as a stand-alone structure, but how it fit into the larger streetscape, a term referring to "visual elements of a street, including the road, adjoining buildings, sidewalks, street furniture, trees and open spaces, etc., that combine to form the street's character," which I learned about in one of those aforementioned community workshops. Part of that streetscape is the alleyway I live on. Not one of those overgrown alleyways, forgotten and forlorn, but a busy and highly visible passage running alongside my house and yard. By the following summer of 2016, my 8' x 20' alley-adjacent wooden fence became my next project. A simple coat of paint or stain would have spruced it up but I had a different idea. On my many walks and bike rides throughout the city, I had admired artwork on my neighbours' garage doors, in other alleyways and on buildings downtown. As a long-time admirer of street murals from around the world, I wondered if I could have my very own piece of public art to share. The adventure that was about to unfold has become a highlight of my short time in Hamilton.

I had no experience with the arts before I came to Hamilton, besides being an avid spectator. It has been my good fortune to live and travel throughout North America and overseas from a young age, and I always sought out contemporary art in those places. As I grew older, the art I was really drawn to was seldom found in an art gallery or museum – more often it was found on the streets. I love art galleries but they can be very stifling and the pieces they contain don't usually affect me the way outdoor public art does. I have a childhood memory of lying on the living room floor in front of the fireplace, flipping through the pages of one of those Time Life art encyclopedias that were popular back then, looking at the works of Cézanne, Degas and Vermeer and wondering why these people were so revered. From my young and limited perspective, these artists who became the stuff of ubiquitous, mass-market prints hung in cheap frames or emblazoned on drinks coasters were surely not all that the world of visual art had to offer. I have no doubt that early disconnect with what was "establishment" art motivated me to seek out art, not just in visual form but also film, dance, theatre and especially music, from the fringes – outsider art that emerges from disillusionment, disenfranchisement, protest and political struggle.

My love of travel and a burgeoning interest in politics fuelled my fondness for murals, graffiti and other forms of public art. So many of my trips featured pilgrimages to see art in neighbourhoods that were not on the radar of the average tourist. While most folks would have their top five must-see museums, galleries and cathedrals, I would frequently take three or four buses or walk for hours to track down a piece of street art or even graffiti on an out-of-the-way wall somewhere. The appeal of street art for me is that it is hard to commodify

– it is for display but not consumption or private gain. A trip to Belfast at the age of twenty-one had a big impact on me, not least because the history and strife of Northern Ireland and their socio-economic and religious struggles are depicted in giant murals across the city. Those images and the stories they tell stuck with me. And so began a long and winding road around the world, looking for inspiration from artists along the way.

That long road eventually brought me back to Hamilton and later, to that fateful summer of 2016. Armed with a pretty good imagination, but no artistic talent and very little spare cash, I set about to make my fence mural idea a reality. Months went by, and that no-artistic-talent plus no-money combination proved to be a big problem. I reached out to a number of mural artists, but they were either not interested or set a fee too steep for my meagre budget. Some artists weren't interested solely based on where I live, telling me that mine was an undesirable area to put their artwork. Then through a very lucky community connection in October 2016, I was introduced to staff from Hamilton's Centre[3], an artist-run centre for print and media arts. They were looking for community-based arts projects with a focus on collaborative creative experiences, and together we began hatching a plan to make my fence their next canvas.

As the possibilities for the mural unfolded, and during countless hours of meetings, my participation in the collaborative process was encouraged. I was sure of one thing: I had a theme in mind. The mural should honour Indigenous culture and acknowledge that we are living on traditional territories. Hamilton is home to some great public art, but little of it pays tribute to Indigenous people and the vibrant cultural community they are a part of. I also wanted to connect with young and emerging artists in the city. Our discussions about weaving a celebration of Indigenous culture together with engaging young artists lead to connecting with an after school youth program at the Hamilton Regional Indian Centre (HRIC). A close partnership with Indigenous youth and leaders from HRIC was formed, and Centre[3] held a number of workshops that introduced us to three talented young artists, aged eleven to fifteen years old. Working with them on the mural creation and development process was fascinating. My involvement in this part of the project evolution was relatively minor, but was skilfully facilitated by Centre[3] staff. The guiding principle I asked the group to focus on was honouring Indigenous culture without relying on overused and stereotypical imagery like dream catchers. Dream catchers have become so commonplace in representing all aspects of Indigenous culture, so thoughtlessly pervasive, that they are often relegated to the status of rear-view mirror ornament. Centre[3] staff worked with the young artists to create a series of meaningful images and map out how they would come together to make a mural. We chose seven key images to feature most prominently on the vertical fence slats: a corn husk doll, a jingle dress dancer, a smudge bowl, Grandmother Moon, a tree of life, a boy with a raven headpiece and a medicine wheel. The other element that ties the mural together is a wampum belt painted horizontally on the receding fence slats.

The fence mural project was generously supported by grants from the Hamilton Community Foundation, Councillor Matthew Green and the Canada 150 Fund, and the participation of more than a dozen community volunteers.

All of this hard work, a few setbacks and some unpredictable and inclement weather brought us to early May 2017. Under the leadership of our Centre[3] champions, and with the help of our young artists, youth and staff volunteers from HRIC, as well as a number of community volunteers, we prepped and primed the fence and painted the mural in four days. On May 11, we threw a wrap party for our artists and volunteers and invited the community to celebrate the mural with us.

Located near the intersection of Barton and Lottridge Streets, a stone's throw from the city's industrial and manufacturing sector, this is an area unaccustomed to random acts of beautification. Reactions and feedback from my neighbours and community has been mixed, ranging from unbridled enthusiasm about the project, to complete indifference and even a strong dislike for the mural's bold depiction of Indigenous imagery. Some community members, resigned as they are to the negative stigma of the area, asked me why I bothered. I am immensely proud of the mural and everything that went into it, but I have learned to not be too attached to how other people feel about it. With hundreds of people on foot, on bicycles or mobility devices, and in cars passing the mural ever since, it has now become a part of the scenery. Some people stop and admire the mural, some ask questions and take pictures, and others still go right on by without taking notice at all. In this way, the mural is doing exactly what I hoped it would: infusing into the streetscape. I can't say whether the mural is a political statement on par with any I have seen on my travels, but in some small way, I like to view it as an act of resistance against a dominant narrative about where good things should happen.

Thinking back on the vision and scope of the project three years later, it was an amazing undertaking. From a coffee shop chat with a community developer to sketches of the final mural design spread out across my dining room table eight months later, it was an occasionally frustrating and ultimately wonderful experience. It inspired me to get involved in more community-based arts initiatives, and led me to coordinating two other nearby alleyway mural projects in partnership with Green Venture, a local environmental education organization, in the fall of 2017. I have taken part in many public art consultations, and even bestowed my own clumsy handiwork to a part of the Pipeline Trail project, designed by community members in the nearby Crown Point neighbourhood. In July 2018, I teamed up with Red Tree Collective to coordinate a multi-generational arts program at a local elementary school. Alone and with troops of awesome volunteers, I have participated in many alleyway cleanups and greening initiatives, most notably with Beautiful Alleys, a volunteer group dedicated to improving Hamilton's laneways and alleyways.

Alongside my growing interest in how public art can have a positive affect on its surroundings, I have grown increasingly concerned with the negative impacts of the manufacturing and waste facilities in my area and city-wide. With the support of Environment Hamilton, I have taken up the cause to lobby our municipal and provincial governments to address poor air quality and other detrimental effects of our industrial neighbours. This continual work has become a form of activism for me. It has generated small successes for the community and forged larger community bonds. In October 2019, I began working with Ward 3 Councillor Nrinder Nann as climate action community coordinator, giving me the opportunity to be a voice for residents on issues of environmental concern.

As I reflect on more than five years since coming home to Hamilton, and the fateful role that a fence mural project has played in my return, I'm reminded of how often thoughts of public art, greening spaces and so-called beautification seep into how I feel about this city. Inevitably, the spectre of ever-present issues like gentrification arises. The neighbourhood rumour mill teems with tales that we are poised for big changes 'round here. Some of those changes have taken root – first there was the Bernie Morelli Recreation Centre, which opened in December 2018, and then Bernie Custis Secondary School, which opened in September 2019. Plans are under way to build a large park and soccer field on the former Dominion Glass site and I still hear whispers of a vision for a local creative arts hub. Buzzy terms like *urban renewal* and *regeneration* are often used in wishful discussions about neighbourhoods like mine, leaving me wondering what imprint those economic and cultural forces will leave on its denizens.

I think often about all the privileges I have (including being a property owner), the responsibility of stewardship and the tendency of beautification efforts to be fronts for some kind of saviour mentality. If I am personally invested in the well-being of my community, and the personal is political, then all my community engagement activities are political ones, right? Even if Hamilton is home, do I belong here? As self-indulgent as that line of thinking may seem to me now, it remains true that, for many of us, a sense of belonging makes us more likely to take action for the common good. I'm still on the fence as to whether I belong here, but I will do my best to keep contributing to the common good until I know the answer.

Bringing Congress Crescent to City Hall

Joey Coleman

Today, I like to refer to myself as an "accidental journalist" because it was never a career path I explored. I didn't even apply to be a journalist, following instead a few years of passionate blogging on student affairs. *Maclean's* magazine called me out of the blue and offered me a job. A decade later, I held one of the most competitive and coveted places in Canadian journalism: Southam Fellow at the University of Toronto.

My story is that of a Hamiltonian who was a child during our industrial peak, coming of age during the tumultuous transition from industrial powerhouse to something that isn't quite defined yet. Hamilton shaped me, and today I'm helping to shape Hamilton.

Another reason I refer to myself as an accidental journalist is that I'm the socio-economic exception. I've endured overwhelming odds as someone who lived in social housing, was abused as a child and became a Crown ward. Born a decade later in Hamilton, my journey would have been impossible.

The journey really begins with a daily van ride.

It's 1985, and each morning a van picks me up in front of 30 Congress Crescent. The van's Variety logo is my second oldest memory. Each weekday, it took me to child care at the corner of Gage Avenue North and Beach Road.

This simple memory encapsulates my Hamilton journey. I lived in a Hamilton housing survey but had enough connection to the outside world to feel a part of the city around me. This sense of connectedness was enabled largely by United Way donations from Hamiltonians from all walks of life, many of them hard-working people who spent their workdays in the industrial plants that I'd pass in the van that took me back to Congress Crescent each afternoon.

I was always amazed by the length of Procter & Gamble on Burlington Street, all the workers crossing at Burlington and Depew Street, and the flames flaring out of the steel plants during their peak of the 1980s. Even today, when I ride on the 4-Bayfront bus along Burlington Street, I see the now demolished Procter & Gamble building with its overhead pedestrian bridge and the small waves of workers pouring in and out of gate 6 at Dofasco. While I couldn't appreciate it at the time, this early childhood experience would set me on a path out of Congress Crescent, a path that's taken me more than halfway across the world as a journalist, on long Greyhound trips across Canada, to Massey College in the University of Toronto as a senior resident of the college and to exciting adventures yet to come.

East Hamilton's Congress Crescent is a pretty typical and bland social housing survey. Isolated from the surrounding community by low fences, there are only two entrances into the complex where over one thousand people live. To the east of the complex is the Red Hill Valley, on the north a Canadian Pacific Railway line and to the west Mount Albion Road. I never crossed Mount Albion except to wait for the HSR bus. To the south was a street of large homes that backed onto the creek.

To those who live in Congress, it's just "Congress," without crescent. Starting in the mid-1990s, the city tried to market Congress as "Pine Grove Place." Even today, the residents of Pine Grove Place still call it Congress.

Congress had its own parks, and at age five, there were two that I could go to unsupervised – the one directly behind my building, 20 Congress, and sometimes the one beside the building. During the day, the survey was pleasant. I'd play at the park, adults would be hanging outside and occasionally, a snake would appear from the Red Hill Creek to make things exciting. At night, it was different. People returned to their apartments, and sometimes I'd hear one of the fights outside. I related taxis to nighttime, because they were so common as I looked out the windows at night.

Once a month, everyone would gather in the lobby. With around one hundred apartment units, it was crowded. People opened their mailboxes and waited for the postman to arrive. It was exciting. As the postman slid welfare cheques in each mailbox, mothers (every family I knew was led by a single mother) would quickly grab theirs and thus began a race along Mount Albion Road walking to the Fortinos Plaza at Greenhill Avenue.

The one-kilometre walk was my favourite adventure. About half way to the plaza, there was a house with a raised stone driveway. I loved running along it, which frustrated my mother because she wanted to get to the grocery store early enough to avoid the long lineups, and to cash her cheque after making the minimum purchase. It is funny, today a kilometre seems barely worth noting. For a young child, it's quite the distance. I always enjoyed the walk.

The next day, there would be a trip to either Eastgate Square or Centre Mall. There was a long wait for the 11-Parkdale HSR bus. I loved the big steps getting on board, and that I was always age four if the driver asked (to ride free). The trolley buses of the 1-King and 2-Barton were thrilling as well, I'd run to the back of the bus to look out the back window and see the city. The 1-King and 2-Barton ran every few minutes; I always enjoyed watching the sparks when another bus was close behind.

Centre Mall, with its water fountains, always excited me; the food court was well lit, and there was an interesting mix of people, many of them workers from the industrial plants on their lunch breaks. Eastgate Square was less interesting. Other than getting my hair cut there, I can't remember much of note about the square.

My grandmother lived on Queenston Road overlooking the Red Hill Valley. She worked in the trucking industry, and whenever we had to go to her office, there was a trip to Van Wagners Beach and Hutch's. I was fascinated by the structure in the lake – Hamilton's water intake – and especially the fountain outside the pumping station. The landmark Hamilton Globe didn't really interest me. My grandmother took me to Red Hill Library to get books; it was here I was introduced to Robert Munsch's books and my love of reading was sparked.

Each summer, I went to Camp Marydale. My Camp Marydale weeks were funded by the *Hamilton Spectator* Summer Camp Fund. This was the highlight of my year, and my first introduction to kids from outside of Congress.

Camp Marydale was just over the Wentworth-Wellington county border, and the bus to camp travelled along Highway 6. When I started day camp in 1986, there were few landmarks on the highway and the traffic seemed light. As the decade I attended passed, I marvelled at the massive pace of development of what was once rural Hamilton. Today, I'm grateful for having seen Highway 6 before it developed; it gives me an appreciation of the significance of change in our rural areas.

Within Congress, I had three primary friends. Today, one of them is in jail, another I lost track of and the third still lives in Congress with her kids and grandkids.

It was in my seventh year that things changed. My biological mother was able to get CityHousing to give her a townhouse near Upper Ottawa Street and Limeridge Road. I would return to Congress two more times before I was fourteen, living at 20 Congress again, and then 30 Congress. In 1989, Upper Ottawa and Limeridge was the edge of the city. There were open spaces, farmers' fields, and I was free to roam in all directions.

Trips to downtown Hamilton now became frequent. November 1989, to me, is when Hamilton reached its peak. The excitement downtown was palpable in the week prior to the greatest Grey Cup game of all time – the nail-biter between the Hamilton Tiger-Cats and the Saskatchewan Roughriders. In front of Jackson Square there were street merchants selling pins and various items celebrating the Ticats being in the Grey Cup. Noisemakers provided the background chorus for Oskee Wee Wee cheers.

Hamilton was at its pinnacle, our downtown had no vacancies, there was nightlife and the streets bustled with people and shops.

The 22-Upper Ottawa bus stop beside Gore Park's Cenotaph was a great observation point to watch city life. Late at night, downtown was boisterous with young men coming in and out of the bars at all hours. Oliver's was always busy. There were two arcades, with large lights, emptying people's pockets of quarters. (A few years later, in grade eight I'll be assigned to "alternative education" and suspended for nearly the entire school year, giving me the chance to spend much time in the arcades.)

The new Eaton's had opened earlier in 1989, and the Eaton Centre was under construction. We took a school trip downtown at one point to marvel at the construction. It opened in 1991/92 with three floors of great retail, and I was amazed at the model rockets sold in a shop on the third floor at the top of the north escalators.

Thanks to Big Brothers, free tickets to Tiger-Cat games often came my way; the end-zone seats in Ivor Wynne Stadium were the funniest seats in the house. In 1996, my foster home was near the stadium and I got free tickets as they tried to fill the stands. Booing the Argos at the Snow Bowl (so named because of the amount of snow that fell during the game) is a prized Hamilton memory.

In late 1996 I spoke to a council committee supporting an expansion of the Hamilton East Kiwanis Boys and Girls Club. The following year, I got involved in writing letters against the 1997 round of cuts to our public transit agency, the Hamilton Street Railway. But the 1997 teachers' walkout and opposition to education reforms by the Ontario Progressive Conservative Party led by Premier Mike Harris became my first real political involvements. I opposed the reforms and let Wentworth North member of provincial parliament Toni Skarica know. Skarica is an honourable man, and sadly one of the last politicians of his kind in Hamilton. He attended public meetings across Hamilton, getting blasted for the proposed reforms. Calmly he explained why his government was pursuing the changes. In the process, at the Club Continental on Gertrude Street, I gave him a yelling earful during a public meeting.

Much like principled Hamilton Progressive Conservative politicians Skarica, Lincoln Alexander and Ellen Fairclough, the Club Continental is a fond memory of a Hamilton that no longer exists. The residential neighbourhoods in the shadows of the steel mills were littered with social and veterans' clubs that are no more.

In winter 1998, I was part of a group of students who'd built the Glendale Secondary School computer network. The city and county school boards merged on January 1, 1998, and a memo was sent out to schools stating that new system-wide policies were being created by transition committees, and that included a policy for then new computer networks and Internet access.

I could spin you a tale of nobly volunteering to serve student interests, but I really joined transition committees to protect my tiny little piece of turf. See, the Internet was still a new concept, and the teachers knew just as much as we students did about how to manage a computer network. We students administered the network, and I knew there was no way that would be allowed to continue forever. My high school principal placed a great deal of confidence and trust in us, and we took our responsibilities very seriously.

Formal schooling was difficult for me, not because it was hard, but because it was too easy. In grade three, I was tested for the gifted program. My results came back: I was two per centile below the gifted standard. I failed the test because I could not complete large sections of it; my inner-city school had not taught me the concepts. See, Prince of Wales had to teach to the classroom, and most of my peers were struggling. I was too young to understand concepts like poverty and the social determinants of health. The gifted test had no considerations for circumstances at the time. Thus, instead of recognizing how exceptional my result was, I was left to my own devices as my teachers tried to figure out what to do with me in a regular classroom.

Today, there is a review committee for similar circumstances. Had that existed, who knows what I would be doing today. But while the life journey would've been easier, I doubt it would be so interesting.

In grade four, I completed classwork in minutes and despite my reading books at my seat, I was a distraction to the rest of my class. My teacher found a way to solve this problem, letting me use the computer lab. One of the IBM computers was equipped with a 1400 baud modem. I dialed CompuSpec, the *Hamilton Spectator*'s bulletin board service. Yes, the *Hamilton Spectator* was an online leader before online existed as we know it today. It was on Hamilton's BBS I connected with others and learned the basics of computers. I became a self-taught computer nerd. (I didn't even have a computer at home until I could afford one in my early twenties.) So in the latter half of grade eleven, I ended up at a school board transition committee about school networks. It turned out I was the only student who joined a committee. Ray Mulholland, the chair of the new

Public Board, approached me and asked if I'd serve on a variety of transition committees. It seemed interesting, and I started my political path.

I wasn't the only one motivated by self-interest. Most of the committees were split fifty-fifty between county and city factions; I was often the odd man out. My ideas – those of a sixteen-year-old who didn't know "we've always done it this way" – were often opposed by both factions who each wanted the new board to operate like their old board.

Mulholland, a trustee from the city, and board vice-chair Reg Woodworth, a trustee from the county, proved to be masterful politicians and great mediators. They were committed to creating the best possible new school board, and to preventing the tense feelings of amalgamation from becoming scars. They succeeded; we don't talk about a city/suburban divide in local education decisions.

The most important learning moment for me was a boundary review that proposed to have students living across the Ancaster border attend the Hamilton-side Sir Allan MacNab Secondary School. MacNab is a short walk from the Ancaster border, and to a sixteen-year-old like me, changing the boundary made sense. Students were being bused to Ancaster High School, and changing the boundary provided clear savings. I recall a woman, appearing to be in her early forties, yelling at me, "I moved to Ancaster so my kid wouldn't have to go to a Hamilton school!" I stood by my views; the politicians watered down the proposal such that they officially changed the boundary but offered busing to Ancaster High School. Effectively, nothing changed, but that's politics for you.

I learned politics at the Public School Board, and I learned leadership at the Catholic School Board as a volunteer sports referee with the Catholic Youth Organization. I started with flag football; I loved football. When winter arrived, I took up scorekeeping basketball. Basketball's rule book is complex, and many of the calls are extremely subjective; it is a very challenging sport to referee. I was quite happy to stay on the sidelines.

A long-time mentor pushed me the next year to become a referee. I later heard there was some sort of disagreement in the system, I never learned what, but many senior referees had left, and my partner was a rookie as well. Sheldon and I made it work. I was a by-the-book thinker in my young age, having gained nearly all my knowledge from books; I could quote the rule book like nobody else. Sheldon's officiating was informed by having played the game.

Sheldon taught me about relationship building in the gym; he was a natural people person. I remember thinking we were an odd couple when we began working together. He showed me how not to be robotic in applying rules. I learned from him the importance of proper exercise of responsibility and power.

The most important lesson of refereeing? Handling the bad call, the call you make by mistake, or the call you miss. At first I tried to compensate for this, making a balancing bad call or letting a call go to try and fix my error. This is the wrong way of handling mistakes. Learning to accept my mistakes and their impacts upon others was the strongest character-building element I gained. I learned to cope with mistakes, and how to regain my composure and focus.

It didn't take long for the convener to see my ability to work under pressure. I started to regularly get assigned to games with problematic parents or teams. I learned a lot about working in stressful situations, and self-control.

I remember one decision well. The basketball rule book forbids any contact between players; obviously, the literal interpretation is not the correct one. The amount of contact tolerated is always to the interpretation of the referee. In this game, two players were making regular contact with each other, some of which was starting to border on stiff-arming and pushing – the prelude to a fight. I verbally warned the two players multiple times, then after about two minutes of play with continuing contact, I called a double foul. Both players responded with frustration, I vividly remember the one player yelling, "What!"

and turning towards me. In almost unison, both coaches shouted at their players, "The referee warned you." I took my time calling it into the table, seeing that both coaches were using this as an opportunity to manage their players. There were no further incidents with either team for the rest of the season, and in subsequent games, I loosened the reins significantly.

Over fifteen years later, in 2016, at the height of city council's attacks on my character while I was reporting on city politics, a man sat across from me in Gore Park. "You don't remember me, but I remember you. You refereed my daughter's games at St. James. I know the claims about you are not true. I know your character, and many others do. Keep up your great work."

I met many great parents over the year, many good coaches and players. Being a sport official is great training for journalism, but at the time my eyes were set on politics.

I lived on my own at age seventeen. I had a steady foster parent for two-and-a-half years, but as her health failed, I would be placed into group homes regularly. I had two incidents in short order in group homes that pushed my CAS worker to move me out on my own. One group home had a strict 8:00 p.m. curfew, and the home operators (I wouldn't call them foster parents, housing Crown wards was a profit-driven business for them) punished me for violating curfew. I had explained that I was the key holder for my gym and as an official I had to be there on Wednesday nights, but the police were called. Nothing came of their involvement, and the home operators kept my meagre allowance that week. Thankfully, all my experiences, and anger management training, kept me from lashing out, though I gained a deep understanding of how Crown wards come to transition from the institution of the group home to institutionalization in jail.

In the late spring of my seventeenth year, I became ill with shingles. I was under extreme stress in many regards both socially and academically at school. One of the group homes I ended up in at this time made me sleep beside an air conditioner as I was struggling with the illness, and barely mobile. My condition worsened, I was transferred out of that group home, and once recovered, the decision was made to transition me to "extended care and maintenance." That meant that CAS paid my rent, and – because my mouse- and pest-infested unit was cheap enough – utilities, and I was responsible for the rest of my living and school expenses.

As I remarked often at the time, I had all the privileges and responsibilities of an adult.

Being in foster care, officiating sports, being on school board committees, along with attending and engaging with city council prepared me for my 2000 run for school board trustee in Ward 5. Or at least I thought so.

On my eighteenth birthday, I went to city hall to register to run for school board trustee. I didn't have the $100 filing fee but got my paperwork, and returned my next payday to officially register as a candidate. I was the first to register for public school trustee in all of Hamilton. Campaigning was an eye-opening experience. I started very naively trying to "educate" voters about the role of school board trustee. The number one question at the door was "Where do you stand on the expressway?" I thought voters misunderstood the role of school board trustee.

Finally, on the Beach Strip one day, a voter explained to me that I misunderstood the voter. "Look, kid, I'll listen to your school board positions once you've told me where you stand on the expressway. I'm not voting for some punk who is opposed to the expressway, it's too important!"

Living at King and Quigley, and walking across Centennial Parkway often, I understood the importance of the Red Hill expressway to removing traffic from my neighbourhoods and was fully in support of the project. I told him I favoured the expressway, then shared my positions on school board matters. I hope I secured his vote. The expressway was divisive across the city, but on the east side of the Red Hill, it enjoyed wide support.

Campaigning was mostly uneventful; other than some sign vandalism. One of my opponents accused me of orchestrating teenage vandals. My other opponent, and eventual winner, Wayne Marston, was a noble campaigner. One day, walking home after campaigning in Rosedale, I saw Wayne trying to remount one of his extra-large campaign signs that been knocked down. It was a two-person job, and he was on his own. I helped him with the sign, he offered me a ride home, and we almost got side-swiped during the drive. We joked about what the ensuing headlines would've been.

In the end, I spent just under $500 on my campaign, each of my opponents spent over $5000. I was in third place, but managed to secure 23 per cent of the vote; I was very happy with my first political campaign.

Many expected that I would pursue university after high school. In fact, I applied to Mohawk College for computer programming late, and was accepted, but the acceptance came by mail the day after I left for basic training with the Canadian Forces, and by the time I returned home from basic training, I had missed the acceptance deadline. Having had shingles, which cost me a job, added to my fears about turning age twenty-one. At twenty-one, CAS would no longer pay my rent, and I had to be completely self-supporting and secure. I had applied to universities for political science, York University had made me a great offer of financial support for first year, with promises that – provided I did well in my courses – further support would be forthcoming. I fixated on the risk of losing a term to illness, and the consequences if this occurred after my first year.

I chose a career in the army, determining that I would pursue education part-time by correspondence and take leaves of absence whenever possible. I spent three years with the Canadian Forces, becoming full-time after the 2001 9/11 terrorist attacks. During this time, as required by the National Defence Act, I had no political involvements whatsoever.

In May 2003, the National Road Cycling Championships were held in Hamilton. The Canadian championships were a trial run for the Fall 2003 Road World Championships. The day before the nationals, I was assigned to the military operation supporting the race. My role was limited. I would be with the major commanding the operation and was to inform him when a dignitary was approaching. As I knew all the city councillors, my assignment was a wise use of me as an asset by the military.

I showed up the next morning to find an operation that was disorganized at best. The army was short-staffed, and next thing I knew, I was assigned to "Sector 1," handed the operational plan to read and told my primary task was to secure the race route at the start-finish line. Secure meant keeping civilians from jumping the crowd control barriers onto the race route, watching for suspicious activity and preventing people from overhanging the barriers. My sector was Main Street from Bay Street to MacNab Street. A few minutes later, my sector expanded to James Street, then to include James Street from Main to Jackson Street. I was promoted to corporal from private (but didn't get corporal pay), and I was assigned fourteen civilian volunteers to assist in securing this area of the race route. The whole operation was poorly planned, with master corporals and sergeants taking sector assignments far from the crowds and junior soldiers assigned to the difficult lower city portions of the race route.

I was excited by my assignment, assisting with a major event in my hometown! As I was trying to read the operational plan, standing in front of city hall, the media sighted me in uniform and a media scrum was set up. A reporter asked the first question, "Why are you here today?" I responded, "Because I was ordered to be here, ma'am," then caught myself, and joked about that not being the answer the media was looking for. I tried to buy myself a bit of time by apologizing for my nervousness. A Canadian Forces public affairs officer behind the media signalled me to continue speaking. Not knowing the operational plan, I told the media we (the military) were present to provide our expertise in communications, logistics and coordination, then spoke about my pride as a Hamiltonian being at the event. My past experiences paid off; the PAO commended me for how I handled the media.

People were forbidden from crossing the race route; they hurled insults at me and the volunteers who informed them they would have to walk to the CP tracks at the GO station to cross James Street, or to Queen Street to cross at a manned checkpoint. At the corner of James and Main, a group of anti-military protestors greeted me with fury, placards overhanging onto the race route. It was very tense as I explained they could not have placards overhanging onto the race route; they wanted a confrontation. Their yelling at me attracted a large crowd of media, and two plain-clothed military commanders. I was horrified, thinking about what would come next, remaining gentle in my voice, calm in my demeanour and repeatedly acknowledging their right to protest. Internally, I was thinking this was my "Oka moment," that my military career was about to come to an end in a blaze of media coverage showing me in a standoff. I took up the relaxed posture I learned as a referee to appear non-confrontational and waited in the hope that something would happen to end the situation.

I recall one of the protest group leaders defused the situation by asking if it was okay for them to stand behind the barrier holding up their signs during the race. I responded this was their Charter right, pointing them to an area where they wouldn't block the view of spectators behind them.

Midday, the race organizers decided to change the track configuration on Main Street to two lanes from four. The change in track size was obscured by the old Bank of Montreal Building. My previous experience as a referee was handy in this situation; I foresaw the risk of bicycles, travelling at nearly seventy-five km/h, crashing into the crowd control barrier on the turn. On the first lap of the next race of the day, around two dozen bicycles were involved in a pileup that pushed the barrier back at least four metres. There were no onlookers in the area of the crash; I'd closed the area to spectators with yellow caution tape.

The rest of the day was spent dealing with people jumping barriers to cross the street; as the *Spectator* wrote, the volunteers in my sector took "abuse from pedestrians in stride." Around 10:30 a.m., a pedestrian was struck at Bay Street on the side in my sector. Police then set up a crossing at Bay Street for the rest of the event and manned it with auxiliary officers.

By the end of the first day, a Friday, people became much more relaxed about the race. Saturday and Sunday went without a hitch; people adjusted to the crossing points and started enjoying the event. Sunday saw thousands of people in the downtown. It cannot be emphasized enough that Hamilton's downtown had reached bottom in 2003 with the vacancy rate at its highest. For many people, this was the first time they'd been downtown for years. The crowds were vibrant and cheerful; it was a very exciting moment for Hamilton.

I trace the "revival" to this moment, civic pride was back!

I was sad when it all came to an end on Sunday, but not before I would get a story to tell. Races ended over an hour late, people could not cross their cars back into the closure area at 5:30 p.m. as scheduled. James Street Baptist Church had rescheduled its 11:00 a.m. Mass to 7:00 p.m. As 6:30 p.m. approached, the races were coming to an end, and I started to assign my team to barriers for removal. Main and MacNab, James and Main, James and Jackson, James and Hunter were my four barriers. The barrier at James and Main could be dismantled early, police barriers prevented traffic from reaching it due to one-way streets. I safely took down the MacNab barrier. Hunter was also closed at John by police, but I didn't dismantle this barrier as a few cars had used Hughson to access Hunter and wait at the barrier.

The vehicles queued on Jackson Street extended past John Street. An elderly man was the driver of the first vehicle in the line; I chatted briefly with him, and after small talk, I told him that I would be dismantling the barriers but I needed him to wait until I was allowed to open the road before he could cross. He agreed. Myself and three volunteers dismantled the barrier, and I sent them to await the command to dismantle other barriers when roads reopened. The all-clear didn't come as expected. After about five minutes, the third vehicle in the queue on Jackson turned on their engine and pivoted their tires to try using the opposing lane to get to James Street. I was able to shout a strong command to them, and they turned off their engine again. The old man in front then turned on his engine, slammed his horn and started pushing me with his vehicle. Shouting obscenities, the man yelled about how he was now late. I commanded him to stop, his wife was telling him to calm down, and I was now pushing against his car, mostly to feel the tension and dive out of the way if I needed to. In my mind, I was thinking "no good deed goes unpunished" and that I would deserve the forthcoming reprimand as this guy drove onto the cycling route.

Eventually, in his yelling, the old man said, "I'm only going across the road to park, I'm going to be late for Mass!" In my mind, I laughed at the irony; he clearly needed Mass, and shouted back, "I'm sure the Mass won't start without parishioners." The commotion had brought the pastor of James Baptist out. He defused the situation, explaining how "the soldier has his orders" and citing Scripture to the member of his flock. The old man kept repeating that he only wanted to cross the road, the pastor kept repeating the soldier must follow his orders. My radio announced the opening of the roadway and I moved to the middle of the intersection and did traffic control for a few minutes.

At the end of it all, I took my volunteers out for dinner and drinks at the then new downtown restaurant Acclamation. Many of the volunteers commented on not knowing about the changes in downtown Hamilton. I told owner Patricia Roque to keep the pitchers and food coming, I would settle the bill at the end of the night. Patricia asked if I'd prefer an invoice, I told her it was out of my pocket. The volunteers were not compensated for their time, I was getting time off in lieu (being paid) and they'd served well. Patricia charged me $200 for the night. I know that was a steep discount, but that's how those of us in the downtown take care of each other.

I'd leave the military a year later. A series of events led to my unexpected decision. I'd been doing part-time correspondence courses with the University of Manitoba and applied to take on-campus courses in the summer of 2004. My summer application was mistakenly processed as a regular year application and I received a generous offer package for full-time studies. I called to explain the error and the university immediately approved my summer course registration on the phone. I asked them to cancel the offer package. The university said it would automatically expire in two weeks and no further action would be needed. The next day, my captain denied my request for an unpaid three-month leave of absence, stating that it was not in the interest of the military to allow me to pursue an activity that would lead to my leaving the forces. I contacted the university, took the fall offer and when my military contract came up for renewal, I informed my captain I was leaving at the end of my contract.

The decision was not planned. I saw the university package offer as a signal and opportunity. I'd grown much less risk-averse during my time in the army.

I moved to Winnipeg in May 2004 to attend university, an "accidental" choice that remains one of the smartest decisions I've ever made. I had just launched joeycoleman.ca. Blogging was new, and I thought I'd learn programming by running a blog on my server. Turned out I had to write in order to have a website to code. Getting involved in student politics I found a subject to write about.

Winnipeg was a more expensive city to live in than Hamilton back in 2005, I had better employment prospects in Hamilton, and decided after a year in residence at Manitoba that I'd return to online studies combined with classes as a visiting student at McMaster. I continued blogging on student politics and university affairs. In March 2007, *Maclean's* magazine called me out of the blue and offered me a job covering post-secondary education for them. That day, I "accidentally" became a journalist. I had "reporter/blogger" on my business cards at *Maclean's*, I insisted on blogger instead of columnist because I wanted to emphasize that I thought blogging was a noble pursuit when done properly.

This worked out for me. As a Crown ward, I couldn't afford the living costs of university, and OSAP made no allowance for that reality.

I quickly became one of Hamilton's Toronto commuters. *Maclean's* was great to work at when I started. I had a large national audience. Nobody else was competing against me. I accounted for about 20 per cent of daily traffic on their website, just my blog on post-secondary. I would be blogging six or seven times a day with a lot of interesting content and many short snippets. I did one or two long posts a week. Then I would do a news article every other day with some depth. I worked twelve-hour days and I loved it.

As I commuted more and more to Toronto, however, I came to rely solely on the *Hamilton Spectator* to know what was happening at Hamilton City Hall. I started to realize that I was losing touch with my community because the *Spectator* was not covering it – they weren't there at every meeting. And a lot of the stuff they were looking for had drama but not the substance.

After a few years at *Maclean's*, the publication and I diverged on direction.

I had been covering First Nations education funding on a story about provincial and federal cuts to the First Nations Technical In-stitute – a post-secondary institution – on a reserve just outside of

Belleville. The institute had been doing phenomenal work and had great graduation rates. The federal government cut it because it was education, and education belongs to the province. The province cut it because it was First Nations, and First Nations belongs to the federal government.

It wasn't clear who cut funding first, cuts were announced at the same time. FNTI had 250 students, a record of success, but nobody in Toronto or Ottawa was covering the story; only the local newspaper. It's near Belleville, on a reserve, and those in power did not seem to care. It was in my beat and my editor and I decided we were going to press hard on this story. But the executive editor and bean-counters at Rogers weren't supportive of covering the story as it took a lot of time, and readership was very low. Meanwhile, unpaid contributors were blogging about the latest online outrages and driving a lot of traffic to the site.

At the end of my contract a few months later, I left *Maclean's*, planning to leave journalism.

The *Globe and Mail* approached me with a freelance gig writing once a week for them, which kept me in journalism, but I continued to look for an exit. *Hamilton Spectator* editor-in-chief David Estok and I met at an event early in 2009 and I was in contract talks with the *Spectator* when a hiring freeze came because of the great recession.

The recession is the pivotal moment in my journalism career. I watched good smart people being laid off. The senselessness of those layoffs bothered me. The lack of a plan among legacy media managers to fix journalism frustrated me, and their demands to produce clickbait enraged me. My Hamilton roots were showing: bullshit, which is effectively what clickbait is, is not tolerated in East Hamilton, bullshitters quickly get socially ostracized. Another important piece of blue-collar Hamilton culture is that you don't get to complain about something unless you are fixing it.

Fundamentally the crisis facing journalism is the collapse of local news. It is the loss of connection to local communities and the loss of public trust resulting from the lack of coverage of and disengagement from where most people live – the communities outside of Montreal, Toronto and Vancouver.

In 2010, I took leave of my contract at the *Globe*, and stepped into a summer position at the *Hamilton Spectator*. My plan was to recharge locally and then head back into national journalism, reigniting myself, overcoming the burnout that I was feeling and then work to find an opportunity to engage in entrepreneurial journalism.

It did reignite my passion and love for journalism. But I loved it again because I loved being in my hometown. There was no turning back. I was going to make local journalism work here in Hamilton. I, a lowly Crown ward, had taken up the task of addressing what I feel is the great challenge of our age – saving local journalism!

It took me two years to find my way to crowdfunding. In 2012, joeycoleman.ca became crowdfunded and it morphed into what is now ThePublicRecord.ca. Hamiltonians supported this new idea. We were first to use crowdfunding to create local news. My mission was simple – produce the journalism necessary for citizens to be informed so they can fully exercise their responsibilities of citizenship in a participatory democracy.

Hamilton is a great place to experiment and fix journalism. There is a dynamic and ongoing story to cover that is of both local and regional interest in the ongoing gentrification, and because of our people. Hamilton welcomes people who come to the city with the intention of becoming part of the community. The story of the late Dave Hanley is a great example. He arrived in 2015 from Kitchener, and quickly became part of the community. Hanley ran Pop Up Hamilton, which held event dinners at various locales in the city. He was also involved in Food4Kids and other Hamilton-boosting activities.

Hanley died suddenly in September 2017 and a "pop-up" memorial was held days later in Sam Lawrence Park on the same day he had been planning a pop-up dinner at the park. As I sat there, I thought about how important Dave had been in creating our new better Hamilton. Dave helped get Hamilton past its red tape to allow for this type of spontaneous event. The contributions of people like Dave Hanley matter, and they are stories that local journalism must share.

Famed documentarian Ken Burns says the greatest find in his extensive research for the seven-part PBS miniseries *The War* was the writings of Al McIntosh. McIntosh was editor of the *Rock County Star-Herald* of Luverne, Minnesota, during the Second World War. He told the stories of the people of the community. Nearly seventy years later, his plain writings give us a vivid and comprehensive look into how people were affected by the war. I remind myself often that covering the "common story" is important in local journalism – the first draft of history, as they say.

The Public Record covers city hall in-depth. Currently, I'm a one-man operation. I record every meeting at city hall and post it to the Internet for people to be able to see what their government is doing. I also do it to hold myself to account: I can't misreport the story, or misquote the participants, the full recording is there to fact check me. It's also there for others to use.

There are limits to what I can do. It's hard to find time to, for instance, view a new planning application and follow that application from planning to approval. If the week isn't too busy, I can go to the planning division at city hall and ask to see what files were submitted that week. This happens less often than I wish, maybe once a month now. I go when I learn of specific high-profile applications, but that kind of "shiny object" journalism is not all I want to be doing. People voluntarily fund The Public Record, because they know I am going to be covering issues at city hall. But if all I did was cover city hall it wouldn't be enough. It wouldn't be enough because people want more than just city hall. They want to feel connected to their community. That's why coverage of people's lives, the people who do good things that build community every day, is important.

They fund The Public Record because it is a community good. There is no paywall. A paywall limits who can be involved. Journalism behind a paywall is no longer a public good and without being a public good, what would be the purpose of journalism?

A paywall doesn't work in local journalism. The open monthly patron model can work, but it takes time to become sustainable. Local journalism requires sacrifice by journalists, not just short-term financial sacrifice but personal sacrifice.

My character is regularly attacked by the powerful, those on council, in the media and beyond. You cannot really be popular if you're doing good journalism.

Hamiltonians, due to our city's blue-collar history, appreciate this, and value direct honesty above many traits.

One of the primary attacks I regularly face is the charge that I'm involved in my community. To a blue-collar Hamiltonian such as myself, it's hypocritical to complain, as journalists often do, that people are not involved enough and don't vote and then turn around and state that, as journalists, they do not have to engage in the hard work of civic engagement because "I have to be neutral."

There is no such thing as neutrality.

The idea that writers such as Desmond Cole should stay quiet in the face of carding and racial profiling, or just write for the *Toronto Star* about it, instead of taking an active role in addressing it, fails to recognize that Cole, by his hard work, has found a platform where he can do something about the problems facing his community. Cole is speaking on behalf of the people he grew up with, the people he knows. And if all Cole did was write about the topic or discuss it at cocktail parties, he wouldn't be effecting the change his community needs.

When Cole stood up at the Toronto Police Services Board meeting against carding, and was removed from the meeting, he did not end up in a police cell. He got heard. On the other hand, if a young Black man who was not Desmond Cole had done the same thing, that young Black man would likely have spent the night in a cell for his troubles. Journalists from working-class backgrounds live differently in our communities; our involvements are not on boards of directors, it is in our communities. We're clear in our bias; we don't claim to be "neutral and unbiased" because we don't have the luxury of "neutrality."

I've regularly stated to people, "Here is where I'm coming from and here's my view. Here is why I have this view. Here are the full video documents for you to decide for yourself." Journalists traditionally get somebody else to express the view that they themselves hold. They say, "Oh I have no opinion – I'm a journalist." That's why many people have lost a lot of respect for journalists: they know the journalist has a viewpoint and has a bias, but they have other people in their stories speak for them. We choose our sources!

In late 2012, after my first crowdfunding campaign, I started livestreaming and videotaping every public meeting at city hall. Council and some in the local media took it as a novelty – they thought, "Oh this guy will disappear." I wasn't a threat to their collective. However, people started watching the videos and the meetings, increasing civic engagement and upsetting the status quo. Eventually, perhaps in the hope of undercutting my reach, the city itself started videotaping council meetings. However, they used a very low-quality video that often crashed and they edited out parts of meetings. I continued to post the full meeting video to YouTube. This radical transparency changed everything.

Prior to this, city councillors controlled the news narrative. Mainstream journalists would only cover full council meetings, and sometimes not even those. When asked, councillors told the journalists their version of what happened at meetings. Suddenly, the dynamic of council changed from a very comfortable old boys' club of "we'll decide what the people need to know" to people being able to learn exactly what happened.

Mainstream journalists now attend about 50 per cent of council standing committees. There were complaints that I was filming in a non-designated area. My camera used to capture the media row in the background during standing committee meetings and the public could see that the media row was empty. I was told to film pointing away from media row in the chamber. We finally have media back at city hall for standing committees because they must compete with my coverage. This diminished council's control of the public narrative, and some councillors seemed particularly upset.

The Accountability and Transparency Committee in particular appeared to take extreme offence to this new transparency. It was a committee that did nothing, spending seven years trying to not create a lobbyist registry. Once people could see for themselves how dysfunctional this committee was, change occurred. For many, my videos were their first exposure to how city hall worked, or in this case worked on not working.

I focused on the Accountability and Transparency Committee because of its name, but there were all sorts of other committees that exist that no journalist had covered in recent memory. Councillors would often claim to their constituents, "Oh no I fought against such and such a proposal." Now people could see if their councillor was saying one thing to their community and another thing at council.

The council seemed particularly nervous leading up to the election in 2014 because there was a sharp rise in civil engagement. This was a recent phenomenon. In the 2000s, Citizens at City Hall (CATCH) tried to get more people engaged, but they were ahead of their time in many ways. The challenge CATCH faced was that, because they came out of the anti–Red Hill movement, large segments of people saw them as just the Red Hill "activists." They couldn't get traction as a journalistic outlet, despite the excellence of their ongoing work.

THE "SHOVING" INCIDENT

There were attempts to discredit me, here and there, as I followed city hall council meetings and subcommittee meetings. They finally culminated into what many refer to as the "shoving incident." Councillor Lloyd Ferguson didn't shove me – it was an assault, let's call it what it is. He grabbed onto me and held on.

His loss of control happened in February 2014, on Pink Shirt Day, after a meeting in which he lost a closed session vote.

The day of the assault, he came up to me in the middle of a council meeting, threatening that if I kept writing about Accountability and Transparency there "would be consequences." The meeting had to stop because he was towering over me in the council chambers. Committee members told him to sit down and he sat down. The media behind me went – wow he's pretty angry. That was two hours before the assault.

It felt clear to me that he was angry he had no leverage over my coverage of his role as chair of the Accountability and Transparency Committee. In early 2013, Ferguson had approached me looking to make a deal, he sought a typical access journalism arrangement – he would provide me insider information, and he would hope for favourable coverage in return. I had no interest in making a deal. I don't play access journalism. The fact he was not in control is what seemed to anger Ferguson, a privileged man who is able to control everything in his life. I am of a lower socio-economic class and there is an age difference, but the power dynamic that he appeared to expect to have was not present.

The Accountability and Transparency Committee is responsible for accountability and transparency to improve government. There were around 165 subcommittees in city council and each of these subcommittees has important agenda items. I chose to focus on the Accountability and Transparency Committee for obvious reasons.

After the meeting, I left the council chamber and was walking in the public foyer to a room where a press conference was being held. Ferguson was walking out as well; he buttonhooked back, stating to a city staff member, "I need to talk to you about something." Ferguson looked at me, told me to "get the fuck out of here," and a half-second after that he shoved me. Then, he took two steps towards me, grabbed my arm and jostled me around.

The public foyer has four security cameras, and according to City Manager Chris Murray, three of the four simultaneously failed for a few minutes when the assault occurred. The city had to "recover" video from a camera in another room, and couldn't export the video, having to play it on a computer monitor and record the video from the monitor using a Blackberry smartphone. The recovery was only fifteen seconds of video, which the city then further edited by blurring the video for "privacy reasons."

The city's edited video ends with Ferguson moving towards me. The city's official version of events is that Ferguson then suddenly turned and walked away, and that I had to be restrained – that I was out of control. Funny how they didn't keep video of that!

Ferguson was not only chair of the Accountability and Transparency Committee; he was also chair of the Hamilton Police Services Board. The police board met in closed session and chose not to investigate the matter. City council quickly removed the Zero Tolerance for Violence signs from city hall.

I knew immediately after the assault that I would be smeared in the court of public opinion. Sure enough, the next morning, former mayor Larry Di Ianni took to Twitter to attack my character.

I remain proud of how I handled the assault: I didn't push back, I didn't pull away and I didn't retaliate. I did everything right. I was in a public lobby. I was in the right. The reality was if I'd pushed him back, I would have been arrested immediately for assaulting Lloyd

Ferguson, and it would be a more serious assault charge because of his being the police board chair.

Earl Basse, the integrity commissioner, reported to Councillor Lloyd Ferguson as chair of the Accountability and Transparency Committee. Basse was assigned to investigate his boss, the very man who would decide if he would be renewed as integrity commissioner weeks after the report was completed.

Earl Basse stated that because Lloyd Ferguson felt I was "eavesdropping" and that I had a history of "eavesdropping" on public meetings Ferguson's actions were excusable. He stated that "Joey Coleman had sensitive recording equipment with him." The integrity commissioner also said it was odd that I was still at city hall after the council meeting. It was eleven minutes after the meeting.

Basse's investigation did not involve interviewing any of the witnesses. Basse determined, based upon a "gut feeling"[1] (Basse's own words), that I was involved in a conspiracy against Ferguson. He interviewed multiple people looking for this conspiracy, finding no evidence to support his gut feeling.

Nonetheless, Basse reported to council that he felt I had conspired against Ferguson after the incident by not stopping people from filing Code of Conduct complaints. "The Complainants deny that they were acting in concert and that the two (2) day difference in filing the complaints is a coincidence only," Basse wrote of his investigating into his gut feeling of "collusion" to have Ferguson investigated.

Basse was particularly critical of me for requesting the city preserve neutral security video of the assault.

CCTV security video is normally saved for a period of 14 days only. The complaints against Councillor Ferguson were not filed with the City until May 27, 2014 (#1) and May 29, 2014 (#2), a full three (3) months after the incident and both within two days of each other.

Had Mr. Coleman not informed the City on February 27, 2014 that a complaint had been filed, the security tape would not have been available for inquiry purposes on May 27, 2014 when the complaints were actually filed with the City. It is interesting to note that at the time of Mr. Coleman's email, a private citizen had not filed a complaint with the City in this regard.

City council endorsed Basse's report in a 13–2 vote on Pink Shirt Day 2015, after delivering speeches claiming their commitment to ending bullying. Immediately, my media credentials were revoked, and I had no access to the press room. I lost access to agendas, and the Internet connection I used on media row was disabled.

André Marin, Ontario's ombudsman learned of the situation, read the integrity commissioner's report and tore it apart. He called it one of the worst reports he had ever seen.

"To be fair, there is great value in the #HamOnt IC report,"[2] Marin tweeted. Marin vowed to use the report as a "model of how not to write a report." The ombudsman reviewed the report, graded it an "F"[3] and ended his review tweeting "I would have sent the #HamOnt IC report back to the drawing board. And not the grade 3 one it appears it was written on."[4]

At the time, the ombudsman had no jurisdiction over municipal governments in Ontario. Mayor Fred Eisenberger stood by Basse's report, declaring it to be the final word on the incident.[5]

On May 25, 2015, in a closed session, the council held a "security session." The contents of which, and decisions made, remain secret to this day.

A few days later, the city revoked all my access, and without recourse, I was not able to cover city hall for the remainder of 2015. On January 1, 2016, the Ontario ombudsman finally gained oversight of Ontario's municipalities. The city lifted all the active restrictions, but passive ones were left in place. I wasn't allowed to plug into electrical outlets during committee meetings for "safety reasons" as people might trip over my laptop power cord (that was tucked under my chair). As I was no longer "media" following the revoking of my credentials, I was not allowed to use the media room, and as a member of the public, I was not allowed to leave my bag or anything in a public meeting room when I went to the washroom during a meeting. Many times, I left my coat or bag sitting on a chair, and the city quickly moved the items to the lost and found. City staff knew they were my items, and they were not lost, it was just petty harassment in the hope I'd get frustrated enough to either lash out or quit covering city hall. The city stopped seizing my items late in spring of 2016 when I finally spoke to the ombudsman's office about the "lost and found" practice.

Again, my experiences growing up prepared me well for this bullying. One must put up with harassment when one comes from the lowest socio-economic classes. I could not complain about the bullying, due to socio-economic dynamics. If I did, I would be called a "whiner," *whiner* being the politest of the various attacks I would receive for speaking up.

In March 2017, the city clerk created a new "broadcasting policy" to address "bloggers" who were "broadcasting" by tweeting during meetings. The policy stated that "broadcasting" by bloggers during public meetings was strictly forbidden at subcommittees and non-council committees.

I didn't know about the policy, the clerk waited to announce it on a day when two committees were meeting at the same time. I attended the beginning of one meeting, and the clerk started the other meeting by announcing to an empty public gallery that this new policy was now in effect. I happened to walk into this meeting room with only my cellphone, leaving my laptop and other gear in the other meeting room.

It was serendipitous that I happened to only have my cellphone in hand. I sat down and started tweeting with my cellphone. A city clerk stood up shouting, "Are you secretly recording this meeting with an unauthorized recording device?" Having been subjected to this harassment in the past, I ignored the clerk and continued tweeting. The clerk declared that I was engaged in a violation of city policy and stated the committee needed to leave the room to receive legal direction from a lawyer in the city solicitor's office.

The chair of the committee and the clerk came back to the room and ordered me to hand over my cellphone. The lawyer from the city solicitor's office came in and demanded that I swear an oath that I had no secret recording devices on me, that I remove the battery from my cellphone and that I place all my items on a table in the middle of the room to prove I wasn't secretly recording the meeting.

I sat in the chair in the public gallery ignoring them and the lawyer warned me that if I continued to ignore her, security would be called and I would be banned from city hall under the Trespass to Property Act. I continued to tweet. The city's lawyer then declared that because of the risk that I was "eavesdropping" on this *public* meeting, the meeting would be cancelled and all the citizens who came that day to speak would have to return at a later date when "Mr. Coleman is more respectful of the rules." At this point, with security staff present, I asked the city's lawyer to confirm I was being removed under the Trespass to Property Act, which she confirmed, and I left the room.

A representative from the Canadian Civil Liberties Association was attending the meeting that was occurring in the other room. They joined with Canadian Journalists for Free Expression (CJFE) in filing a complaint to the Ontario ombudsman. CJFE and I also sent the city a list of demands and cautioned the city we were prepared to go to the Divisional Court to get the trespass order declared a violation of the Charter of Rights and Freedoms' press protections.

Thankfully, because the room had a security camera, and I was wearing a very light T-shirt and tight-fitting pants that day, it was clear I couldn't be hiding any items on my person. The body language of the city's clerk and lawyer were clearly aggressive, whereas mine was not. CJFE and I stated we were prepared to go to the Law Society of Upper Canada regarding the lawyer's behaviour.

The city had overreached in their harassment, CJFE demanded that the city lift all punishments imposed by the *Basse Report*, that I be granted full media privileges again, the trespass order be removed, the city manager issue an apology for the trespass order and the Broadcast Policy be revoked.

Much to our surprise, the city manager accepted the conditions except for recognizing me as a journalist. City staff resumed giving me copies of public agendas, I could use the media room again and it would be two years before staff harassed me again.

The city manager has no control over council; councillors regularly attack me on Twitter; the mayor still likes to imply I'm the Fox News of Hamilton by mocking my coverage as "fair and balanced," the Fox News tagline; and Ward 8 councillor Terry Whitehead continues to push for licensing of "citizen journalists."

I continue covering the stories city hall doesn't want covered, filing frequent Freedom of Information requests and providing the public a lens into what our government is doing in our name.

NEIGHBOURHOOD ASSOCIATIONS AND THE NEW ACTIVISM

Covering municipal affairs day to day as an independent journalist is not glamorous, far from it. There are few noteworthy moments; stories happen over time, change is slow.

My work is succeeding because I'm still at city hall, and engagement in the community is increasing. Standing my ground and still being at city hall is a significant victory. Reading the archives of the *Hamilton Spectator* from the 1980s and '90s, there is a recurring theme of the citizen who tries to improve civic governance and policy. They engage with council, rally public support, but only for a couple of years before being ground down and burnt out.

The media has been part of the problem by traditionally deciding that anyone not part of the existing political structure is a "fringe candidate" and effectively ignoring them. Coverage of council races has been basically non-existent when there is an incumbent politician running. Prior to the Internet age, this effectively ruled out any change to council.

In 2014, this tradition continued amongst the mainstream outlets. I did something different. On the first day of registration, January 2. I set up my camera and went live all day interviewing every candidate that registered. During the election, I livestreamed numerous debates, but only two of those debates were in wards with incumbents – Ward 2 and Flamborough.

The Flamborough Chamber of Commerce debate is a tradition; the Ward 2 debate was noteworthy and new. Organized by neighbourhood associations, it represented the growth of political engagement in Hamilton. This did not go unnoticed among Hamilton's political class; the first crack in their control of the narrative appeared. There were attempts in other communities to organize debates, without success.

In 2018, I significantly improved my coverage by launching *The 155 Podcast*, so named because there were 155 registered candidates in all the races. I interviewed 102 of the candidates, excluding acclaimed candidates, a white supremacist and two candidates who sent inappropriate messages to female candidates.

The podcast was brilliant in its simplicity. Candidates answered fifteen questions related to the public office they were seeking, and voters had the opportunity to judge candidates at their convenience. There were over four hundred thousand downloads of the podcast, with the Ward 15 race being the most popular of the council races. People tell me they used the podcast to decide how they voted, but the impact of this cannot be quantified. We can quantify the Ward 15 results however. In that race the incumbent barely kept their seat, winning by a 216-vote margin. Considering the thousands of listens to the Ward 15 challengers podcast interview, it is likely the podcast impacted this race. It's part of the reason why the mayor, councillors and mainstream journalists regularly malign "social media" and "social media activists"; they no longer control the message.

People seeking election to council used to be frozen out by an inability to be heard, which often meant they couldn't reach potential donors. With the rise of grassroots civic engagement, it is now possible for new candidates to be heard, for small donors to pool enough funds to create a viable campaign and to be heard using online platforms.

In the past two years, we've seen four or five new neighbourhood associations on the Mountain, a new one in downtown Stoney Creek and nearly every neighbourhood in Ward 3 has a neighbourhood association. There are loose associations of people in Dundas, which could lead to a formal neighbourhood association. This is happening outside the control of councillors, and poses a threat to their ease of re-election.

Councillors regularly complain to me about my open licensing of videos of city hall meetings. People are using the videos to advance their arguments on social media, to hold council to account and to show when councillors are voting one way, but claiming another position in the community.

I do enjoy much support under the surface at city hall. Many city staff support my journalism, but staff cannot be seen to support me. It would be career damaging for them. Their spouses are some of my biggest crowdfunding supporters. Councillors have been known to micromanage careers at city hall, a staff member who is seen to treat me with respect risks career consequences and losing promotions. It should not be the role of council to decide who gets promoted, to decide which potholes road crews will fill. A councillor's work is to oversee governance and policy. This is one of the reasons that Denison surveys at the city have found significant dissatisfaction by city staff in their jobs and poor corporate culture results.

Staff who fail to abide by city hall culture are publicly maligned during council meetings. In other municipalities, politicians do not malign the professional public service because the civic culture does not allow for it. In Toronto, if a politician attacks the integrity of a staff member, the senior staff member present immediately intervenes, and if it is the senior staff member who is being impugned, the chair of the meeting intervenes. Here in Hamilton, bullying of staff is normal and we don't even realize it is bullying. Often, I'm the only person who is defending our public service staff, arguing for proper separation of politicians from operations.

Twice a year I go to a Burlington City Council meeting and just sit in the back of the public gallery. Each time I attend, a staff member will bring me a print copy of the agenda. The last time the mayor of Burlington actually acknowledged and welcomed me publicly, although that attitude might change if they had to put up with me every day.

The City of Guelph and the City of Toronto have invited me to be present at their public engagement sessions. In 2015, while I was kept out of Hamilton City Hall, the City of Guelph invited me to speak at a staff learning session about relationships with media, citizens and what the future of public dialogue will be. Ironically, the panel was scheduled to include the editor of the daily newspaper, the *Guelph Mercury*. Three weeks prior to the panel, the paper's parent company, Torstar, closed the paper.

In many communities there is a concern that soon nobody will be covering their council, and this will increase their local democratic deficit. They realize the importance of a free and adversarial press. Citizens trust in government declines without independent account-ability and for cities this is a problem. Local politicians cannot fulfill their mandates without public trust.

The Guelph staff learning session was open to the public, the dis-cussion was frank, staff asked uncomfortable questions and I was able to give uncomfortable answers. In many ways, the opposite culture at

Hamilton City Hall is unique. I've gone to many municipalities to discuss open data, open government and to speak at public engagement sessions.

Hamilton has a much more secretive bureaucracy because the council has become entrenched. Many councillors have been at city hall for over twenty years. We lose good staff to other municipalities and the private sector. As I often note, as much toxicity as I get, I still have a platform and I still have some freedom. I hate to imagine what some of the staff are going through.

The good news is that all this could change if the new culture of neighbourhood activism helps bring fresh blood, new ideas and a different approach to city hall. As for me, I'll keep on doing my part: continuing to work to address the crisis in journalism and to build a better Hamilton.

Endnotes

1   Andrew Dreschel, "Integrity commissioner Basse speaks," *Hamilton Spectator*, February 27, 2015, https://www.thespec.com/opinion-story/5451025-dreschel -integrity-commissioner-basse-speaks/.

2   André Marin, "1/2 To b fair, there is great value in #HamOnt IC Report," Twitter, February 27, 2015, 12:36 p.m., https://twitter.com/Ont_Ombudsman/status /571363312706965507.

3   André Marin, "Page 1: My marked-up marking of #HamOnt IC report," Twitter, February 27, 2015, 1:20 p.m., https://twitter.com/Ont_Ombudsman/status /571374284309987329.

4   André Marin, "If #Bill8 had been in effect, I would have sent #HamOnt IC report back 2 drawing board. And not the grade 3 one it appears it was written on," Twitter, February 27, 2015, 12:53 p.m., https://twitter.com/Ont_Ombudsman/status /571363318067277824.

5   Dreschel, "Integrity commissioner Basse speaks."

Making Art in a White Town

Seema Narula

O n a hot August summer evening on the second Friday of the
month James Street North is bustling. Sidewalks are starting
to fill up with people. Vendors and musicians line the street
trying to get in on their share of Hamilton's art scene. They've been
staking out their claims on a few squares of cement in front of stores,
the armoury, restaurants and the few remaining vacant buildings since
mid-afternoon. The vibe is that of a Wild West free-for-all frenzy, which
is increasingly becoming the norm for the busier summer art crawls.

It's a far cry from over a decade ago, when the crawls had their
humble beginnings. At that time, a few galleries had opened on James
Street North along with a handful of shops. They decided to join forces
to start the monthly crawls, which were held in tandem with gallery
exhibition openings. The point of the crawls were to encourage people
to check out the multiple art openings, and to give people an excuse to
get out and rediscover this little stretch of the city.

These early crawls were what created the first rumblings, especially
for people outside of the city and the downtown core, of a new type of

Hamilton emerging – an arty one filled with "potential." It preceded the more recent tidal wave of gentrification, along with its large-scale condo developments. Catch phrases like "Art is the New Steel" and "You Can Do Anything in Hamilton" took hold of the city. That was in 2009. The landscape of the city has continued shifting physically, socially and economically as Hamilton continues its rebirth as a post-industrial city. But who is the city changing for and who are the changes benefitting?

Although Hamilton is a city that is ethnically diverse and seeing a growth in its population of young visible minorities – one in four according to the Social Planning and Research Council of Hamilton – some would say that Hamilton still operates as a white town. In 2014, however, Hamilton's Ward 3 city councillor Matthew Green was elected. He broke the city's over forty-year-long institution of an all-white city council and happens to be Hamilton's first Black city councillor. Yet still, when looking at our larger institutions like city council, school boards and our bureaucratic systems, there is no reflection of our changing population. So, should it really be a surprise that Hamilton's newish claim to fame of having an "ultra-hip" art scene happens to be for an art scene that is predominantly white?

Many of the artists of colour that I interviewed for this project shared the same feeling of having to go to Toronto to attain success. Their encounters with racism or the experience of a lack of success in Hamilton was quite resounding. The artists strongly want to remain in Hamilton and foster communities similar to those that exist in Toronto. There was an acknowledgement from all that white artists – predominantly white, male artists – dominate the art scene. Those artists are promoted, nurtured and given opportunities to develop and grow.

For people of colour there is often a need to have to work much harder to have those same opportunities. Imagine having to hone one's own practice as an artist and then to additionally feel the need to create and develop institutions like a record label that promotes and records *your* music, a gallery that promotes *your* art, a theatre company that will perform *your* plays, a fashion show that celebrates *your* fashion designs, a music festival that celebrates a variety of music genres and an organization that promotes *you* because no one else will.

Many of the artists I interviewed were doing just that. Creating their own communities and agencies to support and promote their own art, while also helping to champion other marginalized artists around them. Instead of just focusing on the success of their own artistic careers, as other artists might, they are putting extra energy and time into developing and building a supportive scene – one that they feel Hamilton is lacking. Although many of the racialized artists I interviewed directly experienced the negative affects of discrimination in their artistic careers, other marginalized artists that I interviewed did not. Discrimination is a complex entity and is not experienced the same way by everyone.

Enter COBRA.

Formed in 2016, COBRA, the Coalition of Black and Racialized Artists, is a Hamilton collective that champions racialized artists by providing opportunities for people of colour to partake and become included as active members in Hamilton's arts community. COBRA essentially pools networking and resource connections together to build a positive creative community and environment that empowers each of its members in a way that racialized artists often do not have access to.

≡

Kojo Easy Damptey (K.E.D.) is a musician, a filmmaker and a founder of COBRA. Born in Accra, Ghana, he's been in Hamilton since the early 2000s, actively contributing to the city's music scene, creating music in the genres of hip hop, funk, soul and Afro-soul. For many years, Kojo's work with COBRA was integral in supporting racialized artists. He was dedicated to mentoring, promoting and sharing with the city, and the larger arts community, the talent coming from musical genres reaching beyond Hamilton's touted indie rock scene.

I first met Kojo at a panel discussion about Hamilton as a city in transition for CBC Hamilton. As the panellists moved through topics from increasing real estate prices and affordability, to gentrification and awe of the pace of these changes – all the new shops and places opening in the city – the thing that stood out for me was Kojo's answer when asked about how he thinks the city has changed. He responded, "Ain't nothing's changed," and added that for people of colour in the art scene "you can't just be yourself." He continued, saying that it's "not just the arts. It's everything. Until people are willing and are able to change then we won't get any gender diversity, diversity of women, women of colour. They never want to talk about that in the arts scene."

When Kojo spoke with me about his struggles as a racialized musical artist he gave the music we hear on the radio as an example. It's on the radio "because someone made it happen. Not because it's the best song. If my music was pushed in the same way as other successful musicians, I'd be in a different place than I am now. That's where we are lacking, we don't have the pull to make things happen." Kojo was hoping to create just that kind of traction for other racialized artists with COBRA by sending an artist's work on to places like CBC Radio as well as promoting and connecting musicians with the greater music community and industry. The success of this approach can be seen in up-and-coming musical artists like Shanika Maria, who have been featured on CBC in part because of COBRA.

If Hamilton doesn't celebrate and acknowledge the existence of genres of music beside indie rock, Kojo was concerned that these less favoured music scenes will not stick around. He feared Hamilton was "going to lose the cache and scope of enjoying other musicians in the city, and other musicians who want to stay in the city" as these artists leave in search of communities where they will be more recognized or appreciated.

Besides writing, producing and making his own music, Kojo has been putting on the Renaissance Music Festival. This is a festival in Hamilton that has been running since 2012, which celebrates music from Africa and the African diaspora with genres ranging from hip hop, soul and R & B to Afro-jazz. Although no longer an active member of COBRA, he is currently the interim executive director of the Hamilton Centre for Civic Inclusion, where he continues to do anti-discrimination and equity work. Kojo is a tireless crusader in challenging inequality and addressing social issues through his music and community involvement in the arts scene to motivate change.

▤

Radha S. Menon, playwright, actor, designer, producer and owner of Red Betty Theatre, has had a similar experience in Hamilton. In 2012 Radha created the Red Betty Theatre, a company that helps to support, develop and mentor actors and directors from marginalized populations. Radha helps promote and enable actors in ways that were definitely not accessible to her when she was an actor, working in film and before she moved on to theatre. With the Red Betty Theatre, Radha's vision is "to create a theatre culture in Hamilton that includes stories with deeper and more complex themes, a thriving and diverse scene so that artists and artists' audiences don't have to commute to Toronto to experience eclectic art."

Radha Menon was born in Malaysia, grew up in Birmingham, England, and has been calling Hamilton home for about ten years. Her plays have received much acclaim: she was a finalist of the Woodward/Newman International Playwriting Prize in 2012 for *The Washing Machine*, while *Rukmini's Gold* won the 2015 Toronto Fringe Festival's New Play Contest and the Critics' Choice Award for the 2015

Hamilton Fringe, and in 2016 she was the recipient of the Hamilton Arts Award for Theatre.

Despite Radha's success as a playwright, she has had to overcome many challenges and obstacles as a woman of colour. As a result, she is certain that her success has taken much longer to achieve. "The stories that I want to tell do not resonate with artistic directors," she says, and then spells it out for me: she means predominantly white, male directors. She adds she has to fight even harder than the white feminists. Radha's stories are rooted in her South Asian heritage, and have a narrative that encompasses her life and history. Her plays are not light and fluffy; they have complex stories to tell and characters to reveal. According to Radha, this cannot be said for plays that she finds are "superficial and ethnically cute; more suitable for digestion." These types of "cute ethnic" plays, Radha finds, are typically more apt to receive mainstream exposure.

For the most part the Hamilton theatre scene caters to a white upper-middle-class audience. Radha points out that Hamilton Fringe is when there is the most diversity in the types of plays shown in the city. The plays selected to be produced during Fringe are picked via a random lottery, which removes any bias that an organizer might have. Radha is trying to build a home for all women of colour in theatre that lasts longer than the season of the Fringe Festival, and she's trying to build that community here in Hamilton.

Although Radha has written countless plays, and is certain to write many more, she laments on the struggles and difficulties of becoming a published playwright. Without being published there is no documentation of existence and no legacy to leave behind: "Our voices and stories go untold, they disappear, are wiped out as if you never existed . . . when we're undocumented, then we don't exist." This is the cultural invisibility that marginalized artists suffer from.

In the summer of 2017 Radha was asked by the new programming director of Theatre Aquarius, Jennie Esdale, to teach playwrighting to a group of youth. Instructing alongside Radha was Cliff Cardinal, an acclaimed Cree actor and playwright. Radha attributes her and Cliff, along with a roster of other, diverse POC instructors, being asked to teach as an effort made by Jennie Esdale to make connections within the theatre communities, and to actively seek out accomplished instructors reflective of our culturally and ethnically diverse community. More people in positions of artistic decision-making power need to make efforts like this.

▤

Stylo Starr is a printmaker, graphic designer and visual artist whose artwork celebrates Black culture. She brings to the public realm conversations about beauty, invisibility and legacy. Stylo was born and raised in Hamilton, a "Black girl that grew up in a white city," as she says. Over the past decade, Stylo has had many exhibitions of her artwork at Centre[3] on James Street North and most recently has had a large and lengthy exhibit at the Art Gallery of Hamilton titled *89Dames*. She is, without a doubt, a Black female artist in a predominantly white arts scene.

When I asked her about the impact of her exhibit at the Art Gallery of Hamilton, Stylo answered that she felt it opened a space and brought a level of comfort to people that might not have previously felt connected to the gallery or felt it was a space where they were welcomed or belonged. I have to agree, having a local, contemporary artist that is a person of colour exhibit their work in a place like the AGH really opens the doors for other marginalized communities and artists to feel welcome, and to feel like having their art hang in the city's largest gallery is a possibility. The impact of having eighty-nine Black female portraits up on the gallery walls of the AGH is immeasurable. People of colour could connect with and see themselves reflected in the art – especially in forms that are not cloaked in traditional or stereotyped historical colonial depictions and settings. Stylo's *89Dames* exhibit is scheduled to open at the Art Gallery of Burlington in fall of 2020.

Stylo is one of the founding members of COBRA, and attributes her opportunity to exhibit her series *89Dames* at the AGH partly to that. For Stylo having an opportunity to exhibit on the main floor of the gallery is a true testament of COBRA's success in helping make the right connections by helping promote and profile artists of colour. It is with conscious decisions to exhibit artists like Stylo that the art scene can start to shift.

Exhibits that coincided with and then followed Stylo's exhibit at the AGH included Hamilton local and Iranian-born artist Abedar Kamgari. Abedar's exhibit featured her film *The Journey West*, a retelling and re-enactment of the artist's experience as a refugee and immigrant. During that same time, Indigenous artist Shelley Niro exhibited her artwork *1779* as a response to Canada 150. A reflective examination of the history of the Six Nations of Haudenosaunee and the depletion of the land originally given to them in the Haldimand Proclamation of 1784, Shelly Niro's *1779* was shown in juxtaposition with selected works from the AGH's permanent collection of historical colonial art.

▧

Filimone Mabjaia is the executive and artistic director of the Matapa Music Festival. He has been living in Hamilton for seven years but originally hails from Mozambique. When Filimone first moved to Hamilton, he found himself with some extra time on his hands – an unsurprising result of his employment limitations during his immigration process. Being a lover of music, Filimone visited all the clubs, bars, pubs and musical venues and got to know the Hamilton music scene.

Although he appreciated what Hamilton had going on, he longed for something that reminded him of home. He would always have to go to places like the Lula Lounge in Toronto or to clubs in London, Ontario, to experience the kinds of music that he enjoyed. So, he decided to create a scene for the music he loved right here in Hamilton and in 2012 Matapa was born. Filimone launched Matapa with the Hamilton World Music and Roots Festival in 2013. During this time he felt the challenges of being a new immigrant, a Black man, a new citizen to Hamilton and a visible minority: "Every day you are reminded that you're Black in Hamilton and that you have to prove your worth three hundred times as hard, municipally, federally." Filimone felt this whether he was trying to get the grants and funding or the support and guidance he needed to get a new music festival off the ground. A festival that would bring world-renowned musical guests from all over the world to play here in Hamilton.

Filimone worries that Hamilton "will risk losing out on the massive potential to be a better and more culturally rich city because people will feel that they must leave to go to Toronto because the platform is not being provided here." He believes that as a city we need to create an environment where everyone feels safe and adds that "as minorities we need to step up, express our beliefs and not be silenced. We exist!"

In 2018 Filimone felt that the time was right for the removal of the word *world* from the festival title. *World music* in the loosest sense means music from somewhere else besides here, it sets apart non-Western music and "others" it. It was time for the festival to simply be about music – the Matapa Music Festival – featuring music of all kinds, not just for people of colour but for everyone. Another aim for the festival will be to move its location to the downtown core. This will bring Matapa's presence to the centre of the city to say "we are here!"

Filimone is full of enthusiasm and hope despite the constant uphill struggle. His passion and love for music keeps him going. It is Filimone's dream to have a space in the city "where everyone's music is respected, where people who are afraid that there is no room for them are given a voice." Future plans for Matapa include bringing artists to schools to educate youth about music in a way that raises awareness of all music. Filimone is determined to be successful no matter what obstacles he has to overcome.

≣

George Qua-Enoo is a commercial and editorial photographer and the founder of the online lifestyle magazine *Locke-Taylor*. He moved from South Africa to Canada in 2004, but he's only been in Hamilton since 2012. Still he affectionately says, "It's my home, my family." I first met George just after he launched the magazine.

Although George loves Hamilton, life for him here has not been easy. Back when he lived in Pietermaritzburg, South Africa, he was a brand manager; when he first moved to Canada he struggled to find work in his field. He was told time and time again by numerous agencies that he just didn't have any Canadian experience, and he wondered what exactly Canadian experience meant?

He added wryly that in South Africa when people are racist they don't beat around the bush about it – they just straight up say it to your face. In Canada he found that racism was polite, and codified. He couldn't figure out whether people weren't actually aware of their racism or whether even racist tendencies were just more proper. We joked about how if someone was going to be racist, you'd rather they just come out and say it than subtly hint at it, leaving you wondering whether there's some other reason why you can't land a job or make the connections you need to break into an industry.

Overcoming that self-doubt is challenging. Having to constantly question one's worth as an artist, and wonder why your work is never enough despite all the efforts can be disheartening. Among the numerous artists of visible minorities that I interviewed this feeling that one has to work twice, three times, ten times as hard to move ahead was consistently mentioned.

George is a self-taught photographer, but this did not come by chance. His uncle was a photographer and owned his own film studio; when George was in high school he picked up many skills there. When he moved to Hamilton in 2012 he'd already been dabbling in a career as a professional photographer and was trying to make it his full-time gig but in this new city he didn't know anyone. We all know, as George says, "It's all about who you know. You have to know people." He got a break after he did a photo project for Hamilton Youth Poets about their identities – many of the HYP are people of colour. The *Spectator* picked up on the story and wrote about him. After that he says, people started saying, "Hey, I know that guy George." Since then he has shot portraits of William Shatner, and gathered a long list of clients including the *Globe and Mail* and *Cosmopolitan*. George believed – as did numerous other artists of colour – that many of these issues were not as prominent in Toronto. There, George has been able to establish himself more easily as a commercial and editorial photographer. Not to say that a bigger city does not still have its issues with discrimination but are they more accepting and open to hiring people that aren't white than Hamilton?

But perhaps there is a shift starting to happen within Hamilton's art scene. Recently George did a series of thirty photographs for the Hamilton Arts Council's *I Am an Artist Project*, which was created "to celebrate the diversity of Hamilton's Artistic Community." It featured banners of artists' portraits along King William Street and outside the Seedworks Urban Offices on Catharine Street. There were over thirty artists featured on those banners and more than half were POC – yes, I counted.

There are also galleries like the Workers Arts and Heritage Centre and You Me Gallery who have long maintained exhibits from artists that represent diverse cross-sections of the Hamilton community. Bryce Kanbara, the owner of the You Me Gallery, is a Hamilton arts veteran. He's one of the original founding members of the Hamilton Artists Co-op, which later became Hamilton Artists Inc., and his was the first gallery to open on James Street North. I asked if his choice of exhibiting artists of diverse backgrounds was a conscious decision. Bryce says he exhibits artists influenced by his connections within the community he surrounds himself with. He stressed that his community and his connection to it has always played an important role in being an artist and curator. When I asked Bryce about what it was like for marginalized artists in Hamilton's art scene in the '70s he noted that it was essentially non-existent besides a small handful of people that he knew of.

In July 2016 the McMaster Museum of Art hired Indigenous curator Rhéanne Chartrand as its inaugural resident curator of Indigenous art for a one-year period. At the end of that term she was hired into her current full-time position. Her exhibits have helped to bring a contemporary view of Indigenous art in a way that has broken free from traditional, historic and colonial representations.

Twenty seventeen saw the creation of the New Committee; a committee branch of Hamilton Artist Inc. that was established to actively decolonize the Inc.'s space and programming. They have continued to make large strides in challenging and changing their institutional and organizational structures through programming and community engagement.

In November of 2019 Centre for Margins (C4M) emerged as a new Hamilton artist collective formed in response to the absence and underrepresentation of BIPOC artists in the Canadian arts community. They threw a hugely successful launch event called The Reception. This free two-day symposium featured artist performances and workshops led by BIPOC artists and community members that explored the Truth and Reconciliation Commission's calls to action, activist burnout and strategies for enacting structural change.

Amidst the growing awareness of anti-Black violence that was heightened by the violent death of George Floyd, there has been a recent flood of statements from historically white arts organizations proclaiming solidarity with the Black Lives Matter movement. For many, these are performative gestures; empty statements that include no strategic plan or action towards dismantling the structures of their organizations, which historically and currently continue to uphold and perpetuate racism and exclusion. There has been support in the amplification of marginalized artists' voices and experiences that has resulted in growing public pressure in attempts to hold these organizations accountable.

With changes like these, along with the ongoing effort of arts groups such as COBRA and C4M to bring marginalized artists to mainstream awareness, perhaps that cultural shift will start permeating more fully through the city's art institutions and art scene.

Dodging Demolition in Renaissance City

Shawn Selway

Within the urban "built-up area," as cities are termed by planners, rising land values eventually render every structure obsolete from the perspective of the landowner, though not necessarily from the perspective of others who are affected by the landowner's choices. However this rise in value is not continuous, and the ups and downs over the years provide an array of opportunities for different users. In Hamilton these changes in building ownership and use have been most evident along the older commercial main streets, like Barton, James, King, Ottawa or Kenilworth.

During the second decade of the twenty-first century the full range of possibilities could be seen on Barton, where ground-floor commercial premises are often accompanied by two or three floors of apartments. The businesses range from medical supply outlets and restaurants through convenience stores, second-hand shops and bars to a school uniform outlet, a bookstore and a martial arts studio, many of which depart after a year or two to be replaced by others. The crucial point occurs when reinvestment capital abandons a building altogether, leaving a maintenance deficit that can be filled from below by raw labour power. This is when young, eager and willing new owners, let's call them Samir and Nadine, apply themselves to hanging drywall and stripping out dud wiring in an old building, forgoing wages for their work in hopes of being compensated in the sweet by and by when capital finally returns to their street.

Once the young hopefuls have sweated the premises into presentable shape they then deploy their expertise to develop symbolic capital. These entrepreneurs often display, and impart to their customers, a specialized knowledge and refined appreciation of some scarce commodity or service. By and by their business attracts others to attempt the same and the aggregation, through the magical power of market confidence, draws financial capital and even produces an increase in underlying land value. How this magic can occur is best left to the anthropologists, but that it does occur is an observable fact.[1]

The earliest moment in this process, when labour is briefly more decisive than capital, is an inversion of the normal state of affairs, and cannot last because the thirst for autonomy felt by enterprising individuals like Samir and Nadine is nothing compared to the voracity of Capital, which looking back over its shoulder as it rampages through Toronto's Parkdale neighbourhood or the greenfields of Ancaster and spying the revived opportunity, dips its snout back into the abandoned place and gobbles up a few things on the "revitalized" street for digestion later. No more bootstrapping to independence for those of little means, who return to their usual station in life as renters. However, this repurposing may fail to occur at all, in which case the structure continues to decline and a once changeable situation may become rigid and lasting. This can happen when the building is internally subdivided and the residential rents that accrue from operating the property as a rooming house become more profitable than offering the space to either commercial or long-term residential tenants. At this point the owner has no incentive to reuse the commercial portion of the building, nor to sell, until other owners in the vicinity raise all values by bringing their properties back up the maintenance ladder – and into compliance with zoning and property standards bylaws.

This sort of blockage can happen at all scales. For example, after 2012 David Blanchard and his associates froze activity along half a block of the Gore by taking the buildings off the rental market, apparently judging that the properties could not attract rents adequate to the costs of retrofit and repair. It would be difficult to argue the converse, although not impossible, since there are enough businesses operating around the core to allow a comparative study and some tentative conclusions, but who would perform such an exercise? Similarly, when the public school board refused to entertain the interest of a potential developer in converting Sanford Avenue School to residential use and demolished the extensive structure instead, it seemed to many that a fine opportunity was lost – but again, the potential of an adaptive reuse of Sanford can only be speculative.

But it is not only devaluation that can produce chronic disrepair. A strong *rise* in the value of a property may also slow or stunt improvement or delay redevelopment indefinitely. This was the fear among James Street watchers in the spring of 2015 when council, setting aside the objections of planning staff, approved an application from the owners of the Tivoli Theatre property to build a twenty-two-storey tower on the site, previously zoned for a maximum eight storeys. The effect is to oblige other property owners in the vicinity to reconsider their plans, since the city has signalled that the existing zoning may no longer be considered the "highest and best use" and the door has been opened for changes that may substantially increase the value of their land. This in turn tends to devalue the existing structures and deter additional investment in them, while at the same time raising the assessed values, which increases the taxes and so the rents. This will necessarily alter the commercial character of James Street – depending on how quickly the Tivoli gets built and occupied.

In any case, though the path to demolition day may be long and winding, eventually a choice must be made whether or not to clear the land of its buildings in order to realize the increased value of the underlying asset, and it is then that interesting troubles begin. Cultural concerns other than the economic come into play.

These concerns are generally expressed in two lines of argument. One is that the return on investment accruing to private interests from the change in use or the increase in tax revenues consequent on a rise in assessed value (which is the municipality's share of the value that it has conferred upon the private interest through its zoning processes) should not be the only considerations in land use decisions. Municipal government is not a business, the argument goes, but rather the custodian of the greater good.

The second line of argument is that the calculation of the return on investment is incomplete, that there are values not being counted. These costs and benefits are either externalized or not entered in the ledger at all. Some are difficult to quantify; others are being wilfully ignored. If all factors were entered into the balance sheet, the final calculation would lead to a different decision.

Over against these broader cultural concerns is a privileging of growth, progress and market forces, grounded in the tax regime. This legacy of the social and technological optimism of the mid-twentieth century is now reinforced but not entirely supplanted by the obsessive reductionism of neo-liberal doctrine. When it comes to killing a building, however, the two neatly support each other.

Of course, on paper, market forces remain well subordinated within Ontario's centralized land-use planning regime. At least to the extent that local authorities choose to exercise the considerable powers delegated to them by the province. In the words of Ted Tyndorf, chief planner of Toronto in 2006, "Land value is supposed to be driven by the bundle of development rights attached to the ownership of the asset. Those rights should be predicated on the highest and best use as set out in the Official Plan as prescribed in zoning."[2]

Clearly there may be differences of opinion as to what constitutes the "highest and best use," and who shall define it. The province attempts to reconcile private and public interests by providing negotiating tools at the lowest level of decision making, that of the individual site, with things such as Section 37 of the Planning Act (density bonusing for benefit) and inclusionary zoning rules (allowing affordable housing quotas) while also dictating certain restrictions at the highest level, that of the metropolitan region, by way of the Greenbelt and the Growth Plan legislation.

I want to discuss the politics of disinvestment/reinvestment as it unfolded in 2017 around three strongly contested moments in the cycle, namely the public school board's decision to launch a West Hamilton "Pupil Accommodation Review," whose opening gambit was the proposed closure of Hess Street Elementary School; David Blanchard's drive to clear away a stretch of Gore Park frontage much cherished by built heritage advocates; and the attempt by Kevin Green, president of Greenwin Inc., to increase the number of rental units in his portfolio by subdividing a portion of the apartments in his downtown Robert Village property. This last proposal was not a wholesale demolition, but since it involved the elimination of most of the three-bedroom apartments in those buildings, it came to the same thing and drew opposition arising from notions of equity that are often voiced when democratic sentiment runs up against pure economic calculation.

HESS SCHOOL

Unlike other buildings, schools continue in the same use under the same owner and the same management for the entire life of the structure, and in theory with the same draw on funds for maintenance and rehabilitation. This being so, the task of determining the point of obsolescence is not simple.

When a school board in Ontario wishes to conduct a Pupil Accommodation Review, it must follow a procedure stipulated by the Ministry of Education. This begins with the production of an initial report and the selection of an initial option for the geographical area under consideration – in this case, a chunk of the lower city dubbed "West Hamilton City" by the school board, which was actually a portion of central Hamilton well east of what everyone else calls West Hamilton. Once the report is done, the board must proceed to public consultation with the residents of the affected area, including several sessions of detailed discussion with an advisory committee of parents, teachers and interested community residents, who together with the relevant trustees and staff constitute the "working group."

West Hamilton City has the benefit of nine elementary public schools, and the initial option was the closure of Hess Street Elementary School and an elaborate redistribution of students between four other schools. This idea made for much unhappiness among Hess school parents, and in January of 2017 they and others came out in large numbers, about 150, to say so. Along with the parents came many interested observers – not only members of the advisory committee drawn from the other schools, but neighbourhood activists and the politically engaged of various stripes. Enough representatives of all groups were on hand to fill the gymnasium of Sir John A. Macdonald Secondary School. Translators were supplied, and people sorted themselves to one or another table of Somali speakers, Spanish speakers, Vietnamese speakers, etc. It was patriotically thrilling, and very loud.

Hess was widely known as a newcomers' school, sharing with Sir John A. the reputation of being a sort of mini–United Nations. Hence the general suspicion abroad in West Hamilton City that Hess had been selected for closure because Hess parents, coping with linguistic and other challenges, were less able to fight for their school than, say, the administrative and professional cadre whose kids attend Earl Kitchener in the southwest corner of the district, and who have a healthy sense of their own significance in the scheme of things.

The meeting was turbulent, with staff obliged to reassure the attendees several times that no decision had yet been taken, and ended early when a fire alarm went off and the building had to be cleared. From the perspective of the members of the advisory committee, I was told, this was a pretty good start: staff had been shown that their preference would be no cakewalk, reinforcing a message already delivered in *Spectator* op-ed pieces. NDP leader Andrea Horwath wrote, "The funding process put in place by the Ministry of Education means that this school is seen as a potential cash cow, instead of as an integral part of a community." Hess parent David Heska said, "For decades the school has been a neighbourhood community hub where cultural and religious differences blend together as a wonderful example of unity."

The reader of the twenty-four-page *Accommodation Review: Initial Report: West Hamilton City* is made aware of the existence of a forbidding number of complementary and qualifying documents, such as the Long-Term Facilities Master Plan (itself co-ordinate with the Community Planning and Facility Partnership initiative and the Joint Property Asset Committee) and its guiding principles, along with supplementary criteria and facility condition indices prepared by VFA Canada and additional facility feasibility studies prepared by a local architectural firm. Crucial are the provincial School Board Efficiencies and Modernization Strategy (SBEM), the School Consolidation Capital program (SCC), the School Operations and Renewal Grant (SRG) and the School Condition Improvement funding pool (SCI). The report contains detailed tables of comparisons between the schools in the study area, and has six appendices. Evidently many, many minds must meet to obtain a result in the education business.

After one has wandered in this maze for a while, the importance of separating the pots of money appears: it has the effect of forcing choice by making deferred maintenance the decisive factor in calculations. This is because the larger the sum of those projected costs becomes, the closer that number approaches the total current replacement cost of a school – about $10 million, exclusive of land purchase, for a building able to house about five hundred junior kindergarten to grade eight students. The way money is allocated seems to promote replacement over repair. A school closure also yields the value of the land beneath it – various sales are expected to bring in about $65 million from 2017 to 2022 for the Hamilton-Wentworth District School Board.[3] School for five hundred is the preferred optimal size at the moment. The fact that the recently built Dr. J.E. Davey and Cathy Wever Elementary Schools are even larger implies a preference for a wider catchment area (i.e., bigger schools farther apart).

One also begins to appreciate that this administrative machinery of many interlocking parts has been assembled by bureaucrats whose roles are to patiently edge the trustees, the public, the parents and the inexpert committee selected from among them toward the desired conclusion. The problem for the inexpert committee is to determine whether this conclusion is in fact the better choice, or merely the most robotically rational. Compounding the problem in this case was the fact that the whole exercise was voluntary. The province had lured the board into trying a closure in order to tap into a fund otherwise unavailable for improvements.

As an advisory committee member pointed out to me early in the shepherding process, the laymen involved had a double goal: (1) they had to hang together, despite a difference in interests between the parents of the various schools, and (2) they had to make sure that there was a reinvestment commitment of some sort from the board if any school were to be closed. No commitment, no closure. In other words, there could be no question of simply boarding-up Hess and reallocating pupils to empty places at Bennetto, Dr. Davey, etc., an option which David Heska characterized as the wish to "bus my daughter, along with over 250 other students to an expanded 700 student megaschool in the North End." As it happened, both goals were achieved – after five months of deliberation, including two public meetings and eight meetings of the advisory committee. On decision day, the trustees voted to close Hess and Strathcona, the two smallest schools, but only if the province would agree to pay for a new replacement school, along with a community hub, to be built on the land occupied by Sir John A. MacDonald Secondary School, across the road from Hess.

This was in June. In August trustees voted to move the New Hess proposal up in the priority ranking of a six-project list going to the province for funding.[4] If the ministry refused the money, then Plan B, on a motion of trustee Christine Bingham and contrary to the staff recommendation, was that all nine schools remain open. The community hub proposal was for a $22 million structure with any leftover land going to possible housing on the site.[5] It also entailed, for reasons unknown, the demolition of Sir John A., a building that would seem a very good candidate for adaptive reuse. The province subsequently refused to fund either the hub or the new school, but the school board retained the land. Meanwhile a development consortium, whose spokesperson was lawyer Jasper Kujavsky, made public its interest in acquiring the land as part of a proposed entertainment district encompassing also an existing shopping mall and the hockey arena. Subsequently the group attempted to gain a voice in Ottawa by running Kujavsky as the liberal candidate in the riding of Hamilton Centre, an NDP stronghold, which in the event did not pass into the hands of this particular batch of land speculators.

Since the key factor impelling accommodation reviews is the optimization of pupil distribution across existing facilities, I want to consider these metrics more closely. As mentioned, board staff had somehow determined that the optimal school capacity is between five and six hundred, in a kindergarten to grade eight facility, which allows for two or three classes for each grade. The optimal site size is six acres. Note that this is an operational definition. Geography – including looking at the area served and the age and proximity of the student and his or her parents to the school – is not considered, although the enrolment projection software that staff use to model eventualities is no doubt capable of absorbing such a data set and spitting out a handsome graph to illustrate the results. In the words of the initial report,

> Planning staff apply historical student yields (by unit type) to municipally approved development forecasts to project the estimated numbers of students generated by housing units. The yields are broken down by housing types which include single-detached, semi-detached, townhome and apartment. Each community has its own unique yield . . .
>
> There are a number of . . . school specific assumptions captured in the projections as well. These assumptions can include programming (i.e. French Immersion), Board policy (i.e. Out of catchment) or new Ministry initiatives (i.e. full day kindergarten).

It is possible to knead in plenty more variables, but one begins to suspect that all is well with these methods as long as all is well (i.e., proceeding in the usual way at the usual pace). Downtown Hamilton is not proceeding in that way at all. A period of decline and slow, steady population loss is ending, but the future is not quite determined yet.

It emerged during working group discussions that no predictive modelling seemed to have been done for enrolment increases arising from impending large-scale development in the area, nor was there much understanding of the changes unfolding in the existing housing stock as reinvestment-induced displacement occurred. For example, as we will examine in detail later, Greenwin property management, in repositioning its Robert Village properties by emptying the bulk of the three-bedroom units in those buildings, had probably caused a dip in enrolment at Dr. Davey. Similarly, elevated vacancy rates at Hamilton

Housing's Jamesville townhouses in the north end had caused a drop at nearby Bennetto Elementary School.

After distributing a map of West Hamilton City, which indicated student origin as dots, staff were asked to produce one that scaled density with dot size, and returned with a "Students per address" version that clearly showed the importance of the towers of Queen North as a contributor to Hess enrolment but also that of other towers to other schools, especially in Durand. But how stable were these projections during this redevelopment phase? Not very, seemed to be the answer. If unstable, the effect would be serial cannibalization: a string of Pupil Accommodation Reviews like this one, which would generate turmoil as students were shuffled about, with no idea of how long the fix would last, entailing loss of schools, which would in turn discourage family resettlement into the area.

This line of thought suggests another approach, one that would dovetail with the provincially imposed imperative to intensify land use in the "built-up areas." How about looking at schools such as Dr. Davey, and its operationally optimal enrolment figure, and then surveying the residential land use within the immediately surrounding area with a view to seeing what kind of use might be required to meet the optimal number? Since new builds in West Hamilton City are mostly multi-residential, owing to the land values, and mostly above four storeys, the question becomes one of unit suitability for families with children. Are developers building units with enough bedrooms? In order to get some notion of what was planned, the working group invited Chris Phillips, Senior Advisor, Planning & Economic Development at the City of Hamilton, to come along and talk to them about these matters. His remarks were reported as follows in the summary minutes of the meeting:

The City of Hamilton does not micro forecast population growth. We are given information from the Province. The City then allocates the forecast. From there we have to ensure there is adequate land to support and accommodate the growth city-wide. What we do not do is drill down to specific regions of the city to decide on allocation. We then zone and plan for certain properties depending on development applications.

From a City perspective there is growth in this West Hamilton area, however, there is growth throughout the city, including south mountain, Ancaster, Dundas, Waterdown, and along the lake in Stoney Creek. It is pretty easy to predict the type of growth in these areas – based on what is already developed – low-rise family residential housing. The growth we are talking about in this West Hamilton City area is somewhat unpredictable as we haven't had growth like this in this area for quite some time. It is more difficult to project the growth than the suburban areas.

In this area there are considerable re-development parcels to work on including Pier 8, Barton/Tiffany, City Housing/Jamesville complex and the Pier 6/7 commercial village. We don't expect the neighbourhood to change in the form and style as it is today. You may see some singles turning into semis, triplexes or even quads but you probably won't see any major changes in residential neighbourhoods aside from the large parcels that the City actually has.

This is a backward-looking perspective that assumes that a certain conception of financial and social maturation will rule indefinitely. Currently it is expected that in the nature of things, individuals will progress from student life to independent apartment living and automobile ownership, and thence to marriage and family raising in the no-rise well-trimmed and watered outer reaches of their city. But this is not the whole story anymore, as younger persons in Vancouver and Toronto are finding it difficult and sometimes even undesirable to leave the central city to raise their children. Nor has it always been the main story. Back in 1964 when Hamilton council lifted a six-storey height restriction from forty-six blocks of the downtown, the rationale was, in the words of Alderman and Controller Jack Macdonald, that the city would be needing about 1,500 "family living units" a year for the next twenty years, and that "we can't afford to keep on pushing services out to the suburbs."⁶ High-rise living was touted as providing a high level of amenities: the pool, the party room, etc. This expectation that some families would prefer downtown living was still very much alive in 1975, when Robert Village was built with 125 three-bedroom units (on the lower floors), 129 two-bedroom units and even 4 four-bedroom units. Obviously the builders anticipated demand from families with children – although perhaps not the families that were living there forty years on.

Secondly, there is a kind of bland diffidence on the question of the composition of density and size of units, as shown by these exchanges from the Q and A session that followed Phillips's presentation:

Q. Do you have specific numbers right now for Barton/Tiffany and Jamesville developments?
A. We don't project on one bedroom units, 2 bedroom units etc. We do have unit projections but cannot tell what form those units will be in. The numbers of units for Barton/Tiffany are around 1100 and the number of units for Jamesville is around 330. . . .

Q. When planning future projects overall are you looking to see if families with young kids are moving to [the] area? Do you have an overall demographic area?
A. We do not use that information to forecast. We look at what is currently in the area. We look site by site and at planning applications.

Of course, Phillips can only do what he has been instructed to do, namely move city-owned lands in the West Harbour to market by steering them through all the required planning processes, during which passage the lands accumulate, from the perspective of developers, a lot of encumbrances in the form of design guidelines. However, the city's indifference to unit composition, and therefore actual population density, is hard to square with the provincial emphasis on compact urban form as we build to accommodate population growth.

Ontario Greenbelt and Places to Grow legislation is a last-ditch attempt to keep Southern Ontario's land base from becoming an unfillable money pit for road construction and an overflowing sink for our wastes as we negotiate the transition to environmentally safer cities. If it is to succeed, then density must be achieved by infill and redevelopment of existing residential, commercial or post-industrial sites. Some of these spaces will feature tall multi-residential buildings, and these must accommodate families with some two- and three-bedroom suites and include affordable units (measured by comparing housing cost with income). Presumably the city will have to produce a policy on unit mix at some point – just as Vancouver and Toronto are doing.[7]

Similarly, Phillips's assertion that existing neighbourhoods won't change much is difficult to reconcile with the provincial drive for density. It does correspond to the land use designations of the secondary plan for the West Harbour area, and perhaps to the preferences and prejudices of many residents in the "stable areas," as the older areas of single-family housing and row housing are termed in the secondary plan. "Stable area" is a misnomer at any time, but a soothing one in periods of rapid change. The issue of incremental intensification is one of the most difficult we face – perhaps the most difficult. Rejection of laneway housing, secondary units, small apartment blocks and the rest is expressed as preserving the "character" of neighbourhoods. However, it is not generally acknowledged by character-savers (of any class) that in an area of rising land values homeowners cannot preserve both the built form and the social character of the neighbourhood. If the built form is kept widely intact then those with strong professional or business incomes will outbid all others for the coveted detached houses with large yards. If the mixed social character, that is to say, the broad affordability of this or that area is to be maintained, then the built form must change – lots must be used more intensely, though how much more intensely varies from neighbourhood to neighbourhood. Densification will be less in areas where prices are already in the upper registers, and more in areas of rapid appreciation, although of course affordability is always a relative quantity. In East Vancouver in 2017, so-called secondary housing (e.g., a small detached structure in the rear of an older house) would run you six or seven hundred thousand dollars for a thousand square feet – the price of a decent full-sized house in one of Hamilton's more expensive neighbourhoods.

From what has been said, it would seem that there is a disjunction between land use and education facility policies at both the municipal and the provincial levels. At present, only those directly affected – that is, displaced renters with children, and the parents of students displaced by school closures – are paying much attention to this disjunction.

THE GORE

The Gore, named for its triangular shape, was the commercial and ceremonial centre of the city for many decades. Our second instance of disputed obsolescence occurs here, in the row of buildings at the southwest corner of the Gore. The four structures of stone-fronted brick, which form a continuous facade, bear the street numbers 18–28 King and were built between 1848 and 1880. Number 30 King, once the easternmost member of the group, was demolished by the same owners, Hughson Business Space Corporation, around the same time that they decided to empty the other buildings of their tenants. I want to concentrate on the cultural contest over the fate of these structures, all of which are at least 130 years old, although they, and their surroundings, have undergone many alterations in that time.[8] Here we have the inverse of the Hess school case. There, the ministry and the board are trying to cut costs; here, council is trying to gain a stream of tax revenue by accommodating a developer, although somewhat reluctantly at first.

When the Hughson Business Space Corporation, an organization operated by David Blanchard and his associates, was first preparing to demolish 18–22, 24 and 28 King back in 2012, the city got into discussions with the owners and agreed not to impose a heritage designation on the properties if the demolition permit holder would revoke the permit. Municipal grants were then made available for the conservation of the buildings, but there was no uptake. In November Blanchard and company demolished a three-storey office building at 20 Jackson, near city hall, without announcing any plans to build there. In December council voted to designate 18–28 King under Part IV of the Ontario Heritage Act. The owners appealed that decision to the Conservation Review Board, a sister tribunal of the Ontario Municipal Board. Plywood and scaffolding enveloped the buildings and there they sat for the next three and a half years, looking very poorly, casualties in a war of attrition that the owner cannot lose.

Although the do-nothing tactic is usually termed "demolition by dereliction," it might better be called "salted earth" as the result is, often to stop redevelopment and growth in the surrounding area until the eyesore is removed. In this case much of the land was in the same hands that were making the eyesore, and had already been razed and paved. Blanchard's removal of the Permanent Trust building from this block in 1999 had in fact provoked a city bylaw prohibiting demolitions for mere surface parking. This has led to our scattered legacy of neat black rectangles and weed-choked lots bordered with large blocks of concrete, each adorned with its loop of rusted wire rope.[9]

During the intervals between December 2013 when council passed the "intention to designate" motion and June 2015 when the parties began talking about a solution to the impasse, and between June 2015 and April 2016 when Hughson Business Space returned to city hall with a new proposal, an alternative approach to dealing with old buildings gained ground in the core. Steve Kulakowsky and his partners at Core Urban completed the rehabilitation of the Empire Times edifice and the Templar Flats, both one block off the Gore in a long-troubled stretch of King William Street. Admittedly in the matter of the Templar Flats Kulakowsky's hand was forced. Soon after the Empire Times was completed – including a spiffy external elevator-with-a-view and yoga-ready rooftop patio – it was learned that an organization linked to methadone dispensing was looking to buy into the Templar Flats block. This prompted a pre-emptive purchase to protect the Empire Times investment.

Core Urban was also lining up its ducks in order to take on a couple of underused beauties on James, just around the corner from the former Mills China building, which had shed its shroud of metal grillwork and pigeon dung to show the Gore its original facade of pressed tin, carved wood and grand fenestration, soon all nicely polished and painted. This comeback was the more pleasing as it occurred directly across from the ruin-in-progress at 18–28 King, and heritage advocates made lots of hay with it when canvassing support for their battle against Blanchard's new proposal, which was to do away with all but the stone facade of 18–22 King and build new structures to the rear, with a fresh, context-sensitive front elevation at 24–28.

Ironically, Blanchard's group was an early adopter of the adaptive approach, and in proof could point to the sophisticated late neoclassicism of the former Bank of Montreal building, currently housing the law offices of Gowling WLG, and the massive Corinthian statement made by the Landed Banking & Loan building, each holding down their respective corners of Main at James. There is also the example of the former Public Health building nearby on Hunter, once a very suave modernist swerve across from the old TH&B rail station, though arguably that design has been so disfigured by energy-saving changes to the building envelope as not to count as conserved. Did these instances lend plausibility to the contention that 18–28 King were beyond salvation? Arguments to that effect from architect David Premi and Hughson Business Space lawyer Tim Bullock certainly cut no ice with those who were campaigning hard to keep the buildings standing. In a brief to the Municipal Heritage Committee the Friends of the Gore complained that

> the developer has succeeded in framing the discussion in a self-serving, all or nothing narrative: "demolition and redevelopment or desolation."
>
> After evicting its tenants, allowing the buildings to deteriorate alarmingly, sustain water damage and be boarded up, after drawing the matter out for four years, the owners now expect the City to be so desperate for development that it should squander this unique and precious part of our history.[10]

Moreover, "This choice is not between development as proposed or no development at all; the choice is between responsible stewardship or irresponsible surrender."

As Premi had told the *Spectator* some months earlier, "These heritage issues often become polarized and emotionally charged. What we've come up with is a really great compromise."[11]

To which the Friends of the Gore replied:

> The proposal to save only *one* façade, is phoney stewardship at its worst. It ignores the importance of the streetscape, ignores the issue of stewardship, the wastefulness and arrogance of demolition, the backs of the buildings which create a unique heritage street wall and alleyway facing Main Street.
>
> Façadism ignores the light-bringing courtyard that is built into the pre-electricity William Thomas building – which is large enough for a charming outdoor restaurant patio. There is so much potential in

the totality of these buildings and talking about saving a façade of one or two of them, misses the point of heritage preservation altogether.[12]

Maybe so, although some comparative discussion of engineering details and costs might have been in order to demonstrate to investor-friendly councillors that the Friends of the Gore were aware of the complexities facing the owner.

I want to look at why these threats of loss arouse such strong emotions, beyond the sense of betrayal and exasperation at the political shift toward the developer that was occurring at the city. Hughson Business Space had first made their pitch public at the General Issues Committee, but their presentation was unscheduled, so that opponents could not prepare to attend, and the councillor (Jason Farr) made it clear that he had gone over entirely and was promoting the "compromise," that is, complete demolition.

The fabric of the world is knit up with that of our own being. Each of us has a thousand attachments to persons of all degrees of relation to oneself from near kin to the market stallholder who sells you your carrots and cabbage. These attachments, and our intimate connection with the local weather and with the whole natural and built world within which our daily experience unfolds, are what gives exile its deep pain and also causes us to feel an injury when tall trees and familiar buildings, long a part of the backdrop of our lives, are abruptly destroyed.

By the same token, the effrontery of those who remove cherished elements from the landscape can be enormously offensive. Many feel, in some obscure sense that they would not care or dare to articulate, that the privately held property of others also belongs partly to them, because they belong to it, and so they should have some influence over its ultimate disposition. This proposition, when it is not seen as an infringement on private property rights, is generally dismissed by politicians as nostalgia, or a reflexive and harmful refusal of progress, or an attempt to usurp control over someone else's wallet, or all three.

That the ward councillor was inclined to accept Hughson's proposal was no surprise, although the reverse certainly would have been. Council rarely opposes demolitions, on any grounds. It should be noted however, that in this particular instance, councillors Matthew Green, Aidan Johnson and Brenda Johnson did cast no votes. I want to lay out why council generally takes this position, which is fatal to so many buildings.

Blanchard and associates bought 18–28 King in the conviction that money could be made from them, either by rehabilitating them, or by persuading the city to increase the value of the land by upzoning, or by doing something else. There is no obligation on anyone else to supply Blanchard with the anticipated gains. The city does not owe him a return on his speculation. However, the city and its myriad property owners are codependents. The property owner needs the city to bestow value on the property (and protect that value going forward) through the zoning regulations as well as through service provision, and the city needs large property owners to build and provide development charges and a stream of taxable occupancy. Council has no more incentive to protect any particular building than the owner does. Unless the proprietors of nearby structures feel that their interests are being injured by the introduction of a building that is too large, too new or somehow detrimental to the value of their own holdings; or unless there is an appetite to assume a stewardship role with respect to the built environment. Hamilton councillors have almost never accepted this role; certainly it is not part of their ongoing conception of their duties and responsibilities. Councillors wish to be able to point to things built during their time in office, not things kept; I believe they reflect the views of the majority of their constituents in this.

Heritage activists seem never to have quite grasped that the political route is not really open to them. Those who have the power under the Ontario Heritage Act to intervene have almost no desire to do so, and pay no penalty for ignoring those who come to the defence of old buildings, no matter how well argued their plea. This lesson has long since been absorbed by environmentalists, who couple their appeals to politicians with attacks on the enemy's finances, urging disinvestment from oil companies, and engaging in the occasional direct action against the expansion of physical assets. I am aware of no attempt by advocates for the well-being of the built environment to attack their opponents' sources of credit, either on grounds of the duty of care to the built past, or of environmental protection. Without credit, there could be very few new structures when the old were removed. Of course there are municipal grants and loans and other incentives to encourage reinvestment even when no demolish/rebuild option is contemplated, and among these are funds directed specifically to heritage facade rehabilitation.

What preservationists have learned, however, is to emphasize to politicians and the public the wastefulness of sending old buildings, reconceived as deposits of "embodied energy," to the landfill site. Given the polarization that can occur during land-use disputes, the province has provided some mediation tools. One is granted under section 37 of the Planning Act, which is as follows:

37. (1) The council of a local municipality may, in a by-law passed under section 34, authorize increases in the height and density of development otherwise permitted by the by-law that will be permitted in return for the provision of such facilities, services or matters as are set out in the by-law.

(2) A by-law shall not contain the provisions mentioned in subsection (1) unless there is an official plan in effect in the local municipality that contains provisions relating to the authorization of increases in height and density of development.

Although Hamilton's Official Plan does meet the condition, with section F.1.9, there are no guidelines in place and the city seems not to use this tool. In Toronto, where development pressure has been high, downtown councillors have for many years made liberal use of Section 37 to obtain money for parks, works of art and other things generally described as "community benefits." Evidently Hamilton council has not wanted to place any impediment in the path of a proponent, though the reluctance seemed to be fading in mid-2017 as the pace of construction quickened and applications to the planning department multiplied. However, as of June 2020 the provincial government was preparing to change the framework within which "community benefit" charges could be levied.

Some months of agitation and editorializing over the Gore Park buildings culminated in a Planning Committee meeting on January 17, 2017, held in council chambers, at which many delegates addressed Hughson Business Space's request for demolition permits.

David Premi's role as Blanchard's architect on the project was disappointing to many in the room, but his design for the front elevation of the replacement building at 24–28 King seemed thoughtful enough to me, hinting at the precedent on the site yet detailing so as not to falsely elide the difference between old and new. However, Catherine Nasmith, a Toronto architect and activist who founded the indispensable web-based circular "Built Heritage News," had made the trip down the highway to speak on behalf of the Architectural Conservancy of Ontario. She put up some slides to show that the Premi/Hughson proposals did not conform to the directions provided in the Downtown Hamilton Secondary Plan with regard to height and detailing. Premi's was a difficult balancing act to perform, and I took no pleasure in watching him being questioned by Councillor Donna Skelly, who wondered if maybe he could do this and that to tweak the design, rather as though she were rearranging the furniture in her living room.

Granted the last word, the proponent's lawyer, Tim Bullock of Simpson Wigle, took up a few of the delegates' charges for refutation. Demolition by dereliction? Not at all. In fact, before deciding the buildings were not marketable and expelling the few sitting tenants, the owner had spent $100,000 on a roof, and $100,000 on other improvements. With an air of patient resignation before the inevitability of misunderstanding, Bullock explained that the city requires that services be cut off when obtaining a demolition permit. Which seemed reasonable enough, since one would not want to be bulldozing live gas lines or electrical wiring. Of course, no one had the opportunity to ask why, if his client were not attempting to destroy the building, services were not restored when the demolition permit was voided.

The structures are in very poor condition, Bullock said, and hard to work with, as they are long and narrow and can be lit only from the north. This is misleading. Many old commercial structures along the east side of James North are at least as deep and narrow as 18–28 King, and yet are home to successful businesses; and it is simply not the case that the Gore buildings can be lit only from the north. They have a rear, to the south, on an alley, and can be lit also from the east, where there is a narrow vacant lot from which Blanchard has removed a building. And also, owing to the presence of an interior courtyard, from the south, east and west.

To sum up: on the one view, the buildings are dark, narrow, unmarketable dumps; on the other, rather typical examples of antiquated downtown commercial premises, susceptible of being filled with light from all sides and reanimated with the joie de vivre of youthful new Hamiltonians, depending on whether you are selling truckloads of fresh concrete, or Hamilton's "renaissance."

No one asked city staff why, if council had deemed the buildings possibly worthy of conservation, the city had not obliged the owners to treat them accordingly during the ensuing thirty-six months. The answer is that the city has no means to do so, other than expropriation.

Nor, of course, does council wish to acquire any such means, or it certainly would have done so after the long, sorry war against the Lister Block waged by LiUNA. (Trespassers during LiUNA's campaign for years posted to the internet videos of dripping surfaces and falling chunks.) Though most councillors are entirely opposed to the retention of any building whatever, many will offer some lip service to the concept of historic preservation. Today it was Councillor Farr's turn. He reminded the room that he had authored the motion of intention-to-designate, and termed the owner's current position – the complete demolition and removal to the landfill of all but the stone facade of 18–22 – a "compromise" and pledged his troth once more to heritage.

This remark, and its root form – "We can't save everything" – is pronounced with pious fervour whenever a building is to be destroyed. In truth, almost nothing is kept in Hamilton. Between 2012 and 2017, precisely two structures survived attempts to destroy them. One is the Jimmy Thompson Memorial Pool at Scott Park, a legacy of the 1930 British Empire Games. The other is a style moderne Pigott Better Built house in the vicinity of Saint Joseph's hospital, which parking lot enthusiast Victor Vary wanted to level. King George school, at Gage near Barton, was also on the survivor list, but lacked a new user and so was still endangered. During the same period the following structures were cleared away: the Rheem building at Barton and Tiffany, which went down in January of 2012; the aforementioned office building at 20 Jackson; a stone church at Jackson and James; a stone church at Queen and King; the former Sisters of Saint Joseph orphanage at Queen and King; Sanford Avenue School at Sanford and Barton; Scott Park Secondary School; Parkside High School in Dundas; and the Hamilton Education Centre at Main and Bay. This list is not complete but I make that nine major buildings in five years. "We can't keep everything" indeed. Scheduled to join them in the landfill were the original theatre of the Tivoli complex, the Gore buildings and the former Kresge's store, also on the Gore.[13]

At the end of the day, the Planning Committee voted to accept the developer's plan, with councillors Green and Aidan Johnson opposing, but only after Councillor Judi Partridge had made some amendments evidently intended to ensure that after all this Blanchard actually delivered a building or two in a timely manner, and not just another in the series of vacant lots that he has made in the core. A few days later council ratified the Planning Committee decision.[14] In November Hughson Business Space announced that there had been a change of direction, and that the facades of all buildings would now be kept, pretty much maintaining the historic street wall. As of June 2020 no discernible further work had been done on the properties, which continue to moulder under their protective coverings.

"Historic preservation" means preservation of the historic form and the historic materials of a built structure possessing "character-defining elements," as the Parks Canada Standards and Guidelines for the Conservation of Historic Places terms them. This means *all* of the historic forms and *all* of the historic materials that are deemed, after specialist examination, to be compatible with public safety and the long-term stability of the historic forms and materials. Lead-based paint, for example, is not compatible with public safety and must be sealed or removed. The conservation process is the close inspection of the form and materials, followed by the preparation and execution of a detailed plan to clean, stabilize and preserve some of those materials and revise the rest.

The announcement of an intention to designate without specifying any particular features as character-defining implies that all must be kept intact until a thorough examination identifies priorities. In theory. In practice, of course, it is just a delaying tactic, and during the delay, the city does nothing to ensure essential maintenance to prevent further costs from accruing through further neglect. Long-time observers of the local situation know the drill. The bottom line is, council never intervenes to save anything, and demolition by neglect is therefore tacitly encouraged.

As mentioned, Blanchard and associates have a record of adaptive reuse. What they had not demonstrated, until they advanced their second-round scheme for 18–28 King, was an interest in what I will call additive re-urbanization, which is what results when adaptive reuse and newly built forms and landscaping are coupled, and that procedure repeated. The result is a landscape of ever-increasing variety and interest as examples of construction techniques and architectural fashions accumulate.

The local flagship for this approach is the John Sopinka Courthouse, formerly the post office. Here much of the old Dominion building was retained, and an additional new structure erected beside it. Unfortunately, security precautions have made the gorgeously detailed interior of the postal hall off limits to the general public, much reducing its value as propaganda for the additive approach. Another good example is the Witton Lofts condominium on Murray Street, formerly a public school, whose entire exterior with its rug-brick envelope and carved gargoyles remains intact, while several extra storeys have been placed above the original roofline. Similarly, the older buildings at the corner of King William and Hughson, Templar Flats, have been supplemented with a taller infill structure whose limestone facade politely refers to its neighbours without generating confusion as to what came when. This sort of thing is the reverse of what went on in the past, when rituals of renewal were repeated every decade or so on commercial facades. At 24 King, for example, modernizers went so far as to remove the brick entirely from the front of the building all the way up to the third floor.[15] The play of signs that results from additive re-urbanism can be rather shallow. At the moment, historic interiors are so scorned that even fine, intact lime plaster is sledged off the walls to indulge the fashion for exposed brick. At the LiUNA/Hi-Rise Group student residence on James, the William Thomas–designed stone facade of the building that used to stand there is being reinstalled on the pediment of the new tower in a parody of the equally superficial gestures that in the past would have seen facades of that sort covered over with a bolt-on steel framework supporting sheet metal cladding and plastic signage.

The gradualist, incremental approach to reinvestment by adapting the old and inserting the new alongside it offers a true compromise in the cultural clash, one for which the planning framework and even the administrative structure and financial support is already in place. They are there to be used, should council ever become persuaded of the long-term comparative advantages of the additive approach for *all* property owners, large and small, and choose them rather than prioritizing the site-by-site requests made by owners with access to large chunks of capital.

ROBERT VILLAGE

Robert Village is a four-building complex on a block bounded by John, Hughson and Robert Streets, with commercial buildings to the south. Announced in 1975 and built just as illustrated in the rendering, 181 John and 192 Hughson and their companion low-rise structures went up near the end of a surge of downtown high-rise construction that began around 1965. Buildings of this type – which stretch in a long arc from Scarborough through central Toronto and around the end of the lake to Hamilton and beyond – currently house about a million people, and their continued usability has become a matter of concern in the GTHA, or the "Greater Golden Horseshoe" as some prefer to call the region. These buildings have also become of great interest to real estate investment trusts and other large players in the multi-residential housing game, who have developed aggressive strategies to reposition them in the market. This means engaging a property management firm that will employ sharp tactics to encourage turnover – that is, to persuade tenants to give up their lease and go elsewhere while also carrying out a program of renovations in the so-called "common areas" and on building exteriors and then applying to recover the costs through an "above guideline increase" in the rents. This is an amount over and above the inflation-offsetting "guideline increase" set by the province each year – usually around 2 per cent, which the landlord can apply without having to make any representations to the Landlord and Tenant Board that oversees these matters.

Beginning in 2015 Greenwin Inc. undertook a strong drive to achieve turnovers through "buy outs" at its Robert Village complex. These were offers of cash payments to tenants willing to surrender their leases early, accompanied by dire descriptions of the inconvenience and mess that would be experienced during upcoming renovations. At the same time, according to tenants, there were protracted delays in responses to maintenance requests, especially anything involving work within the unit.

In an analysis of numbers released by Statistics Canada in February 2017 by geographer Rob Fiedler and published on Hamilton civic affairs website Raise the Hammer, Fiedler looked at what numbers from the 2016 Census showed about population trends at several levels of detail: for the whole city, for a few of the units called census tracts and for three of the smallest reporting units, the "dissemination blocks," which sometimes correspond to large city blocks. As it happens, Robert Village is reported as two dissemination blocks that together account for the entire resident population of the block bounded by Cannon, Roberts, Hughson and John. Fiedler notes, "There we see an enormous population decline in absolute terms between 2011 and 2016: 581 people or 50 percent. That may be explained in large part by a significant increase in unoccupied units from 17 to 150."[16] In short Greenwin was achieving turnover – emptying the units to refresh them and return them to the market at a higher rent, although clearly with a lag that must have been financially painful.

Having started at the top, the renovators reached the lower floors toward the end of 2015, where the makeover work was complicated by the presence of three-bedroom units, many occupied by tenants who were determined to stay in them. Greenwin's next move was to seek the planning permissions it needed to reconfigure the floor plates of the lower storeys and change the unit mix. In the spring of 2016 an agent for 181 John Street Inc. and 192 Hughson Street Inc., representing Kevin Green, applied to the Committee of Adjustment for minor variances from the site zoning that included building alterations. These would increase the number of units on the sites from the currently permitted 190 dwelling units per hectare to 260 units per hectare. The alterations involved the conversion of three-bedroom apartments into one- and two-bedroom units. Citizens taking an interest, which included members of the Beasley Neighbourhood Association and the Hamilton Tenants Solidarity Network, were troubled by the potential loss of accommodation for larger families entailed by the application, but did not grasp the full import of the proposal until almost a year later, on the eve of a second scheduled Committee of Adjustment meeting at which the decision was to be made.

A good deal of grinding, grassroots, democratic politics ensued.

This application was to go before the committee on May 19, 2016, but was withdrawn after the applicant's representatives went to see Ward 2 Councillor Jason Farr requesting support, and were directed by him to first pay a call on the Beasley Neighbourhood Association (BNA).

Members of the BNA were not well disposed toward Greenwin, because of what they had been hearing about the way the company had been attempting to persuade tenants to leave. However, the association agreed to hear a presentation from Greenwin managers at a BNA membership meeting – attended but not addressed by Kevin Green and Green's local lobbyist, former mayor Larry Di Ianni, as well as by six-term mayor and later citizenship judge Bob Morrow, whose presence astounded everyone who knew who he was. Morrow had never before been seen to attend such a presentation/lobbying effort that anyone could recall. Encountered some weeks later in the lobby of city hall and asked why he had been at the BNA meeting, he replied that he had come as a courtesy, simply because Di Ianni had asked him.

Greenwin's people allowed as to how they had gotten off on the wrong foot with the neighbourhood, and would like to restart the relationship. The three-bedroom apartments were awkwardly laid out, some on two levels, and needed to be redone by current standards. After they had said their piece, they were roundly scolded by those attending for their past treatment of tenants, but the BNA declined to either support or oppose Greenwin's application as an organization, leaving it instead to individual members to communicate with the Committee of Adjustment as each saw fit.

In April 2017, the application was resubmitted, with changes that included the retention of ten of the currently existing three-bedroom units.

Then on May 10, 2017, the BNA changed its stance and voted to support whatever position the tenants might adopt. This was in response to efforts being made by the Social Planning and Research Council of Hamilton to mediate between Kevin Green's representatives and the tenants. In the event that a package of benefits agreeable to the tenants was negotiated, the BNA did not want to stand in the way of their getting it by opposing Greenwin at the Committee of Adjustment. This caused some grumbling from BNA and Tenants Solidarity Network members who wanted to insist on the principle that family accommodation should not be stripped out of the building. Apart from the ongoing need for larger units, there was the problem of the precedent that removing existing units might set for other landlords.

Greenwin did produce an offer, consisting of several items, the most substantial of which was an undertaking to pay the difference between their current rent and the new rent for five years, for any tenant who agreed to relocate to a three-bedroom apartment in another building. Ultimately, at a meeting in an apartment at 181 John, the tenants declined the proposal, preferring to oppose any conversions of the three-bedroom units.

At this point, a difficulty with the form of the tenants' internal organization began to make itself felt. Some of the individuals with whom the BNA and the Tenants Solidarity Network had been working had left the building, and many of those remaining in the three-bedroom units were Somali immigrants led by three or four male heads of households, who required translation services. While they were rejecting Greenwin's offer, through a translator, they were asked if they in fact spoke for the entire Somali community, and they replied, emphatically, yes. One voice. This was fine, if correct, and there was no reason to doubt, but it made communication difficult. It could not be a matter of simply picking up the phone to stay in touch as the situation developed. Translation was always required, and the non-Somali speakers involved had difficulty in assessing whether everyone had the same understanding of what was occurring, and in gauging the level of trust that existed between all participants.

On June 14, a BNA membership meeting was attended by Larry Di Ianni, who told the meeting that his client had made a new application to the Committee of Adjustment and now wished to retain ten of the three-bedroom units, and that the BNA was choosing between "negotiation" and "litigation." He hoped they would not erect a "wall" between his client and the neighbourhood. After Di Ianni's departure, the BNA executive committee discussed their joint willingness to proceed as far as the Ontario Municipal Board if necessary. (Now reconstituted as the Local Planning Appeal Tribunal under somewhat different rules, the board at that time was the last court of appeal for land-use planning matters.)

The allotted time in the meeting room having elapsed, the discussion continued in the parking lot before being brought to a vote. All being willing, it was resolved to canvas for wider support and organize a large attendance at the impending Committee of Adjustment meeting.

Variance requests are circulated to several departments of the municipal administration. A couple of days before the meeting, relevant reports and letters and supporting material were released to interested parties. The planning staff report recommended approval, which was mildly disappointing. The effects, which a strong shift away from accommodation for families with children might have on the planning objective of "complete communities," drew no comment. Indeed, that the proposal was a large change was not acknowledged. Instead, we had this: "The proposal is for the maintenance and rehabilitates an existing residential property, which maintains the existing scale and character of the area and supports the creation of a range of housing options." All true except that it was a radical reduction in the range of housing options, toward a preponderance of one-bedroom units.

What was most interesting among the documents was a letter from the applicant's lawyer, Mark Noskiewicz of Goodmans LLP. Goodmans is a two hundred-lawyer firm with offices in Toronto's Bay Adelaide Centre, a very good address indeed. To the humble neighbourhood association members who were active on this file, Goodmans seemed like a rather serious legal force to be brought to bear on an application for a "minor" variance. The letter also served as a reminder that Greenwin was a very large and well provisioned firm. Noskiewicz's written explanations to the Committee of Adjustment were clear, concise and, for the BNA, revelatory. Up to that point everyone involved had been under the impression that there were 70 three-bedroom units in the buildings. According to Noskiewicz, there were 125!

On June 29, about sixty people came out to city hall for a weekday afternoon meeting of the Committee of Adjustment, enough to fill the room. Among them were tenants from the buildings, members of the BNA and other neighbourhood associations in Ward 2, Environment Hamilton, the Hamilton Tenants Solidarity Network and the councillor. Greenwin's representatives – CEO Kris Boyce, lobbyist Di Ianni and planner Ed Fothergill – made their case, but the committee quickly decided that this matter exceeded their mandate and denied the requested variances "without prejudice," a legal phrase meaning that their verdict ought not to handicap Greenwin's case in any other forum or tribunal.

Greenwin had a couple of choices. They could attempt to obtain a change in the zoning bylaw, which would come from the city's Planning Committee, subject to consent by council, or they could turn to the Ontario Municipal Board. On July 14 Noskiewicz appealed the denial of the variances to the Ontario Municipal Board.

During the week of August 28, 2017, Councillor Farr notified Rob Fiedler, a Beasley Neighbourhood Association member who was advising the BNA executive on planning issues, that Di Ianni was attempting to meet with city planning staff in order to discuss the matter. The Planning Committee was to consider the Greenwin problem at their meeting of October 3. Worried that they might be shut out of discussions going on at city hall, the BNA executive accepted a suggestion that they contact Brad Clark, a former city councillor and provincial cabinet minister, then a principal with the Toronto branch of government relations consultancy Maple Leaf Strategies, and after 2018 once again a city councillor.

Maple Leaf seemed rather a lofty source of advice for a neighbourhood association, but Clark lived in the city and had been a two-term councillor, so it was felt that he might take an interest. And the BNA needed someone who had the same sort of access as former mayor Di Ianni at city hall. Fiedler and BNA co-chair Michael Borelli decided to ask for a meeting. Clark did express interest, so at the beginning of September, at a stand-up meeting around the island in Borelli's kitchen, the BNA executive voted to engage Clark. They then discussed what a negotiated settlement might contain that would lead Greenwin to withdraw the Ontario Municipal Board appeal: the retention of more three- and two-bedroom units than Greenwin contemplated, in order to maintain family accommodation in the central city; and also perhaps some general statement of support from Greenwin for the development of a "complete communities" policy that would prescribe unit mix for new builds. The thinking was that if Greenwin were to proceed to an OMB hearing, the result could only be a decision favouring the corporation or the Committee of Adjustment. The OMB could not write other things into its order, unless the parties were somehow to come to terms in the margin of the proceedings. This was unlikely. Accordingly it would be preferable if the BNA, supported by city planning staff and with the mediation of Councillor Farr, could bring an agreement to the Planning Committee on October 3, because it was possible at this stage to obtain gains not achievable through the OMB process.

A few days later, Di Ianni contacted Councillor Farr, requesting that he arrange a meeting with the BNA.

Still unrepresented at this point were the tenants of 181 John and 192 Hughson, because the meeting called in the week following the Committee of Adjustment's refusal of Greenwin's variance was attended by a single individual and a translator. It appeared that the leaders of the Somali community in the buildings had decided to hunker down and stop trying to distinguish between the various suitors for their attention. Nor did they wish to delegate to others in their community the task of working with the Tenants Solidarity Network or the BNA to learn about the ways in which Greenwin operated within the legal framework of the Residential Tenancies Act and the planning regulations. This made it impossible for the BNA to bring to its discussions with Greenwin the question of benefits for the existing tenants of the three-bedroom apartments. These might have included the renovation of their units or the provision of new appliances, with an agreement that the landlord not seek to recover costs via an Above Guideline Increase application; or an agreement that those tenants have a right of refusal on a renovated three-bedroom unit when Greenwin was done. Unhappy with this state of affairs, representatives of the BNA and the Tenants Solidarity Network got together with an immigration settlement worker who was familiar with the Somali community, and who met with a group of Somali women on a weekly basis. This individual agreed to discuss the situation with the others, and subsequently reported that, yes indeed, they wished to remain in their current homes.

On Thursday, September 14, Rob Fiedler, Jeanette Eby and Brad Clark, representing the Beasley Neighbourhood Association, met with Larry Di Ianni, Kevin Green, Kris Boyce (Greenwin CEO) and Nicole Kirby (Greenwin project manager for construction at 181 John and 192 Hughson) at Di Ianni's offices at the former Hamilton Hotel above the Mulberry Cafe. This meeting and a second on the following Tuesday produced the outline of a memorandum of agreement that stipulated a larger number of three-bedroom units be retained than was proposed in Greenwin's last application to the Committee of Adjustment, and set a limit below which the number of two-bedroom units could not fall. In addition Greenwin agreed to convey to the city Planning Committee its support for a proposal that city staff undertake a feasibility study toward developing a family-friendly housing policy. Finally, Beasley agreed to facilitate a meeting between Greenwin and the tenants after the deal was concluded.

From the point of view of the BNA, this was all heading in the right direction, so one final attempt was made to let the tenants know what was occurring – although there was a narrow limit on the specifics that could be made public until the agreement had been written up and presented to the councillor and to city planners. On Monday, September 25, a member of the BNA and a member of the Hamilton Tenants Solidarity Network, with the assistance of the settlement worker, met with four men from John/Hughson and a staff lawyer at the Hamilton Community Legal Clinic offices, for purposes of informing the tenants about the negotiations, and to discuss things with the lawyer. The anticipated problem was that under the Residential Tenancies Act, tenants can be evicted if the landlord plans renovations so sweeping that vacant possession is required, with or without compensation, and with or without being extended the right of first refusal on the refurbished unit when it comes back on the market, depending on the circumstances. Although Greenwin was now giving assurances that no tenant would be put out, it was not clear how the tenants could protect themselves during the ongoing reconstruction of their building should the company change its mind. For that, the tenants would need a strong, permanent organization of their own. On Wednesday, September 27, Rob Fiedler, Brad Clark and the Greenwin people met with city planning staff, Councillor Farr and the mayor at city hall to finalize the memorandum of agreement, and two days later the terms of the settlement were posted among the agenda items for the Planning Committee meeting.

Finally, on Tuesday, October 3, 2017, the Planning Committee met in council chambers and a small gallery looked on while the committee, after twenty minutes of perambulation, voted to endorse the settlement, which would now proceed to the Ontario Municipal Board. Introduction of this item kicked off a mini-festival of congratulations, beginning with Brad Clark's presentation of the terms of the deal, attained, he said, by early agreement with the negotiating partner to stick to planning issues only. Clark praised the magnanimity of Greenwin, who had agreed not to displace any tenants during their unit conversion campaign, and explained that his work was not quite done, as he and the BNA had agreed also to facilitate a meeting between Greenwin and the tenants, in order to explain the deal to them. He returned several times to the notion of a family-friendly housing policy, just as his clients would have wished. "Questions?" the chair asked. Councillor Farr wondered, "What was the mood of the negotiations?" "Friendly," said Clark, as many issues were parked at the first meeting and Greenwin had been very receptive to the family-friendly policy idea.

Councillor Farr suggested this deal might serve as a site-specific example of the policy. All in all, he remarked, a very welcome outcome after two or three years of a roller-coaster situation. Councillor Matthew Green had a question: Having in view the complexity of these situations, what had Mr. Clark taken away from all this? Well, said Clark, negotiations had gone well. It had been a learning situation for the BNA. Greenwin was sincere in wanting to improve their buildings and relations with the community, and had seen the usefulness of a policy going forward, which could be helpful when it came to questions of inclusionary zoning. Councillor Green countered that perhaps there was some learning required of the developer too, who would have to grasp that there were not just financial but also social considerations. Clark reiterated that the BNA recognized that the financial component must be considered, and the whole project needed to go forward and make money. Clark then stepped aside and Rob Fiedler took the microphone on behalf of the neighbourhood association to thank Greenwin (especially for the commitment not to displace any further tenants from the three-bedroom units), as well as Councillor Farr and Mr. Clark for their efforts. Farr then thanked Fiedler and asked him to report briefly on his recent trip out west, during which he had spoken directly with planners in North Vancouver and New Westminster about the genesis of their family-friendly (i.e., unit mix) guidelines. Fiedler complied, after which Farr moved the necessary motion. Vote done, Farr circulated a notice of motion titled "Family Friendly Housing Policy," which read as follows: "That the City of Hamilton conduct a feasibility study with appropriate public consultation for the development of a 'Family Friendly Housing Policy' that would explore means of incorporating consideration for families in future development proposals for rental units, condominiums and affordable housing." The various participants in the deal then repaired to the lobby to shake hands all around.

A couple of years went by. As of June 2020, no such policy had been written.

≣

These examples show that the ideological supremacy of the market is incomplete and tentative, since many people continue to believe that economic activity is for something other than itself. The threat of loss felt when a school is to be closed, a long-familiar building demolished or dwellings suddenly removed and their occupants sent down the road brings into confused awareness the continual struggle to reconcile society's two competing conceptions of space. On the one hand space is a swarm of qualities, a complex cultural artifact that is both the condition and the product of much of our experience, and on the other hand space is an abstract volume that can be subdivided into discrete units, each having a bundle of legally enforceable individual rights. From time to time this second aspect comes sharply forward into our awareness. If we are not the owner of the property, the idea that a piece of land ought to be considered entirely separate from the whole fabric of a community may be contested; that is, we reject pure abstraction. From the other side, the owner of the bundle of rights attached to a piece of land generally regards those rights as inviolable. Of course, they can be enlarged, but never abridged. However, the contest may result in that bundle being untied and a few removed, or not, depending on who prevails. For the holder of the bundle, central planning and private sovereignty are difficult to reconcile: he or she wants the value that central planning authorities can confer, but none of the restrictions they can also impose.

Of course, the success possible to the participants in protests and campaigns against the conception of space as a pure abstraction is limited by their isolation from each other. In the three contests discussed above, there was some crossover, but commitment was unequal because interests differ. The deeper common interest, a rationality that balances all factors – that is, democracy – seems not to be well appreciated.

Stopping the removal of Hess Street Elementary School does not in itself ensure that its maintenance deficiencies will be addressed, and the same nasty conundrum faces those who wish to preserve the Gore Park properties or the stock of three-bedroom apartments in Robert Village: Once saved, how are the owners to be obliged to keep them in good repair in the months and years ahead?

≣

The schools problem and the preservation of a varied cityscape are probably less intractable than the housing problem. Within the question of how to plan for complete communities lie two other questions:

1. Diverse unit mix at what price? That is, we must address the affordability problem, which seems not to be amenable to a market-based solution, as the market is currently constituted.
2. Diverse unit mix in buildings of what design and construction? That is, we must address problems of flexibility and sustainability.

Affordability is gauged by the ratio of income to housing cost. Housing cost in turn varies with the ratio of land value to construction costs, and the ratio of both of those to the cost of borrowed money. The affordability problem probably requires for its solution forms of market-independent tenure developed by separating the ownership of land and structure, and assuring the continuous accumulation of a reserve – in short, the treatment of housing as a public utility or as a co-operative venture on a long-term basis. However, under current condominium and co-op regimes, it can be difficult to maintain reserves against pressure to hold down monthly fees or rents. In privately owned rental properties, there is at present no way to compel the owner to hold an adequate reserve particular to this or that building, rather than drawing off the income and investing it elsewhere, with the result that the condition of the building overall, as well as within individual units, can become quite poor. The same situation occurs in those condominium buildings where a large proportion of investors are absentee landlords of units, who tend to resist raising fees meant to service maintenance reserves.

From this one infers that some landlords prefer to avoid fixing capital in any one property in favour of mobility and diversification. The owner simply does not want to wait for an investment in this or that building to be recoverable with a profit, when they can turn over the capital more rapidly in some other asset. This is the origin of the disinvestment phase of the cycle, which more or less rapidly becomes a contagion affecting an ever-wider area. When re-investors return to the derelict properties in the disinvestment zone, they must sink comparatively large sums in order to make up the long-standing maintenance deficit, and then seek to recover the outlay from their tenants. The province is mulling rules to limit the damages, but as the career of the Landlord and Tenant Board has shown, no amount of half-hearted regulation can persuade landlords to a rationality that the system thwarts at every turn. Accordingly, some proportion of housing might best be taken out of the market in order to place it on a rational, sustainable basis

The design problem is to produce housing whose floor plans can be altered cheaply and easily to accommodate changing household size, especially to allow for immigration and refugee reception, and also the need for combined live/work space – the home office or atelier necessitated by the atomization of service provision. This flexible building type, when designed also to be energy efficient both in the materials of construction and in its operation, requires legal and architectural innovation, and may or may not look much like the balcony-festooned multi-residential towers to which we are accustomed.

What I have sketched is a longer-term response to the harms and displacement of market- and climate-driven war, which is producing wave on wave of forced migration, as well as the accelerating reduction in labour's share of the social product, with the resulting problem of weak effective demand, a.k.a. spreading poverty. These problems are insoluble unless the state socializes the basics: food, housing, health care – a program that, as has been repeated so often for so many decades, is somehow entirely acceptable during mass mobilization in wartime, but wicked heresy in peace. The apparent contradiction, of course, is none. In peace as in war, the few insist that the many must exist only to work, suffer and die for their benefit. Property is not always theft, but twenty-first-century financialized capitalism, indemnified by the state, has become criminal through and through.

Endnotes

1   Readers interested in some current thinking about this profound mystery could consult Daniel Miller's *Stuff* (Cambridge: Polity Press, 2010).

2   Ted Tyndorf, "Amenities for Density: Section 37 of the Planning Act" (presentation, *All About Planning* symposium, Munk Centre for International Studies, December 6, 2006). https://munkschool.utoronto.ca/imfg/uploads/88 /tyndorf_amenities_for_density_2006.pdf.

3   Richard Leitner, "$55 million to be spent on school upgrades," *Hamilton Spectator*, February 1, 2017.

4   Richard Leitner, "Demolition of Sir John A. high school now big priority," *Hamilton Spectator*, August 21, 2017.

5   Mark McNeil, "Hub planned for Sir John A. school land," *Hamilton Spectator*, September 9, 2017.

6   *Hamilton Spectator*, November 25, 1964.

7   See Allison Dunnet, *Family Room: Housing Mix Policy for Rezoning Projects* (presentation, Vancouver Housing Initiative, Vancouver, BC, July 12, 2016), http://council.vancouver.ca/20160713/documents/cfsc2-StaffPresentation .pdf; and Jennifer Keesmaat, *Growing Up: Planning for Children in New Vertical Communities – Study Update* (Toronto: City Planning Division, October 2016), http://www.toronto.ca/legdocs/mmis/2016/pg/bgrd/backgroundfile-97982.pdf.

8   For a comprehensive history, see Goldsmith Borgal and Company Architects, *18–30 King East, Gore Block Apartments, Hamilton, Ontario, Cultural Heritage Impact Assessment*, April 2016, revised June 2016. Available through the City of Hamilton.

9   Ryan McGreal, "Negotiation with Gore Property Owner Should Have Started With Designation," Raise the Hammer, August 13, 2013, https://raisethehammer .org/article/1926/negotiation_with_gore_property_owner_should_have_started _with_designation.

10 Friends of the Gore to Hamilton Municipal Heritage Committee, 15 December 2016, reprinted as "Friends of the Gore Statement to Heritage Committee," Raise the Hammer, December 15, 2016, https://www.raisethehammer.org/article/3163 /friends_of_the_gore_statement_to_heritage_committe.

11 Carmela Fragomeni, "New plan for stalled Gore Park project," Hamilton Spectator, April 7, 2016.

12 Friends of the Gore to Hamilton Municipal Heritage Committee, 15 December 2016, reprinted as "Friends of the Gore Statement to Heritage Committee," Raise the Hammer, December 15, 2016, https://www.raisethehammer.org/article/3163 /friends_of_the_gore_statement_to_heritage_committe.

13 The last of the Kresge's building was removed in November 2017.

14 The motion as amended can be found on the City of Hamilton's website among the minutes for the Planning Committee meeting of January 17, 2017. Strict timelines, deposits of security and so on are applied to both the demolitions and the salvage portion of the project, including a provision for the city to enter the property at 18–22 and administer to its facade at the owner's expense if the owner was seen to be failing to secure, protect, stabilize, monitor or restore the same.

15 Goldsmith Borgal and Company Architects, 18–30 King East, Gore Block Apartments, Hamilton, Ontario, Cultural Heritage Impact Assessment, April 2016, revised June 2016. p. 18.

16 Rob Fiedler, "Asking the Right Questions About Hamilton's 2016 Census Data," Raise the Hammer, February 14, 2017, https://raisethehammer.org/article/3211 /asking_the_right_questions_about_hamiltons_2016_census_data.

Train Drain: Inside the Seemingly Endless Campaign to Bring Light Rail Transit to Hamilton

Ryan McGreal

I have spent the past decade and then some engaged in a citizen-based movement to roll a large boulder up a steep hill. As of this writing, the project is *at best* still several years from completion and remains beset by peril and uncertainty. What follows is an inside view of the long, often exasperating and as yet unsuccessful campaign to bring light rail transit (LRT) to Hamilton.

Hamilton's LRT plan may be the most overdetermined civic infrastructure project in the city's history. It is the centrepiece of the city's transit strategy and, indeed, its overall transportation master plan. The city's plan to grow transit ridership is based almost entirely on building out a network of rapid transit lines, dubbed "B-L-A-S-T," which stem from a regional transportation plan announced in June 2007, starting with the east-west B-Line route across the downtown core between

McMaster University and Eastgate Square. LRT is also integral to the city's strategic growth plan. Without LRT, the city will not be able to meet even the minimum targets of the Ontario Government's Places to Grow land-use framework to limit sprawl and encourage more infill development. Research from the McMaster Institute of Transportation and Logistics (MITL) supports the plan and indicates that it can be a transformational tool to grow the city's tax base and shape land use more sustainably if coupled with the right policy.

But LRT is not just a bureaucratic planning exercise. It has the enthusiastic support of every anchor institution and major employer in the city. It has been endorsed by neighbourhood associations and community councils across the city. It also has the support of the property development industry. In addition, literally hundreds of small and medium-sized businesses across the city and particularly along the LRT corridor are on record publicly endorsing the plan. And lest one think this is a business-only initiative, LRT also has the support of a broad cross-section of social advocacy and environmental organizations. LRT also enjoys high levels of public support among Hamiltonians who are paying attention to the issue. There are at least two separate citizen groups dedicated to seeing the project through to completion, and many thousands of Hamiltonians have signed petitions and written statements of support for the plan over the years, with no equivalent expression of opposition.

Most crucially, the provincial Liberal government was fully committed to the project, having confirmed 100 per cent full capital funding in May 2015 and set out a politically savvy but aggressive implementation timeline, with a contract to build and operate the system signed before the 2018 provincial election and groundbreaking in 2019. The opposition parties at the time – the New Democratic Party, Progressive Conservative Party and Green Party – were likewise all on record supporting the project. When the PC Party won the June 2018 provincial election, they stated that they would support the LRT project as long as Hamiltonians continued to support it.

LRT quickly became the defining issue of the 2018 municipal election, with a well-funded challenge to incumbent mayor Fred Eisenberger by anti-LRT challenger Vito Sgro. Eisenberger won re-election decisively with 54.03 per cent of the vote to 38.06 per cent for Sgro. Eisenberger won thirteen out of fifteen wards, most of them with an absolute majority, and 189 out of 222 individual polling districts across the city. In response, the provincial PC reconfirmed its support for the LRT plan.

There is probably no other initiative in the city's history that has gathered such a broad, powerful coalition of support. Sectors that normally fall on opposite sides of an issue – environment and business, residents and developers – are lined up together on the same side. It should be a shoo-in. And yet despite this unprecedented level of harmony, every major council vote to move the project forward has been an agonizing convulsion of fear-mongering, hand-wringing and grandstanding. Again and again, LRT advocates have had to rally huge shows of support with hundreds of emails, packed council galleries and arrays of citizen delegations just to remind council of why they had already voted literally dozens of times to move the project forward. Indeed, council's ongoing reluctance to embrace this project – a project in which all the cost and risk is being assumed by the province while nearly all the benefits will accrue to the city – may be the purest case study in what is wrong with civic governance in Hamilton.

The story of Hamilton's current LRT saga began in 2007 when the Ontario Government announced MoveOntario 2020, a grand vision with fifty-two new rapid transit lines connecting the Greater Toronto and Hamilton Area (GTHA). The projects would be administered by the Greater Toronto Transit Authority, later renamed Metrolinx, a Crown agency that also assumed responsibility for the GO Transit regional network of commuter trains and buses that has been in operation since 1967.

Aside from the $17.5 billion in direct provincial capital funding, the real game changer for GTHA municipalities was a new funding model in which 100 per cent of the capital funding would be provided by the provincial and/or federal government. This was a sharp break from the status quo in which capital costs for new projects had traditionally been split three ways between the federal, provincial and municipal governments.

The regional transportation plan announced in June 2007 included two rapid transit lines in Hamilton: the east-west B-Line between McMaster and Eastgate, and a north-south A-Line between the waterfront and the John C. Munro Hamilton International Airport in Mount Hope. These two lines make up the "B" and "A" of the "B-L-A-S-T" network of rapid transit lines, with an L-line running along York Boulevard and Highway 6 between downtown Hamilton and Waterdown, an S-line running along Centennial Parkway and Rymal Road between Eastgate and the Ancaster Business Park and a T-line running along Kenilworth Avenue and Mohawk Road between the Centre on Barton and the Ancaster Meadowlands rounding out the set. In September 2007, heading into a provincial election, the Ontario Liberal Party issued a news release warning that a Progressive Conservative victory "would put rapid transit projects through MoveOntario 2020 – including *two light rail lines across Hamilton* – at risk" (emphasis added).

At the time, the city's transit strategy was to gradually and incrementally upgrade its existing express bus service on the B-Line to some kind of bus rapid transit (BRT) – a system in which buses would run frequently on dedicated transit lanes with upgraded stations and possibly traffic signal priority. The announcement of provincial interest in funding LRT was immediately exciting for transit advocates in Hamilton, who recognized this once-in-a-generation opportunity to make a bold, game-changing investment instead of just poking at the status quo. However, it took a little longer for LRT enthusiasm to take hold at city hall.

In November 2007 I had the chance to meet with Scott Stewart, then the city's general manager of Public Works, as well as a couple of Public Works project managers and a transit consultant from IBI Group, which has a specialty in BRT projects. It was as if the provincial rapid transit funding announcement had not happened. Unfortunately, as the province was taking its cues from cities in regards to their rapid transit needs, there was a real danger that Hamilton would end up with BRT rather than LRT simply because the city hadn't investigated LRT as an alternative. By this time, a group of LRT supporters in Hamilton had formed an organization called Hamilton Light Rail (HLR) – I was a founding member – and was holding monthly meetings to develop a strategy to inform Hamiltonians about LRT and why it was worth taking seriously.

Several early members of HLR had experienced LRT systems first-hand while living in other cities. We carefully reviewed case studies from other North American cities that had LRT, like Portland, Oregon, and Calgary, Alberta, as well as European cities like Grenoble and Bordeaux, France. Over time, we developed a presentation explaining what LRT is, how it works and the various ways it benefits cities. We made the argument that LRT costs more upfront to build than BRT but has a lower per-passenger operating cost, has a much higher peak capacity, attracts more new by-choice passengers and is much better at attracting new private investment around the line, leading to higher density land use with all the associated economic and social benefits. We took our show on the road and began meeting with local civic organizations – business groups, service clubs, neighbourhood associations and so on – to make the case for LRT. Nicholas Kevlahan, another founding HLR member, undertook the lion's share of these presentations and found that people overwhelmingly became enthusiastic about LRT once they learned about it.

One of the first local organizations to endorse LRT was the *Hamilton Spectator* editorial board, which published a glowing editorial on June 16, 2007, written by Robert Howard:

> There are few things that can literally transform a city. Hamilton's share of the $17.5-billion transit plan announced yesterday by the province has the potential – particularly with a push for an "upgrade" – to do that. . . .
>
> [W]hat Hamilton really needs is the next step up – the 21st century solution. The proposed rapid-transit lines for Hamilton would essentially be dedicated routes for better or larger buses. This is the time for Hamilton to push the province, and the Greater Toronto Transportation Authority charged with implementing the plan, to consider light rail transit (LRT) lines for Hamilton that would replace some buses with quiet, environmentally friendly electric trains.

They would be among the first of a whole gamut of civic organizations to formally endorse Hamilton's LRT project.

Meanwhile, recently elected Mayor Fred Eisenberger, who had defeated incumbent Mayor Larry Di Ianni by just 452 votes in a squeaker of a municipal race, was working behind the scenes to create space in city hall for the LRT initiative to be taken seriously. One of the first things he did in 2007 was to change the name of the Bus Rapid Transit Office under the Public Works Department to the Rapid Transit Office – a symbolic gesture, but one that hinted at openness to a more ambitious scope. In early 2008 the Rapid Transit project manager, Jill Stephen, was directed to undertake a Rapid Transit Feasibility Study comparing BRT and LRT on the east-west B-Line and the north-south A-Line. The Rapid Transit Office began studying rapid transit data from other cities and holding public consultations.

City staff published their first interim report in April 2008, and it was somewhat disappointing. They compared the operating costs per vehicle rather than per passenger, which obscured the fact that an LRT vehicle can carry many more passengers than a bus (even an articulated bus). The report stated that BRT costs around $80 per revenue hour per vehicle, compared to $175 per revenue hour per vehicle for LRT. However, since an LRT vehicle can carry nearly three times as many passengers, its operating cost per passenger is actually lower. Likewise, the study compared a $900,000 purchase cost per BRT vehicle with $4 million per LRT vehicle, but again failed to note that LRT vehicles carry more passengers and last at least three times as long (ten years vs. thirty years) with much lower maintenance costs. The study also punted on a comparison of the economic benefits from BRT vs. LRT. Instead, it weakly noted that "LRT is *often thought of* as being more permanent than BRT and as being able to provide greater economic spinoffs than BRT" (emphasis added). Whereas the advantages of BRT were stated in the active voice, the benefits of LRT were relegated to the passive voice.

LRT advocates identified these concerns with the interim report and staff received this feedback with good grace, noting that it was just a starting point for further consultation, analysis and discussion. A public consultation update in June 2008 found that 71 per cent of respondents favoured LRT over BRT. City councillors in the Public Works Committee pushed back against this report, saying that staff needed to talk to more people. Over that summer, staff held several well-attended public meetings across the city and consulted directly with more than 1,600 people. A follow-up report in September found that 66 per cent of respondents favoured LRT over BRT, 8 per cent preferred BRT and 20 per cent favoured either mode. Meanwhile, various civic organizations had by this time begun formally endorsing LRT, including the Hamilton Chamber of Commerce and the Realtors Association of Hamilton-Burlington.

Later that summer, Mayor Eisenberger, Ancaster councillor Lloyd Ferguson and senior city staff went on a fact-finding trip to Calgary,

Alberta; Portland, Oregon; and Charlotte, North Carolina, to study their LRT systems and speak with their local leadership. Ferguson, in particular, came back convinced that LRT was the way to go. In a September 2008 op-ed for the *Ancaster News*, Ferguson wrote, "I am now convinced that we need to look at some form of light-rail system, among other things, to spur our local economy and get Hamilton into the next millennium."

The final report of the Rapid Transit Feasibility Study in October 2008 strongly endorsed LRT over BRT on a variety of measures, including its superior capacity, ridership and per-passenger operating cost, as well as its higher urban land use and economic development potential. It recommended building the east-west B-Line first, while beginning preliminary work on the subsequent north-south A-Line. The report also recommended developing a supportive land-use plan to encourage new urban development along the LRT corridor. Staff urged council to move quickly to secure priority funding from the province under the Regional Transportation Plan funding framework, stating:

[A]s a result of Provincial timelines, which impact the potential funding for rapid transit projects in Hamilton, it has been made clear by Metrolinx that Provincial project priorities, will in part, depend on projects that have strong political support and that can be completed under aggressive timelines. Rapid Transit Team Staff are dedicated, from a technical standpoint and subject to Council approval at a future date, of making rapid transit in Hamilton happen with an anticipated ground breaking scheduled for Spring 2011, subject to Provincial and Federal funding commitments through the MoveOntario 2020 plan.

That timeline would ultimately prove to be optimistic, but at the time everyone seemed to have a shared sense of excitement and urgency about the project. In particular, it was understood that the provincial transportation framework was a rare opportunity to get full capital funding for a transformative investment and it was not likely to last long if Hamilton failed to seize the moment. Council unanimously approved the report, and work began under Jill Stephen's Rapid Transit to develop a B-Line LRT plan that would be eligible to submit to the province for funding consideration. The city also received a $3 million grant from Metrolinx to develop an Environmental Project Report (EPR) for the LRT plan, which is required under provincial law as part of the Class Environmental Assessment process for transit projects.

It was around this time that city staff contacted Hamilton Light Rail and asked us to stop holding meetings. We were told that it was confusing for the public to have an official city organization as well as an independent citizen group holding LRT meetings, and that in any case they were moving forward with the plan and our advocacy was no longer needed. In what may be our single biggest error of judgment over the entire project, we agreed to this request and wound down our public engagement.

When council approved the Rapid Transit Feasibility Study, the decision was made to continue operating the Rapid Transit Office out of the Public Works Department because it was believed that the project would have a more supportive home there than in the Department of Planning and Economic Development. However, in late 2008 the city appointed a new city manager: Chris Murray, formerly a senior project manager who had shepherded the highly contentious Red Hill Valley Parkway construction to completion. Public Works general manager Scott Steward was passed over for the top job, and in late 2008 he accepted a senior management position working for the City of Burlington. This was a significant loss for Hamilton and particularly for the LRT project, since he had become an early champion for LRT and had created a supportive political context for the Rapid Transit Office in his department. The city retained Steer Davies Gleave (SDG), a respected international consultancy specializing in rapid transit projects, to help develop the plan.

In 2009, the Ontario Government decided to shake things up at Metrolinx by replacing its board of directors, which had consisted of the mayors of every GTHA municipality, with an appointed body of transportation planners and project management specialists. At the same time, Metrolinx was merged with GO Transit and the body was granted the power to enter into procurement and service contracts to execute its mandate to build and operate regional rapid transit. The Metrolinx/GO merger was a painful upheaval for both organizations.

Part of the new board's challenge was to find ways to fund the rest of the Regional Transportation Plan (RTP), dubbed "The Big Move" when it was published in November 2008. The original provincial endowment of $11.5 billion, with another $6 billion requested from the federal government, was well short of the $50 billion in projects that had been identified over the twenty-five-year term of the RTP. Unfortunately, every potential revenue source – from highway tolls to business parking levies to regional fuel tax increases – was extremely contentious and carried a big risk of popular pushback and electoral punishment.

The organizational upheaval at Metrolinx also resulted in delays for the Benefits Case Analysis (BCA) on Hamilton's B-Line LRT, which was necessary in order for the project to move ahead to the point where it was ready for a funding request. City and Metrolinx staff were working closely together on the city's plan to ensure that it would meet the provincial funding mandate, and the BCA was the formal approval the city needed. The delays at Metrolinx meant that the BCA was not published until February 2010. It compared three scenarios – full LRT from McMaster to Eastgate, phased LRT from McMaster to Queenston Traffic Circle with a subsequent extension to Eastgate and full BRT from McMaster to Eastgate – and concluded that full LRT cost more to build but provided the biggest overall benefit to the city. It also concluded that the benefits of LRT would be maximized if Main Street and King Street were converted to two-way, noting "the two-way street system is more supportive of the City's objective to create a healthy, more pedestrian-friendly downtown." Regrettably, the BCA fell short of actually recommending a preferred technology, simply presenting the alternatives and noting their respective pros and cons.

In 2010, the Ontario Government delayed $4 billion in Metrolinx projects that had already been announced. For Toronto's transformational "Transit City" network of LRT lines, this would ultimately prove disastrous, since the delay meant that incoming Toronto mayor Rob Ford could tear up the Transit City plan entirely and trigger years of upheaval over that city's transportation strategy. The effect in Hamilton was less dramatic but no less devastating. At the same time that Toronto chose a right-wing suburban populist as its mayor, Hamilton voters rejected Mayor Eisenberger's re-election campaign to pin their hopes on a seemingly affable talk radio host and downtown councillor named Bob Bratina. Bratina had run for election on a pro-LRT campaign, committing to "work with all levels of government to bring light rail transit to Hamilton." When HLR held our first major public event in May 2008, Bratina was actually our emcee.

However, in July 2011, Bratina expressed reservations about LRT, questioning whether Hamilton would receive full funding and claiming the city was "not hearing any kind of clamour from the public on that file." HLR sprung back into action and issued a call for Hamiltonians to write to council and raise a "clamour" in support of LRT. A week later, in a radio interview on CHML with host Bill Kelly, Bratina and City Manager Murray poured more cold water on the LRT plan, claiming that they were hearing no interest from developers, that it was not clear where new development might occur along the LRT line and that LRT was a big risk without any clear return on investment. It was a stunning repudiation of both the city's Rapid Transit Feasibility Study and the Metrolinx Benefits Case Analysis, and it seemed to come out of nowhere.

On another talk radio appearance on July 22, Bratina openly mocked former mayor Eisenberger, who had gone on to take a position as the

CEO of the Canadian Urban Institute after losing re-election. Eisenberger had pointed out that the Metrolinx transit funding model was for the province to pay the full capital cost of approved rapid transit projects, but Bratina was busy claiming Hamilton might have to cover some of the capital cost for its LRT. Talking to CHML's Bill Kelly, he added, "You know, it's interesting though, so many facts are being thrown around that may be myths. So I think that there's probably a 'Canadian Urban Mythstitute' that, from which myths emanate. Because it's myth. It's not fact. I love myths."

Then an email from Murray to council was leaked on July 28, 2011, advising council that the Rapid Transit Office had been suspended and that its resources were being reallocated to push for all-day GO Train service instead, which the province had already committed to provide to Hamilton. This decision was made while Jill Stephen, the Rapid Transit project manager, was away on vacation. Bratina then began claiming that Hamilton would have to choose between all-day GO train service and LRT, a claim that Metrolinx and the province immediately disputed. According to Metrolinx spokesperson Robin Alam: "It is important to remember that both rapid transit initiatives planned for Hamilton – the Hamilton LRT and all day GO Train service from Toronto to Hamilton – are viable and can co-exist. Hamilton's current rapid transit situation is not an 'either-or' scenario." Meanwhile, other councillors were also drifting on LRT. Ward 5 councillor Chad Collins and then Ward 9 councillor Brad Clark were complaining that council was "slowly being backed into a corner" on LRT when they were presented with the B-Line corridor land-use study that they had requested when council approved the development of an LRT plan. They actually complained about the $3 million grant the province had provided to help fund the LRT environmental project report.

On another radio appearance on August 31, Bratina said LRT was "not a priority" and that "if somehow a million people move to Hamilton over the next five years and we have traffic congestion all over the place, we will look at all transit options including LRT." Jill Stephen announced in September that she was leaving her position at the city to work as a senior transportation planning engineer for the Region of Niagara. She had been blindsided by the executive decision to suspend the LRT project and effectively disband her office and it was clear that the excitement and enthusiasm with which the project began just three years earlier had soured.

The full impact of Bratina's obstruction became clear on September 11, 2011, when the *Spectator* published a story quoting then premier McGuinty: "[All-day GO train service] was the number one ask of the city. We've had some important conversations with the mayor, and this is their priority, which made it our priority. Over time, we can enter into other discussions about things like the LRT." This was a dramatic break from just four years earlier, when the Liberals had warned that a PC election win would threaten the two light rail lines in Hamilton that the Liberals were promising to fund. Councillor Clark, who had earlier that summer suggested that LRT supporters were overreacting to Murray's email announcing the suspension of the LRT projects, was now warning that the city's priorities had changed without a council vote and that the mayor and city manager had acted unilaterally. "Did the Mayor and City Manager make that decision? Because council has not made that decision. It was never brought to us to have a discussion." Clark drew a contrast with the Pan American Games stadium (now called Tim Hortons Field), for which the city had to provide 44 per cent of the capital funding: "It is incredibly frustrating that we were promised this commitment and now this Council has jumped through hoops to get the Pan Am Games money, and the entire argument was, 'Why would you turn down 56 per cent of the money?' Well, I'm curious: why are we going to look the other way on LRT when 100 per cent of the money was promised by senior levels of government? I don't get it."

On September 23, Hamilton Light Rail launched a new campaign calling on the city to recommit to its support of the LRT plan and calling on the province to recommit to its promise to fund that plan. The first of thousands of personally written LRT support statements began flowing to the city and province. Councillor Clark brought forward a motion to demand that the province recommit to its funding commitment, while Ward 2 councillor Jason Farr and then Ward 1 councillor Brian McHattie brought forward a more conciliatory motion to reaffirm council support for LRT planning and to ask the province to continue supporting the city's planning efforts to develop an LRT funding proposal. Council approved both motions, and the province indicated that it was still willing to work with the city but that it could not make a funding commitment until the city's design work was completed.

Going into 2012, Public Works staff on the project – who were rolled into the general transportation planning group after Jill Stephen left – continued working on a 30 per cent engineering and detailed design for the LRT route and submitted an Environmental Project Report (EPR) to the Ministry of the Environment as part of the environmental assessment process. The city received a Statement of Completion from the ministry, indicating that the ministry approved the EPR. Transportation project manager Justin Readman assumed oversight for the remaining engineering and design work. Meanwhile, planning staff finished developing a B-Line corridor land-use plan that included a series of public design charettes at each proposed station node along the route.

By this time, the original Metrolinx capital funding envelope had all been committed, so it was not clear from where funding for Hamilton's LRT, if approved, would come. Metrolinx was still trying to develop an investment strategy, and this exercise was still as politically sensitive as ever. In August 2012, then Transport minister Bob Chiarelli reportedly told Mayor Bratina that Hamilton would be expected to cover some portion of the capital cost, a break from the funding model Metrolinx was using for other LRT projects like the Eglinton Crosstown in Toronto and the Hurontario-Main LRT in Mississauga, where local leadership had aggressively pushed for a funding commitment. But instead of demanding the same funding arrangement for Hamilton, Bratina told CBC Hamilton: "It was a relief to finally hear a clear statement from the minister that there will be participation expected from the host community." Ancaster councillor Ferguson objected to this, noting that he had just been told by a Metrolinx official that 100 per cent capital funding "is our model." In November 2012, then Metrolinx CEO Bruce McCuaig once again suggested that Hamilton might be on the hook for some of the capital cost, citing the upcoming Investment Strategy: "I think there's an expectation, there's going to be use of both what are normally considered to be provincial funding tools and municipal funding tools. What those tools are and what the spread between and the rates are, we'll have to see as we come up with our final advice in June [2013]."

In early 2013, Metrolinx created more anxiety by dropping the "L" from its update on Hamilton's rapid transit project, leading many LRT supporters to worry that the project might be downgraded to some kind of BRT system. A February "Big Move consultation" in Hamilton noted: "The city's focus is to implement RT on *King and Main Streets* and to *expand the existing B-Line bus service* to be faster and more efficient. The project will help revitalize Hamilton's downtown core and improve public transit options in the city" (emphasis added). This vague messaging further served to confuse and demoralize LRT supporters while making it easier for Bratina and other LRT skeptics to claim that that province didn't really want to fund the project and that the city should stop wasting time on developing it.

Then, on February 25, staff finally presented their plan, titled *Rapid Ready: Expanding Mobility Choices in Hamilton.* This comprehensive document included the 30 per cent engineering and detailed design that was necessary to assign a budget and request a funding commitment. It also included the Environmental Project Report that had been approved in 2012 and the Nodes and Corridors Land Use plan for the B-Line route to encourage intensification. Beyond that, the plan included a list of other transit improvements considered necessary for Hamilton's transit system – including LRT – to perform to its full potential. After an epic General Issues Committee meeting, council unanimously approved the plan and agreed to submit it to the province for funding consideration. Unfortunately, Metrolinx was still waiting for the Investment Strategy to be finalized and approved in order to receive guidance on whether and how to approve the funding request. Meanwhile, the mixed messaging continued to confound the issue. In March, a Metrolinx vice-president was quoted in the *Spectator* saying, "If a municipality has an ability to present a financial contribution to the projects, that gets bonus points." But on the same day, an article in *YourHamiltonBiz* quoted then Transport minister Glen Murray contradicting this: "I am not looking, and nor do I think Metrolinx will be looking, to be influenced by direct municipal contributions to rate the priority of projects. As much as we, of course, always love to have our municipal government partners as co-investors in these strategies, it is not part of how we rate the projects."

And the project continued to be held back by a lack of local political leadership. Back in mid-2012, McMaster Institute of Transportation and Logistics (MITL) published a study by researchers Christopher Higgins and Mark Ferguson, titled *The North American Light Rail Experience: Insights for Hamilton*, which argued that to be successful, Hamilton's LRT needed to be combined with traffic calming measures to create a more pedestrian-friendly public space; supportive land-use policy to encourage dense, mixed-use transit-oriented developments; and strong political leadership to ensure such a large, complex project is successful. "A political champion can help to realize success by marshaling resources, building coalitions, and resolving disputes. Coordinating institutions, streamlining processes, and minimizing red tape are seen as crucial in implementing TOD projects and are dependent on strong political leadership."

Hamilton had been lacking such a champion in the mayor's office since late 2010, but Bratina had claimed that he could not champion the plan without seeing it. Now, with council's approval of the *RapidReady* plan, Bratina said he was ready to start championing the plan. In a February 28, 2013, email to Raise the Hammer, Bratina wrote: "Council has now provided direction with the expectation of 100 percent of capital funding and that will be our position dealing with the government." Alas, it was too good to be true. On April 27, the *Spectator* reported that Bratina was claiming he was told at a private fundraiser with Premier Kathleen Wynne that Hamilton would have to choose either LRT or all-day GO service. A spokesperson for Premier Wynne denied this, clarifying that the two "are not competing projects" and that "Metrolinx has already committed to providing two-way, all-day GO service to Hamilton." It then emerged that Bratina was not even in attendance at the fundraiser.

By this time, Bratina had already been formally censured by the rest of council for falsely blaming human resources (HR) staff for his chief of staff's pay raise, and for his actions following this event. He was isolated from the rest of council, estranged from senior management and increasingly erratic in his words and conduct.

On the LRT file, Bratina began to insist that the *RapidReady* LRT plan was not actually an LRT plan and was instead a plan to incrementally build transit service so that one day it might make sense to build LRT in the distant future. Council grew frustrated with his continued mixed messaging, and Councillor McHattie brought forward a motion on April 24 to clarify once again that council understood *RapidReady* to be a request for full capital funding for LRT. The meeting was a fiasco, with Bratina claiming falsely that the report did not identify LRT as a priority or even approve the construction of LRT once funding was approved. It made no sense, and City Manager Murray debunked Bratina's revisionism in no uncertain terms, confirming that the *RapidReady* plan was focused all along on the B-Line and advancing the detail of that B-Line so the Province can make a decision on the B-Line....

That's, in essence, the motivation behind the report and that's what we think the report does for you. It puts the ball certainly in the Province's court to make a decision. We've done our homework, we are ahead of everyone else. You know, *we think investing in transit, LRT specifically, in the City of Hamilton is something fundamental to our growth*, and that, you know, it's really at the end of the day up to the Province to make a decision about what it is it wants to invest here in Hamilton.

But *clearly we've been focused on the B-Line*, and by you saying tonight you wish they make the first decision on the B-Line and investment, and if they choose to for whatever reason defer it, then we're saying we're still there wanting to see the other investments made as well. (emphasis added)

Council voted to approve McHattie's motion, with only then Dundas councillor Russ Powers voting against it, on the basis that he had changed his mind about LRT and did not think the province was actually going to fund it. Murray's comments at that meeting prompted Bratina to march over to Murray and yell at him off-mic, saying, "I can't believe you just said that!" Councillor Farr and Ward 4 councillor Sam Merulla heard the exchange and called on then integrity commissioner Earl Basse to investigate the matter. Basse eventually ruled that Bratina had violated the Council Code of Conduct but that he should not be censured again because he had apologized to Murray and Murray had said he did not feel intimidated or threatened.

Metrolinx finally unveiled its Investment Strategy in late May 2013, and it included the following list of "revenue tools": a 1 per cent increase to the harmonized sales tax (HST), expected to raise $1.3 billion a year; a fuel tax of five cents per litre, expected to raise $330 million a year; a business parking levy averaging twenty-five cents per space per day, expected to raise $350 million a year; and a 15 per cent increase to development charges, expected to raise $100 million a year. In total, these would raise $2 billion a year, a steady funding source to pay for the rest of the approved projects in *The Big Move*. The political fallout was almost immediate: municipalities including Hamilton voted to express their disapproval, while the Ontario Government, led by the Liberals in a shaky minority, distanced themselves from the unpopular measures. Instead, they ended up proposing a highly progressive budget for 2014 that included $15 billion in new regional transit investment without adding new taxes, levies or fees. Ontario NDP leader Andrea Horwath led a vote to defeat the budget, dissolving the government and triggering a new provincial election on June 12, 2014. Defying expectations, the Liberals emerged from that election with a majority government and a clear mandate to put its budget into effect – including a new round of transit projects in the GTHA.

Bratina decided not to run for re-election in the 2014 municipal election. The three major mayoral candidates were Brad Clark, who ran on a populist anti-LRT platform on the assumption that the Liberals would not keep their funding commitment; Brian McHattie, who ran on a progressive pro-LRT platform; and former mayor Fred Eisenberger, who ran on a moderate, provisionally pro-LRT platform in which he proposed creating a Citizens Jury to review all the LRT work completed to date and make a recommendation to council on whether to continue to pursue funding from the province. Eisenberger won handily with a 39 per cent plurality and began the work of rebuilding the city's relationship with the province. Meanwhile, Premier Wynne continued to say publicly that the province was committed to full capital funding for rapid transit but Hamilton had to tell the province what it wanted.

During that municipal election, Ward 5 councillor Collins joined Powers, who was not running for re-election, in reversing his position on LRT. Interestingly, both Powers and Collins had been members of the Liberal Party, as indeed was Bratina, who would go on to be elected Liberal MP for Hamilton East-Stoney Creek in 2015. Indeed, for quite some time, the biggest obstacles to the Liberal Party approving LRT in Hamilton seems to have been Hamilton Liberals. Even during the 2014 provincial election, the Liberal candidates for Hamilton Mountain and Hamilton East-Stoney Creek had run on a joint platform arguing that the B-Line should be express buses rather than LRT. They both lost to NDP candidates who supported LRT.

Between the obstruction of local Liberals and the continued mixed messaging from Queen's Park, it sounded rather as though the province was looking for a way to wiggle out of its LRT commitment. Hoping to broker a compromise to break the impasse, senior city management cooked up a Ten Year Transit Strategy with $300 million in capital funding requests to the province to build out its B-L-A-S-T network of express bus routes before even starting work on the B-Line LRT. The Ten Year Transit Strategy had started out as a motion by Councillor McHattie directing staff to identify $45 million in capital improvements to local transit to make while LRT was in development but the recommendation that came back was much larger, and rather than supporting the LRT plan it disrupted it. However, council seemed eager to make the whole exasperating LRT debate go away and fell on this proposal, voting in early 2015 to bolt it onto the *RapidReady* funding request it had already submitted. During this time, Hamilton Light Rail was very active in pushing for the province to keep its LRT funding commitment, and Queen's Park received thousands of LRT support messages. We also prepared a detailed summary of the work completed to date and had it printed and bound and sent to the province, where they were surprised at how far along the city was in completing its due diligence. At the same time, Eisenberger continued to work with the province to convince them that city hall now had a champion who was willing to do the legwork to make sure a provincial LRT project would have local support.

Finally, on May 25, 2015, Premier Wynne came to McMaster University and gave the announcement LRT supporters had awaited since 2007: the province would be providing full, 100 per cent capital funding for LRT. The funding announcement was for a phased hybrid of the B- and A-Lines: a phase one B-Line running between McMaster and the Queenston Traffic Circle, around three kilometres west of Eastgate Square; and an A-Line LRT spur running on James Street between the B-Line and the West Harbour to connect with the new GO Train station. Liberal MPP Ted McMeekin of Ancaster-Dundas-Flamborough-Westdale, then the Minister of Municipal Affairs and Housing, credited "each of the folks who sent me the 20,000 tweets over the past four years." He specifically mentioned Hamilton Light Rail and the "team who came together and worked hard to keep this vision in our minds. To the Light Rail group and others who have been championing this cause for a long time, a very sincere thank you. You literally kept this thing on the rails."

Construction was scheduled to start in 2019 with operation beginning around 2023 or 2024. At the same meeting, Transport Minister Steven Del Duca denied the Ten Year Transit Strategy funding request, pointing out that local transit is the responsibility of municipalities and that Hamilton already receives millions of dollars a year in gas tax transfers for transit. Council voted to accept the funding and to establish a new LRT office under the Department of Planning and Economic Development to coordinate with Metrolinx on completing an updated engineering design and an Environmental Project Report Addendum for the changed route. Council also signed a memorandum of agreement (MOA) and a real estate protocol with Metrolinx, committing the city to work with Metrolinx to complete the project in a timely fashion.

Timing was crucial. The Metrolinx procurement model is to sign a contract with a consortium to design, build, finance, operate and maintain the system (called a DBFOM contract), and the goal was to have a contract signed before the 2018 provincial election in June. That way, even if the Liberal Party lost the election and a different party formed the government, it would be difficult to cancel the contract without incurring cancellation fees and paying a political price (think: gas plants). This project had already enjoyed an extraordinarily long period in which the provincial and municipal funding priorities were more or less aligned, notwithstanding the wasted years during Bratina's term as mayor, and it was seen as crucial to finalize the design, sign a contract and lock in a construction schedule before that political alignment could be jeopardized by a change in leadership at Queen's Park.

Another change that came with the funding confirmation was that people who didn't like the project began to take it more seriously. Prior to this point, there had been no organized opposition to LRT aside from Bratina's idiosyncratic obstructionism. Dundas councillor Powers had come out against LRT in April 2013 on the assumption that the province did not really want to fund it – an assumption that was at least reasonable to make, given the mixed signals coming from Queen's Park at the time.

In the community, a group called "No LRT In Hamilton" was formed by the owners of a specialty clothing store on King Street West. They framed LRT as a "sexy train to nowhere," a phrase that turned up repeatedly among opponents who argued that the crosstown LRT corridor did not warrant such an investment. They tried to argue that LRT technology was unproven and risky, while at the same time comparing it to obsolete "streetcars" that were removed in the 1950s. The leader of the No LRT movement, Carol Lazich, demonstrated the tenor of the group at the March 28, 2017, General Issues Committee when she compared LRT to deadly infectious diseases like AIDS and SARS in her delegation. An apology letter sent to council on November 24, 2016, by Theodore Sares, who had managed the No Hamilton LRT

Twitter account, alleged that the campaign's "strategy has been to stir up as much fear and doubt about this project as possible, to always talk about 'cost' and taxes and damage to the downtown."

Whereas council had been mostly unanimous in its support for LRT, the 2014 municipal election shifted things. Dundas voters elected Arlene VanderBeek, a Powers protege who was skeptical about LRT, while Ward 9 voters elected Doug Conley, a conservative former Stoney Creek councillor who also took a dim view of major transit investment. In March 2016, former CHCH broadcaster and PC candidate Donna Skelly won a by-election in Ward 7, the Central Mountain, after the progressive vote was split three ways. Councillor Skelly had promised during her campaign that she would not go against decisions already made and told the *Spectator*, "To reject $1 billion? I don't think anyone is that foolhardy." Yet she began holding meetings with the No LRT group.

At the same time, Ward 8 councillor Terry Whitehead started attacking LRT in what seemed an all-out suburban motorist assault against transit, active transportation, traffic calming and complete streets in the old city of Hamilton. Whitehead tried to introduce a motion declaring a moratorium on all new traffic-calming projects across the entire lower city. He actively opposed traffic calming on Aberdeen Avenue in southwest Hamilton, attacked staff over the introduction of bike lanes on Herkimer and Charlton Streets in Ward 2, and even threatened a bizarre motion to close the James Mountain Road and Beckett Drive escarpment accesses in response to a housekeeping motion to ratify a decision council had already made to introduce interim traffic-calming measures on Aberdeen. Whitehead also had an office assistant prepare an LRT Report that was immediately and thoroughly debunked by transportation researcher Christopher Higgins, Ph.D., of McMaster Institute for Transportation and Logistics, whose work had been cited and misused in the report.

Meanwhile, other suburban councillors were wondering why they should spend political capital on a project that was not going to directly benefit their constituents. Where council had been more or less united, if weakly, in support of LRT in principle, the prospect of actually receiving the investment and building the system seemed to make several of its members uneasy. The hard core of LRT champions on council was limited to Mayor Eisenberger; rookie councillors Aidan Johnson of Ward 1 and Matthew Green of Ward 3, who had just run on pro-LRT platforms; and veteran councillors Farr, Merulla and Ferguson. The rest of council was either opposed or at best ambivalent, despite most of them having voted repeatedly to move the project forward, accept the funding and start implementing the line. A May 2016 motion by Merulla to reaffirm council's support for LRT caused the rupture to blow wide open into a full-scale crisis. Council closed ranks and voted to defer the motion while Collins proposed making LRT a ballot question in the 2018 municipal election. In September 2016, Whitehead and Skelly hijacked a public consultation on LRT to interrogate staff and politicize what was supposed to be a forum to communicate information about the project.

Glanbrook councillor Brenda Johnson posted a blog entry on her website saying she could not continue to support LRT without knowing what the city's operating and maintenance cost obligation would be – even though she had voted for the memorandum of agreement that spelled out the process for negotiating those very costs once a consortium was chosen to receive the contract to build, operate and maintain the system. At the same time, Flamborough councillor Judi Partridge started claiming that the city's operating cost obligation could be $23 million a year, a number with no basis that was quickly debunked by the city's LRT director, Paul Johnson.

In October 2016, the city solicitor, Janice Atwood-Petrovski, and the integrity commissioner, George Rust-D'Eye, advised council that the rules of procedure would require a "reconsideration motion" with a two-thirds majority to overturn council's previous votes to accept the LRT funding, establish the LRT office and sign the memorandum of agreement and real estate protocol with Metrolinx – hence rendering Merulla's motion moot. That also applied to Collins's motion, since deferring LRT to a ballot question would amount to reconsidering the vote to proceed with the project. Since six of the sixteen councillors were solidly pro-LRT, a reconsideration motion was off the table. However, there were still important votes coming up that council could delay, putting the project at risk.

One of the outcomes of the last round of public consultation was a push by the Hamilton Chamber of Commerce and other anchor institutions calling for an LRT station to be added at Bay Street, where there were a large number of nearby destinations that would be well-served by a station, plus huge uplift potential from vacant lots on three of its four corners. An earlier campaign by a citizen advocacy group called the Hamilton LRT Advocacy had already succeeded in convincing the city and Metrolinx to add a station at Gage Park/the Delta. Council voted 9–6 to reject a motion that would have merely asked Metrolinx to consider adding the station.

A larger milestone was the upcoming vote to approve an addendum to the Environmental Project Report to incorporate the changes to the approved route – specifically, to stop the B-Line at Queenston Traffic Circle and to add a north-south spur connecting the B-Line to the West Harbour GO Station. Since the city and Metrolinx were co-proponents of the project, council needed to approve the EPR addendum before it could be submitted to the Ministry of Environment and Climate Change for review and approval. Councillors received the EPR addendum during an active General Issues Committee meeting on April 19 that included dozens of citizen delegations, most of them in support of LRT. Councillors voted to defer a decision until the April 26 council meeting.

Meanwhile, early 2017, the province de-scoped the north-south spur after a Value for Money analysis determined that it would cost a lot of money to build just two kilometres of LRT and that it would not generate a positive return on that investment. Another contributing factor was that the province was making better progress negotiating with CP Rail to bring all-day, two-way GO train service to the Hunter Street GO station than it was negotiating with CN Rail to bring all-day, two-way GO train service to the West Harbour GO Station. As a result, the Hunter station would receive all-day GO train service in time for LRT to start, and the province wanted to focus on improving the pedestrian corridor linking the Gore Park LRT station with the Hunter GO along Hughson Street. At the time, the province offered to redirect the A-Line funding toward a full A-Line bus rapid transit service to mollify mountain councillors Skelly and Whitehead, who were complaining that the B-Line LRT didn't directly benefit their constituents. Skelly and Whitehead criticized the proposal, calling the A-Line "a joke" and saying they didn't want to lose any lanes of traffic for dedicated bus lanes.

Some councillors were saying they couldn't accept LRT in its current form, stopping at Queenston Traffic Circle. Whitehead in particular decided to make this a deal-breaker in terms of his support for the project, claiming that his votes had been for LRT to Eastgate and that it didn't make sense stopping at Queenston. Hamilton Light Rail began to call for the province to take the money saved from eliminating the A-Line spur and use it to extend the B-Line to Eastgate Square as a way of mollifying enough skeptics to secure majority support for LRT among councillors. At the same time, we stepped up our efforts to get everyone who supported LRT to make their voice heard before it was too late. An extraordinary, unprecedented coalition of LRT supporters unloaded an avalanche of messages on council. Dundas councillor VanderBeek complained that her email inbox was actually broken by the deluge. At the same time, a group of LRT advocates engaged in door-to-door canvassing in select "swing" wards, including Dundas and Ward 6 (east mountain). The canvassers found that everyone they spoke with understood and agreed with the plan once it was explained to them. They were encouraged to contact their councillor and express their support for the plan.

As April 26 approached, a coalition of LRT support organizations including Hamilton Light Rail, the Hamilton LRT Advocacy, the Hamilton Chamber of Commerce, the Hamilton and District Labour Council and others held a rally for LRT outside city hall on a cold, rainy Saturday that nevertheless drew several hundred people. An inspiring slate of speakers included MPP Ted McMeekin and Mayor Eisenberger. Hamilton Light Rail also printed a selection of several hundred of the most inspiring personal statements of support for LRT from its ongoing campaign and had them printed and bound and delivered to "swing" councillors.

Behind-the-scenes negotiations between the city and province produced a last-minute breakthrough: Transport Minister Del Duca agreed that the money saved from the A-Line spur would be used to extend the B-Line all the way to Eastgate. By the time the council meeting began, the outcome was already all but guaranteed: after years of planning, stalling, delays, political interference and civic engagement, and after months of intense debate and advocacy that disproportionately favoured LRT, council finally, reluctantly, was persuaded to support the EPR addendum and move the project forward. Councillor VanderBeek captured the spirit of the vote when she said, "If in doubt, err on the side of progress." Council ended up voting 10–5 to approve the report, with only Ward 7 councillor Donna Skelly, Ward 9 councillor Doug Conley, Ward 10 councillor Maria Pearson, Ward 11 councillor Brenda Johnson and Ward 15 councillor Judi Partridge voting against it. Perhaps the most surprising vote was from Collins, who had been among the first vocal opponents of LRT. He gave one of the longest, most intimate speeches of his political career, speaking for nearly half an hour about how difficult this entire process was and how it was now essential, if the project was to succeed, for council to act together as a team.

The Ministry of Environment and Climate Change approved the EPR addendum on August 2, 2017, freeing up Metrolinx to proceed with the procurement phase of the project. Naturally, this became a political hot potato. The Metrolinx procurement model is to use a public-private partnership (P3) with a consortium to design, build, finance, operate and maintain (DBFOM) the system over thirty years. In cities that already have experience operating rapid transit, like Toronto, Metrolinx will also allow a design, build, finance, maintain (DBFM) contract, with operation being undertaken by the municipal transit service.

In Hamilton, Amalgamated Transit Union (ATU) Local 107, which represents HSR operations employees, launched a "Keep Transit Public" campaign after the EPR addendum vote, calling for operation and maintenance of the Hamilton LRT line to be performed by HSR employees, not private employees of the consortium that builds the system. ATU 107 also asserted that its collective agreement with the city guaranteed the union successor rights for any fixed-route transit service in Hamilton. Supporting this claim, then Ward 3 councillor Green brought a motion to the August 9, 2017, General Issues Committee calling on council to ask Metrolinx to have HSR operate the LRT line, and councillors approved the motion. It's worth noting that most of the votes in favour of the motion were from anti-LRT councillors, who recognized the value of delay in undermining the project.

The request came as a surprise to Metrolinx, which had been operating all along on the understanding that the system would follow the DBFOM model, and it took over three months for them to respond. Metrolinx CEO Phil Verster sent the city a letter at the end of November stipulating that if Hamilton decided to assume operations, it would also be responsible for all the associated costs and risks of that operation: overseeing operations through a control centre; hiring, training, certifying and supervising all staff; operating the safety and security systems; handling all customer service; and assuming liability risk for all commercial claims related to LRT operations. It stated: "The City will also be responsible for and carry the complete and full risk for ensuring that HSR is capable of fulfilling the above accountabilities and has comprehensive plans to achieve that state of readiness."

City councillors formally received the response a month later at a special meeting on December 20, 2017, and decided not to take over operations after all, but to demand that Metrolinx support the unionization of LRT workers by ATU Local 107. However, that decision was not up to Metrolinx to make, as any question about which union should represent the workers would have to be addressed by the Ontario Labour Relations Board.

Thanks in part to this delay, it became clear that there was no way for the project tendering to be completed before the 2018 provincial election. Back in February 2017, Metrolinx had issued a request for qualifications (RFQ), which is an invitation to consortia to demonstrate that they are qualified to build and operate a project of the scope and complexity of Hamilton's LRT line. After reviewing all the RFQ submissions and selecting a shortlist of qualified bidders, the next step was to issue a request for proposals (RFP) to the shortlisted bidders. But that process was put on hold during the almost five months in which the question of who would operate the system was unresolved. If council had decided on a DBFM model, the RFQ would likely have to be reissued as the qualifications and contract terms would change. As a result, LRT was once again destined to become an electoral football.

In March 2018, Ontario PC leader Doug Ford announced soon after he won the party leadership that he supported Hamilton's LRT plan, writing, "I support building the Hamilton LRT because the people [of] this great city deserve a working transit system. This is an investment that will create jobs, countless new jobs and stimulate economic development" in an emailed statement to media. But after Councillor Skelly, at this point the PC candidate for Flamborough-Glanbrook, said she wanted to talk to Ford about the plan, Ford changed tack and announced that Hamilton would be allowed to spend the money on some other transit project if we decided to reject LRT. "Who is Doug Ford to tell the people of Hamilton? It is up to the people of Hamilton to decide." (Further clouding the issue, NDP leader – and Hamilton Centre MPP – Andrea Horwath alarmed LRT supporters when she told the *Hamilton Spectator* editorial board that she would also accept the wishes of council if they decided to cancel the project.)

After Ford's PC Party won a majority in June 2018, the new government suspended the RFP process again and halted the Metrolinx work that was under way, including buying properties that would be needed to build the system. This all but guaranteed that LRT would dominate yet another municipal election. The players quickly took shape: incumbent Mayor Eisenberger ran on a pro-LRT platform, while a well-funded challenge came in the form of Vito Sgro, a long-time Liberal insider and ally of Bratina who positioned his entire campaign around opposition to LRT. His tag line was literally "Stop the Train." This galvanized the anti-LRT group, who fielded candidates in most of the municipal wards and threw their support behind Sgro and his slick marketing campaign of radio spots, social media ads, telephone push-polls and even an airplane banner. The LRT opponents insisted that the municipal election was a referendum on LRT and that the people would finally be heard.

So it came as a tremendous relief to LRT supporters when Eisenberger won a decisive majority on October 22, securing strong support across the entire city, including the mountain and suburbs. Ford responded by affirming that Eisenberger's victory was a clear democratic endorsement of the project. At a media appearance in Grimsby in the end of November, Ford said, "When people democratically elect someone, if he wants an LRT, he's gonna get an LRT. I know that it's a tough issue in Hamilton. That city's almost split if they want an LRT or not. But I go back to democracy. If someone gets elected, let 'em govern."

In March 2019, the province finally lifted the freeze on Metrolinx property acquisition for the line and the RFP was resumed. Bids from the three shortlisted consortia were expected in March 2020, after which Metrolinx would select a winning bid at that time. After that, Hamilton Council would have to cast one more crucial vote, this time for the master agreement with Metrolinx that would finally spell out the details of how LRT costs and revenues would be shared between the city and Metrolinx.

So it came as a shock to everyone when Ontario Transportation Minister Caroline Mulroney came to Hamilton on December 16, 2019, to announce out of the blue that Hamilton LRT was cancelled. Learning of the planned announcement, a large group of residents, most of them LRT supporters, demanded entrance to the press conference. Instead of facing the crowd, Mulroney cancelled the event and called the police to escort her out the building, leaving Mayor Eisenberger to deliver the bad news on her behalf.

Mulroney issued a written statement claiming that an independent third-party analysis conducted for the Transportation Ministry found that the capital cost for Hamilton LRT had jumped from $1 billion to $5.6 billion, rendering it unaffordable. The cost escalation immediately began to unravel. First, on questioning from reporters, Mulroney acknowledged that the number was combining the upfront capital cost with thirty years of operating, maintenance, life cycle and financing costs. Two days later, Eisenberger released a six-page summary Mulroney had provided from the independent analysis. The analysis suggested on page one that the total was $5.5 billion, but all of the detailed numbers on pages 2–6 itemizing the thirty-year costs only added up to $3.65 billion. Even if you included an estimated $950 million in municipal operating costs over thirty years – an implausibly high estimate – the numbers just didn't add up.

An early and vociferous critic was Joe Mancinelli, President of Labourers' International Union of North America (LiUNA), which would have represented the workers building the LRT system. Mancinelli decried the decision and directed LiUNA's property investment division to undertake its own independent cost analysis to challenge the province's numbers. In the face of growing incredulity over her numbers, Mulroney refused to share the full analysis or even the name of the consultancy that prepared it, citing "proprietary and commercial information." However, an internal Metrolinx report leaked to local media and published on January 6 showed that the Ontario Treasury Board had already budgeted $3.66 billion in total thirty-year costs for Hamilton LRT and that the project was only $87 million over budget, attributed to higher-than-expected "professional services."

So the project was cancelled just three months before the consortia participating in the RFP process were supposed to deliver their final bids, and both Metrolinx and the independent analysis found that the total thirty-year costs for the project were only very slightly above the Treasury Board–approved budget. Metrolinx already had a process for this situation: if the final bids came in over budget, the agency would look for ways to trim back the project until it fit the budget. For example, when the final bids for the Hurontario LRT in Mississauga and Brampton came in slightly over the Treasury Board–approved budget, the province decided to trim out a planned loop around Mississauga City Centre, remove a couple of stops and defer a pedestrian overpass. The thirty-year total that was finally approved for that project – $4.6 billion for an eighteen kilometre line – was proportionately identical to the $3.7 billion cost for Hamilton's fourteen kilometre line.

Hamilton was treated differently. The bidders were never given the chance to present their final numbers and Metrolinx was never given a chance to trim the project in order to bring it within budget. Further, in response to a question from Hamilton Centre MP Matthew Green, the federal government said they would be willing to partner on covering the cost for Hamilton LRT – they just needed the province to ask.

As the cost overrun story fell apart under scrutiny, Hamilton Light Rail launched a campaign calling on Premier Ford to "Fix Mulroney's Mistake and Get LRT Back on Track." Over a thousand people participated in the call to action, writing personal statements of support for LRT that were sent to the province. In response, the province announced a "Hamilton Transportation Task Force" composed of Tony Valeri (chair), a vice president at Dofasco and a former federal Transport Minister; Richard Brennan, a retired Queen's Park reporter; Anthony Primerano, a government relations director with LiUNA; Dr. Saiedeh Razavi, director of MITL (which had conducted research supporting the LRT project) and Janette Smith, city manager for the City of Hamilton. The task force was given a mandate to make recommendations to the province on how best to spend the $1 billion capital budget for transportation in Hamilton. Notably, the list of projects under consideration was expanded to include the LRT project itself. This seemed calculated to give the province a face-saving way to put the project – or some version of it – back on the table. In its report, the task force punted the decision back to Queen's Park, recommending "intra-city higher-order transit" that could be either B-Line LRT or B- and A-Line BRT.

In one sense, the most remarkable thing about the Hamilton LRT project is the fact that it has been sustained in any capacity through more than a decade of political turmoil, given the ambivalence of both municipal and provincial leaders – and the tendency of each to be further unnerved by the ambivalence of the other. In another sense, it is remarkable that such an exciting civic investment with such a huge overall benefit and such a broad base of support should be in turmoil in the first place. At many times, it has occurred to me that skittish politicians are not so much afraid of the project failing as they are of the project succeeding and transforming the city in ways none of us can really predict.

From Edge to Centre and Back

Rob Fiedler

There is a vast and growing body of academic and popular writing on suburbs. And that makes sense. All around us now are suburbs and, more importantly, built environments that many urbanists, particularly architects and planners, regard as suburban. That is as true in Hamilton as other places.

The chapter that follows provides a selective exploration of "suburbanisms" and "suburbanization" in Hamilton, which requires some preliminary explanation.

To keep things simple let's start with two concepts found in *Building Suburbia: Green Fields and Urban Growth, 1820–2000*, by American urban historian and architect Dolores Hayden. First, she talks about "the triple dream" of "house plus land plus community" that "encompasses both the public and private pleasures of peaceful, small-scale residential neighbourhoods." Second, she organizes the output of almost two centuries of suburbanization into "historic patterns in the landscape," which gives suburbs as places a historicity linked to their form and dominant period of development.[1]

I want to use these two concepts as analytical lenses to better understand the politics and cultural underpinnings that produce and sustain a kind of suburbanized urbanism in Hamilton. The implications of the triple dream have been explored in detail elsewhere, most notably by sociologist Nathanael Lauster in *The Death and Life of the Single-Family House: Lessons from Vancouver on Building a Livable City*. He notes that in North America there is a deep cultural and psychological attachment to the single-family house as the ideal habitat, particularly for raising children. In that respect, the triple dream is deeply woven into the fabric of urban Hamilton as much as suburban Hamilton.

I must confess that I draw upon the concept of suburbs as historic patterns in the landscape only to complement exploration of the triple dream: to show how the latter influences the former and informs contemporary planning and politics in Hamilton.

The point might be summarized thus: there are different ways to conceptualize or identify what is city and what is suburb (or urban and suburban) and the demarcation can be different depending on who is doing it and from what perspective. A person living south of the Linc (Lincoln Alexander Parkway) might see parts of Hamilton Mountain closer to the brow, particularly north of Fennell Avenue, as an in-between space that is more urban than where they live. Similarly, when I travel east from where I live in the lower city along Barton Street what I see after Kenilworth Avenue gradually becomes less and less urban until it becomes what I recognize as more fully suburban beyond the Red Hill Valley Parkway. But the triple dream, regardless of the specific housing forms and the dominant period when built landscapes were constructed, is fairly constant.

The preceding is not to simply write important differences out of the story. One only needs to observe budget deliberations or debates at city council in recent years over ward boundaries, bike lanes, bus-only lanes and LRT to see urban-suburban fault lines writ large. The intent is to soften the rigidness of the binary opposition that is often constructed and explore how the triple dream is pervasive on both sides of the urban-suburban divide and influences the possibilities for change to increase social justice, improve quality of life, reduce environmental degradation and address climate change.

▬

Several years ago when I served as a parent representative on a pupil accommodation review committee for the western part of the lower city, a senior official from the City of Hamilton was asked to attend one of our meetings to provide an overview of development plans for downtown and the West Harbour area. The purpose was to inform us of what was being planned for the area in terms of growth so we might better understand the implications for future enrolment at local schools. In response to a question from a member of the committee seeking to know how many families with children might be expected to live in developments planned on city-owned lands in the West Harbour area, we were told that families tend to go to areas where new low-rise housing was being built along the outer edges of the city – places like Upper Stoney Creek, Binbrook, Ancaster Meadowlands and Waterdown. The implication was obvious. Family housing is low-rise housing: detached, semi-detached or townhouse. At the time, redevelopment in areas designated for intensification in the West Harbour area was mainly envisioned as mid-rise in scale and apartment buildings in form. Downtown, not unsurprisingly, was being planned for considerable high-rise redevelopment.

The problem that posed for schools in residential neighbourhoods around the downtown core from Wentworth to the 403 east–west and the bay to the escarpment north–south can be grasped intuitively. Despite the promise of considerable intensification in the future, schools in the area north of downtown were underutilized and future enrolment growth was far from certain because there was little expectation that families with children would move into the sort of higher density housing being planned. There isn't the space here to tease out all the details of the situation on the ground, so I'll simply flag that falling enrolment coincided with the in-migration of higher-income, middle-class professionals into ground-oriented housing (detached houses, semis and row housing) combined with the out-migration of lower-income and working-class households from all forms of housing. But a focus on displacement, particularly of tenant families with school-age children, elides a long-term trend in so-called stable neighbourhoods of falling population densities. Average household sizes have been falling for decades in many urban and suburban residential areas, particularly the latter as they mature.

The problem of shifting geographic patterns of enrolment within cities is not new. Providing new schools in areas where rapid residential growth is occurring, while dealing with underutilization of existing schools in mature residential areas, has been grappled with by planners and school administrators for decades. This might seem like a straightforward planning problem. But planners cannot mandate the choices that individuals or households make. They shape outcomes to the extent that they influence permitted land uses and try to ensure proper coordination of those uses with investments in infrastructure and public services. Cultural norms and preferences, as well as the financialization of housing, however, play a significant role in blunting the intentions of planners and their visions.

At present a housing affordability crisis in major Canadian cities like Vancouver and Toronto, and increasingly mid-sized cities like Hamilton, is encouraging a rethink of planning doctrine, particularly with regard to "stable neighbourhoods." At issue is whether rigid protection of the physical character of mostly low-rise residential districts is not only manifestly unjust, but ultimately locks cities into a tall and small dichotomy that limits the full range of housing alternatives that might emerge between these extremes – housing options sometimes referred to as the missing middle and assumed to be a gentler way to add housing and density to existing neighbourhoods. However, attempts to adopt and apply more flexible rules to allow missing middle-housing forms run up against the limits of applying land-use planning tools to achieve social ends.

For example, limiting the scale of intensification permitted to ensure an area's social character is reasonably maintained often results in neighbourhoods becoming more exclusive and achieving higher socio-economic status (social upgrading and/or gentrification), especially in situations where housing costs are rapidly escalating faster than average wages. The practical result is to limit housing diversity and the ability of households to "downsize" their housing consumption to better match what they can afford. There are, of course, practical limits to how far households can downsize their housing consumption. And households with limited means tend to need to trade off both housing quality and quantity to access housing they can afford. Because intensification adds new supply that is generally more expensive than existing housing, by itself it cannot be relied upon to solve an affordability crisis. Indeed, in the short run, market-driven intensification tends to accelerate displacement.

You wouldn't be wrong to ask what all this has to do with the suburbs. The answer involves thinking in terms of suburbanisms. Part of what is driving change in many lower-city neighbourhoods is gentrification in its many guises. But an important strand of that process is driven by the housing choices of middle-income families looking for places to live where they can raise children – the pull of the triple dream of house plus land plus community is considerable. Living in an inner-city neighbourhood is different from life on the suburban edge in important respects, but where low-rise housing is plentiful the opportunity for achieving the triple dream without sprawl is enticing for a growing number of people. From this perspective, there are competing forms of urban regeneration or revitalization under way, though they are seldom acknowledged as such. One consequence is a resurgent politic of protecting neighbourhoods in the lower city as "peaceful, small-scale" living environments.

≡

Provincial plans and planning policy, as well as the Urban Hamilton Official Plan (UHOP), envision building complete communities that offer a range of housing options and a mix of uses to accommodate diverse needs and reduce the requirement for commuting long distances to reach work and routine activities. There is also a stated desire to curtail further outward urban expansion to protect farmland and natural heritage features and reduce the need for costly infrastructure extensions. This is to be achieved by redirecting growth to areas where capacity exists and can accommodate it. For new development on the edge of the city, that is supposed to mean more compact built form, increased densities and a finer mix of compatible uses than was typical of suburban development during the second half of the last century. In existing urban areas, the expectation is that densities in terms of people and jobs will rise via reurbanization (i.e., infilling and redevelopment), particularly in areas designated for growth. For both the goal is creating built environments that are more cost effective to service, as well as more walkable and transit supportive.

If this isn't already familiar, it probably should be. Smart Growth intensification and certain aspects of New Urbanism are now widely accepted by planners, and rhetoric (acknowledged or otherwise) drawn from them is increasingly relied upon to support development approvals. It is hard to argue that we shouldn't seek to intensify within existing built-up areas of our city for the reasons cited or to significantly increase densities where greenfield development is permitted. But I often feel that a comfortable consensus has emerged within planning circles and urbanistic discourse: increased density is seen as both necessary and inherently good. That increasing permitted densities makes land more valuable – all things being equal – is generally left unsaid. Evaluation of the results of contemporary planning is scant because there is a reluctance to assess the efficacy of planning concepts and ideas given they are often only partially implemented and even then only after a long period in which the form they take is contested and negotiated.

Still, the push for denser, more compact development has been asserted for more than a decade now and in Hamilton considerable areas of new suburban housing have been added to the edges of the city in places such as Ancaster, Binbrook, Upper Stoney Creek, Waterdown and areas south of the Linc, particularly along Rymal Road and Twenty Road.

So, how does the housing in the edges of the city stack up? Well, perhaps the best description of what is being created is "compact sprawl." Net densities might be somewhat higher than those of areas built during the postwar years through to the first decade of this century, but in other regards the differences are superficial. Different housing types are fairly segregated from each other and land uses are not finely mixed. If we look at Summit Park along Rymal Road East near the current terminus of the upper Red Hill Valley Parkway as an example, Bishop Ryan Catholic Secondary School is on one end, a SmartCentres power retail node anchored by a Walmart is found on the other, while in between there is housing, a couple of parks, and public and Catholic elementary schools.

Perhaps more telling, the street network takes us back to the early 1950s and the fragmented parallel pattern used at that time to discourage through traffic. While there are no winding collectors and for the most part no cul-de-sacs – hallmarks of the Don Mills model applied generically across Canadian cities until recently – Summit Park isn't a return to the transit-oriented layout of suburban areas built during the streetcar era, and it can't incorporate more than superficially New Urbanism. As former City of Vancouver chief planner and leading urbanist Brent Toderian has said, it is hard to avoid producing sprawl on a project-by-project basis if new projects are plugged into the "big infrastructure" that is really the "suburban genetic code."

So, it is fair to say that Summit Park is a somewhat denser, less spacious-feeling version of the planned suburban community that prevailed across Canada after Don Mills. That hardly seems like a victory for critics of sprawl. And doesn't represent even a modest departure from the car-and-dream-house combination that underpinned postwar suburbanization as a mass phenomenon. Residents appear to get more house on less yard and the car – which is still needed to make it work – reigns supreme in the overall scheme of things. Add in Hamilton's area rating of public transit service and you don't have a recipe for building new areas that function much differently from earlier iterations of auto-dependent suburbanization regardless of their density and possibly more compact forms. Essentially, the genetic code is still intact and producing more of the same, just denser. It should surprise no one that some of the worst traffic congestion in Hamilton is found in newer suburban areas and that it is accompanied by a popular cry for more and larger roads, as well as opposition to changes elsewhere in the city to reduce the dominance of automobility there.

≡

Strange though it might seem to some readers, the North End where I live a short walk from downtown Hamilton can feel suburban to me. The proximity to heavy industry along the eastern waterfront, a storied urban past and a hodgepodge of housing – diverse in terms of time period, condition and style/type – as well as social mix and location to the north of downtown read as inner city. But the strip mall at James and Burlington, the quiet residential streets, long lots, open space and notable presence of housing from the 1960s onward complicate that impression. And the plain truth is that house-dwelling residents in the North End, a majority in the neighbourhood, enjoy a version of the triple dream that differs only by degree from that of their suburban counterparts in Hamilton. This is not to elide important differences, but to say that plenty of suburbanism exists in the North End for those who care to look for and acknowledge it – complemented in an ironic twist by the legacy of postwar urban renewal.[2]

That last bit requires a selective rereading of urban renewal to emphasize attempts to graft aspects of the neighbourhood unit, an early twentieth-century town-planning concept, onto the North End, rather than an overweening focus on the modernist impulse towards destructive large-scale replanning and demolition of the Victorian city and key pieces of its urban fabric during the middle of the last century.

In 1958, Hamilton's first large-scale urban renewal study ranked the North End fourth in priority among the nine areas being considered. The Strathcona and Central neighbourhoods to the immediate west and northwest of the downtown core ranked just ahead of the North End. As a group, the three neighbourhoods were reported to be losing population and possess high rates of juvenile delinquency and relief cases. All three lay in the path of a proposed highway to connect the industrial eastern waterfront to another planned highway, the Chedoke Expressway (Highway 403).

With regard to the North End, scholar Margaret Rockwell tells us in her M.A. thesis, "Modernist Destruction for the Ambitious City": "[The urban renewal enthusiasts] were going to open it up, remove the blighting influences and make it a better place to live."

Of particular interest was the levelling of a four-block area from Simcoe to Wood between Hughson and John Streets that was to extend eastward between Macaulay and Picton across John and Catharine Streets to St. Lawrence the Martyr Catholic church, and the demolition of all but two houses on the south side of Strachan for a perimeter highway that was planned but never built. Urban renewal was about more than this in the North End. But these two components reveal how the renewal scheme sought to superimpose key features of suburban community planning onto the existing layout and built fabric of an inner-city neighbourhood.

Near the end of *A Mountain and a City: The Story of Hamilton,* author Marjorie Campbell notes that closing off Burlington Street at Wellington to isolate the entire area from through traffic was key to the city's urban renewal scheme for the North End. In addition to diverting traffic around the area with a perimeter highway, there were to be changes to the street grid: "Within the redeveloped area traffic movement will be further reduced by closing certain streets, by removing two bridges over the C.N.R. tracks on north-south thor-. oughfares, and by converting many streets into courts and dead-ends. As finally developed, only vehicles bound for a definite area will travel into it."[3]

Without wishing to downplay the disastrous consequences of North End urban renewal for many who found themselves in houses targeted for demolition, we in the present should not assume that a powerful figure such as Kenneth Soble was simply being disingenuous or callous when he lamented that residents opposed to the North End Urban Renewal Scheme couldn't seem to understand that it was "an attempt to preserve a neighbourhood, rather than flatten it."[4]

Looking back we can see concepts drawn from Clarence Perry's "neighbourhood unit" at work in the initial North End Urban Renewal Scheme. Just as planner-architects now talk about the need to retrofit suburban spaces to make them more urban (compact, mixed-use, walkable and transit-oriented), at that time dominant planning ideas encouraged policy-makers to decongest cities and renew older urban neighbourhoods, purported to be blighted or at risk of becoming blighted, by making them more suburban (spacious, functionally segregated and protected from through traffic).

To see this in practice you can use Google Maps to look at the layout of neighbourhoods or communities created by planners and home builders in the superblocks defined by major arterial roads on the Mountain, especially south of Mohawk Road. In most cases you will see green space near the centre of each superblock, with many having institutional uses such as schools, ice rinks, pools and community centres. The other dominant feature is the street pattern. Roads in modern suburban areas are organized according to a hierarchy of intended use, with most designed to be used for local access only. A few roads wind through large sections of a superblock – these are collector roads designed to carry traffic from local streets out to a major or minor arterial road.

Generally speaking, retail and commercial land uses are placed on the outside of the superblock along a major arterial road and especially at intersections. Higher density housing forms are typically found along an arterial road, between land uses that produce noise, traffic and (visual or air) pollution and the lower density forms of housing, including single detached or semi-detached homes, in the area.

To the unfamiliar it can be hard to navigate through the interior of such places. That's intentional. Non-residents aren't supposed to find it easy to drive through these neighbourhoods or communities. The whole setup is predicated ironically on easy, convenient access by car. The corollary is a need to manage "traffic" by moving it through areas, while keeping it off local streets. The result, major arterial roads and highways, is what we now recognize as the big infrastructure, suburban genetic code. The little infrastructure, suburban genetic code – if we might call it that – is the abundant surface space dedicated to parking for vehicles when they are not being driven.

≡

The need to accommodate the car and mitigate its impact on quality of life produces a fundamental contradiction in what becomes effectively a suburbanized city. And you can see it as clearly "downtown" and across the neighbourhoods of Wards 1–3 in the lower city as on the

Mountain and the pre-amalgamation suburbs, towns and rural lands around Hamilton.

In *Cities in the Suburbs*, Humphrey Carver, a landscape architect and influential civil servant at Canada Mortgage and Housing Corporation (CMHC), tried to reconcile the forces of automobility and an increasingly home-centred way of life with the need for community to stretch beyond the scale envisioned by the neighbourhood unit. His aim was to give the automotive city a system for place-making, something the streetcar city seemed to do effortlessly. The town centre, Carver's proposed solution, stripped to its bare essentials and absent a real balance between private commerce and civic functions became the shopping mall.

Around the same time, in *The Death and Life of Great American Cities*, Jane Jacobs argued the "Great Blight of Dullness is allied with the blight of traffic congestion." As she put it, generating diversity and lively streets is impossible "if accommodations for huge numbers of cars get first consideration, and other city uses get the leftovers. A strategy of erosion by automobiles is thus not only destructive to such city intensity as already exists; it also conflicts with nurturing new or additional intensity of use where that is needed."[5]

The rise of automobility started in earnest in the 1920s, but it didn't become a serious problem until a critical mass of people began driving routinely and it wasn't until after the Second World War that designing built environments and organizing space around the needs of the car became an overriding practical concern for planners and city builders. At that point, a gendered middle-class cultural ideal – that the public life of work, commerce and culture in the city should be kept separate from the private or domestic sphere of the home – met with an overweening modernist emphasis on speed and efficiency.

Planner-architect Ken Greenberg calls this a "toxic convergence" in his book *Walking Home: The Life and Lessons of a City Builder* and speaks to how "progress" began to be contested in the late 1960s. He gets to the heart of the problem: full embrace of the car – the reorganizing of more and more space to better suit its needs or mitigate its excesses – destroys those aspects of city life that many people cherish. Nowhere is that more evident than with the urban street, which in the right circumstances can function as a kind of public living room.

Few people enjoy having a conversation over the roar of five or six lanes of fast-moving traffic. So, it shouldn't surprise us that beyond moving around people in cars as quickly and efficiently as possible, turning our streets into urban highways doesn't make them good for much else. What Liberal MP and former Hamilton mayor Bob Bratina once called the twenty-minute city – and Hamilton's reputed competitive advantage – is actually the annihilation of space by time, and it has what the late feminist geographer Doreen Massey called "power-geometries" to it. The benefits of automobility go to those individuals able to partake in it and escape its consequences. While the costs are borne collectively, the benefits are meted out unequally in both social and geographic terms.

≡

The suburbanized city wasn't built by the car alone, however. The car fits into a sequence of technological advances in transportation that have facilitated suburbanization and metropolitan or regional forms of growth and development. Kenneth Jackson's now classic historical survey of American suburbanization, *Crabgrass Frontier: The Suburbanization of the United States,* takes readers back to the first ferry to cross the East River from Manhattan to Brooklyn in the 1800s, then discusses the advent of omnibuses, commuter railroads, street railways and finally the car. Each remade the geography of cities and suburbs, stretching metropolitan growth outwards.

Industrial decentralization and changing employment geographies also played a role. In particular, as University of Toronto historical geographer Robert Lewis demonstrates in *Manufacturing Montreal:*

The Making of an Industrial Landscape, 1850 to 1930 and *Chicago Made: Factory Networks in the Industrial Metropolis*, from the mid-nineteenth century into the early twentieth century industrial suburbs and peripheral investments in infrastructure for new industries were integral to shaping the diverse patchwork of built landscapes and social geographies we now associate with the older parts of cities.

In Hamilton, there is a general pattern of decentralization: with the exception of Dundas (once a separate town), older nineteenth-century industry was mostly located north of downtown in a corridor between Bay and Wentworth Streets that ran down to the waterfront, while during the first half of the twentieth century newer industries, particularly heavy industry, grew along the entire length of Hamilton Harbour north of Barton Street from Wellington Street eastward. Other pockets of industry formed along rail lines, particularly next to junctions and spurs connecting the main lines of Canadian Pacific Railway to Canadian National Railway. In recent decades, as local goods movement has shifted increasingly from railcar to transport truck, new industrial areas have developed further outward on the south Mountain beyond the Lincoln Alexander Parkway and in Stoney Creek, Glanbrook, Ancaster and Flamborough. And the city, to the dismay of critics who see it as sprawl inducing, has big plans and high hopes for industrial development in the area surrounding the John C. Munro Hamilton International Airport, otherwise known as the Airport Employment Growth District.

Certain social patterns in Hamilton fuse together industrial geographies and the development of the pre-automotive city's transit system. Before 1900 the basic divide was the clustering of middle- and upper-class residences to the south and southwest of downtown and the mingling of working-class housing with factories across the city's North End. In the last decade of the nineteenth century the electric street railway made the separation of home and work, as well as travel to shopping, recreation and leisure activities, possible for an increasing cross-section of people. This accelerated Hamilton's lateral spread, especially eastward, in the lower city, while the addition of incline railways at James and Wentworth Streets encouraged the beginnings of suburbanization on the Mountain.

Commentary in Harold A. Wood's essay "Emergence of the Modern City: Hamilton 1891–1950," which appeared in *Steel City: Hamilton and Region*, tells us that a 1945 map of housing conditions produced by planning consultants deemed only one-sixth of Hamilton's population to be living in "sound" housing – much of it either in the "traditional" higher-end residential areas at the base of the escarpment running west of James Street or in newly built areas on the western and eastern ends of the city, in Westdale and around Gage Park respectively.

The solid two-and-half-storey houses found south of King Street from Wentworth Street to Gage Park and in the Delta neighbourhood south of Main Street on the other side of the park stand out as examples of middle-class suburban residential districts built out during the first several decades of the twentieth century – with a few boulevards such as Proctor, St. Clair and Barnesdale standing out as even higher-end. Crown Point, particularly the area south of Barton Street between Ottawa and Kenilworth, represents the working-class equivalent, mimicking some of the features of its southern neighbours such as the green central boulevard at Park Row off Cannon Street, but generally being comprised of smaller, more modest houses – the triple dream scaled down to what its working-class inhabitants could afford.

The same basic processes and impulses that built these parts of Hamilton, which are now considered urban, continue to shape the evolving city and region. Summit Park and new housing subdivisions in Binbrook and Waterdown are one side of the equation, while newer industrial facilities like Canada Bread and Maple Leaf Foods that stand alone at a distance from the urbanized area on the south Mountain or their equivalents around Clappison's Corners at Highway 6 and Dundas Street East or out in the Ancaster Business Park near where Garner Road and Wilson Street meet represent the other.

≡

The takeaway is that automobility is not in retreat, especially on the city's edge. For those that can afford it, moving around these disparate places continues to be most conveniently achieved by car. While much is made about the supposed banality and sterility of post-1945 built environments, if we think beyond cars and houses what is really being critiqued is an entire way of life, particularly debt-fuelled consumerism, corporatism and ecological destructiveness. For some this touches on the "suburban question," a debate that is framed not only around whether postwar suburban forms and ways of life are environmentally and socially sustainable, but also whether they represent a parasitic form of growth, the result of hidden subsidies, or continue to grow because they offer what people are looking for.

I don't wish to fall into a kind of ritualized criticism of "the suburbs" in which the car, the house and the shopping mall/supermarket become a kind of unholy trinity, but there are certain realities that apply. The urban landscape tends to be rewritten regularly. Older, urban areas have been made and remade over the years and reflect the dominant city-building ideas and practices of different times. The areas we typically consider suburbs are newer and have less layering present. In some cases, they are still under construction.

On my block in the North End the houses across the street from me are typical bungalows like you'd find across parts of the Mountain. They were built in the 1960s to replace a Methodist church that was destroyed by fire. A walk around the neighbourhood would reveal many other houses built in styles prevalent from the 1960s forward. The same can be said about the retail plaza at James and Burlington. It is a dead ringer for a suburban strip mall just about anywhere in Canada. Ditto the Food Basics supermarket on Barton Street just across the tracks in the Beasley neighbourhood.

My point is that what we might productively draw from the urban past is that creative destruction of existing urban or suburban fabric is influenced by whether it is more attractive (and possible) to tear down and rebuild, retrofit or just move outward and build on so-called greenfield lands. Planners, architects and scholars interested in suburbs have been discussing and debating the future of older postwar, inner suburban areas for a while. In the last couple decades this has turned into a discussion about suburban decline that considers how suburbs might be retrofitted, which usually means redevelopment that will make them denser, as well as more compact and transit-oriented. I only see fleeting evidence of that in Hamilton now, but in time spaces like Upper James and Lime Ridge Mall could be dramatically remade along more urban lines, especially if the BLAST transit network becomes more than just a plan. Before that occurs, we might look back at urban renewal to learn some lessons. Urban renewal was largely a response to investment flowing outward into new areas and a belief that the older parts of cities were obsolete. Experts and those in positions of power and authority convinced themselves and others that serious changes were necessary to save downtown and the inner city. Some of those plans and decisions continue to cast a long shadow over Hamilton. Indeed, intensification downtown and in the inner city might be more appropriately called re-urbanization, and, while history doesn't repeat itself, it does tend to echo.

≣

Bill Freeman and Marsha Hewitt's book *Their Town: The Mafia, the Media and the Party Machine* provides an overview and political analysis of what happened in Hamilton as the many twists and turns of the Civic Square/downtown redevelopment debacle unfolded and the questionable practices and corruption on the waterfront involving the Hamilton Harbour Commission were uncovered.

They also mention opposition by civic and community groups, but their achievements are portrayed as modest. The Lax brothers' plans for the water lots that are now Bayfront Park were halted; the Durand

Neighbourhood Association fought successfully for zoning changes to halt further high-rise redevelopment to the south and west of city hall and obtained a small park; and a citizens group called Save Our Square (SOS), though not successful in its fight against the First Wentworth plan for Civic Square, brought objections to the project into full public view for a time. Discussion of these modest gains, however, are included in a section entitled "The Failure of Opposition."

To that end, in the book's introduction the authors state that "for us, two symbolic events will mark the beginning of a new and revitalized Hamilton": the emergence of a vigorous opposition group that effectively criticizes the "ideology of business" and a reclaiming of the bay by the people for general environmental restoration, as well as for their recreational use and enjoyment.[6] That would seem to indicate that a 1970s urban reform council, such as those that developed in Toronto and Vancouver at that time, didn't materialize in Hamilton. The present is not the past, but it does feel like the current moment, bound up as it is in big schemes to revitalize spaces that were urban renewed and the promise of transformational changes via big transportation projects, carries with it echoes of the past.

Writing about the Bronx that disappeared to make way for Robert Moses's Cross-Bronx Expressway in the 1950s, Marshall Berman notes in *All That Is Solid Melts into Air: The Experience of Modernity* that Robert Caro's devastatingly critical account in *The Power Broker*, in its emphasis on the destruction wrought by Moses's unsparing ambition and deceitfulness, leaves out an important element: "The Bronx of my youth was possessed, inspired, by the great modern dream of mobility. To live well meant to move up socially, and this in turn meant to move out physically; to live one's life close to home was not to be alive at all."[7] Just as his parents who had "moved up and out from the Lower East Side" believed this, he argues, so did he and his friends. And so, for him what happened to the southern Bronx in the 1960s and '70s cannot be simply papered over with a nostalgic or reductionist rewriting of history. There is a push and pull to local and metropolitan-scale changes for the better or worse.

In Hamilton, people move up to the Mountain or out to Stoney Creek for a complex set of reasons, including until very recently to "move up and out" of the lower city. But there is also nostalgia for what was left behind or how it used to be. Most people also share a common desire to see progress, even though there is usually little agreement on what that means or what it would constitute. This unresolvable tension, sometimes framed as people like the idea of progress but resist change, is often overlooked. But it can be seen in the final chapters of *A Mountain and a City* where a description of Hamilton's new city hall with its gleaming mass of marble, steel and glass, along with its generally modern feel, is contrasted with the taking down of old city hall stone by stone and brick by brick. The demolition could be seen from the new city hall's eighth-floor cafeteria, where it was said to be "frequently attended by the sorrow felt in loss of a close friend."[8] Readers are, of course, given a gentle reminder of the failings of old city hall too.

There is also a tendency to gloss over what is being lost in the name of progress. We can see that in *Pardon My Lunch Bucket*, which was published to celebrate Hamilton's 125th anniversary in 1971. When it turns its attention toward the redevelopment of central Hamilton, then under way, the existing built fabric seems less a friend and more like old carpet and worn furnishings: "With a delicate scalpel, contractors are cutting away the rot of the Victorian age and replacing it with ... the largest single urban renewal project ever undertaken in Canada."[9]

The idea that things are simply old and tired before they morph into being historic and worthy of consideration for preservation obscures that change has always been greeted with mixed feelings because progress comes at a price. It is just that some are more convinced than others that changes are needed and will be worth the cost, while still others stand to benefit directly from what is planned. But the real issue, and the "failure" described in *Their Town*, was not so much that citizens weren't able to influence certain decisions at city hall or root out corruption but that no opposition group emerged or was strong enough to displace the basic ideology and political culture, and little seemed to change, fundamentally, heading into the 1980s with respect to how decision-making power was distributed and exercised in Hamilton. I will leave it to readers to decide for themselves whether the situation has profoundly changed – as opposed to simply taking on new guises – in the four decades that have passed since *Their Town* was published.

≡

You might be asking what does all this have to do with suburbanism?

Well, I think we need to be more attentive to the ways that spaces in Hamilton are being reproduced or remade. Possible futures are not clear-cut or known. They are negotiated. Often multiple urbanisms and suburbanisms rub against each other and contest plans, schemes and infrastructures poised to alter the everyday fabric of life in the city. Varying configurations of urbanism-suburbanism are produced and flow in and out of different spaces, generating new ways of living, even as the old ones remain.

There are recognizable differences and divisions between the city and the suburbs in Hamilton, however they are defined. The 2017 Ontario Municipal Board (OMB) hearings on Hamilton's ward boundaries made some of those plain. The overrepresentation of the communities of Dundas, Flamborough and Ancaster on Hamilton City Council was defended by the city on the grounds that these communities – and especially the rural areas around the city – form a community of interest that needs effective representation on city council. It was an argument that shielded the city's legal counsel from having to directly address a more troubling issue: a thinly veiled resistance from several councillors to any new ward plan that would alter the balance of power between the old City of Hamilton and the (former) suburban and rural municipalities surrounding it.

Since amalgamation in 2001, there has been considerable growth south of the Lincoln Alexander Parkway, which has caused the Mountain portion of the old City of Hamilton to be significantly underrepresented around the council table. In 2015, the City of Hamilton retained the services of Watson & Associates to review its ward boundaries. After public consultation and a review of various criteria including issues such as geography, population and effective representation the consultants produced a report recommending two possible ward boundary plans. Council rejected both options and drew their own boundaries. Two Hamilton residents, Mark Richardson and Rob Dobrucki, appealed the council decision to the OMB (since replaced by the Local Planning Appeal Tribunal or LPAT).

The appellants' efforts seemed to be directed at the voter dilution created by the wide variance in population represented by each ward councillor. That was the case under the status quo and would continue to be the case under the new ward plan approved by council. Curiously, the city's legal counsel tried to exclude council debate and deliberation from being entered as evidence, arguing that city council speaks as one through its decisions. You can understand their resistance to having council debate included if you go back and examine either video of committee or council meetings or the reporting on the process. For example, after a special council meeting held to discuss the consultants' final report, one suburban councillor was quoted in a CBC Hamilton story as portraying the status quo as a "safety net" for the former suburbs.[10] The implication being that adjusting the existing ward boundary configuration to give the Mountain a fourth ward, which would better match its population numbers to political representation on city council, would give urban councillors more power.

During the OMB hearing, maintaining the balance of power on council was bound up with the claim that the status quo, which included a geographically large but sparsely populated ward, provided effective representation for rural interests at council. Rachel Barnett, a Ph.D. student at McMaster University, advanced the proposition based on her academic work that the protection of rural interests at the expense of diluting the voting power of city wards, where many if not most visible minority residents live, has reduced their effective representation. In this light, maintaining the "balance of power" or portraying the status quo as a "safety net" for the former suburbs takes on a different meaning and carries with it implications for political representation and decision-making power that hitherto had remained largely submerged in public discourse.

Full disclosure: I registered as a participant in order to make a statement at the hearings conducted by then OMB executive chair Bruce Krushelnicki and member Paula Boutis. In my statement to the board, I argued that enough time had passed since amalgamation and it was time to reconsider the status quo in order to address population growth and evolving communities of interest in the city.

On the evening set aside for participant statements at the OMB hearings, I was told politely by a Mountain councillor in attendance that no one was pushing for changes to ward boundaries, except a few downtown activists who had been making a lot of noise about it. I replied, "As this is 'inside baseball' that's not surprising." But I've heard similar remarks in relation to a range of policy and planning issues. It is hard to get a representative cross-section of people to talk about the implementation of a traffic management plan, plans to "re-vitalize" the city's public housing portfolio or discuss the implications of an area study or new secondary plan or amendments to Hamilton's comprehensive zoning bylaw. The discussion is often technical and alienating for non-experts or the uninitiated – and too remote from most peoples' daily lives to register as impactful until it is too late and all the key decisions have been made.

I wish it were different. Because what it really means is that most of the business of city hall, for better and worse, rolls on without input from a full spectrum of Hamiltonians and in many cases without much awareness of what is at stake.

There is an obvious asymmetry. To the extent that we are seeing progressive collective mobilization on certain issues in Hamilton it is mostly coming from so-called downtown activists or, as at least one councillor refers to them, aggressive urbanists. While it is probably true that networks of civic activism are densest in the lower city neighbourhoods found in Wards 1–3, engaged people and interest in civic affairs is wider than that. And though the visibility and intensity of interest is lower, hot-button issues and activism that gets labelled as downtown, inner city or urbanist stretches out into the suburbs. It is a mistake to turn issues into markers of urban and suburban difference, even if on balance a socio-political divide exists and registers in the formal politics of city hall.

In Toronto, the United Way's *Poverty by Postal Code: The Geography of Neighbourhood Poverty, 1981–2001* and *The Three Cities Within Toronto: Income Polarization Among Toronto's Neighbourhoods, 1970–2005* by University of Toronto professor David Hulchanski show that geographies of social and economic difference are no longer conforming to old stereotypes of urban poverty and suburban affluence. Indeed, a great reversal has taken place since the late 1970s. Now the areas where poverty and social marginalization concentrate are in the outer parts of Toronto, with sections of the old, postwar suburbs of Etobicoke, North York and Scarborough becoming not just poorer, but places where poverty and disadvantage are increasingly paired with inadequate public transit, city facilities and amenities. They are also the parts of the city with the highest concentrations of immigrants, refugees and people of colour.

Closer to home the evidence is a little more mixed. *A City on the Cusp: Neighbourhood Change in Hamilton Since 1970* finds that Hamilton still conforms generally to the American rust-belt pattern of inner-city poverty and suburban affluence, though that picture seems destined to become more complicated by the decline of inner suburban areas to the east and south and gentrification and redevelopment activity in the lower city, particularly around the downtown core and in neighbourhoods to the north, south and west of downtown.[11] They note the emergence of an increasingly east-west contrast in income polarization, with the west parts of the lower city and suburbs becoming more affluent. That is no doubt informing the public face of resurgent activism around transit, bike infrastructure and urbanism, though it should not imply that activism is limited to these areas geographically or thematically.

For example, organized tenant resistance to above-guideline rent increases evolved into a rent strike in four apartment towers in Riverdale, which is located just east of Centennial Parkway near Eastgate Square and a short distance south of the new GO train station set to open for service to downtown Toronto soon.[12] There are signs of disquiet along the eastern portion of the King and Main corridors where the B-Line LRT project led to expropriations of affordable rental housing – and the development and real estate uplift used to justify the project threatens further displacement.

The sudden and unexpected cancellation of Hamilton's LRT project by the provincial government in December 2019 has put all this in limbo. It is possible that a social movement may coalesce around demands that affordable housing be returned to the corridor regardless and that better protections be put in place for tenants should an alternative transit project ultimately go ahead. But that would require a dramatic rethink and revisiting of the economic development rationale that drove the LRT project as a city-building initiative. One can support LRT and still recognize that land-use planning directed at leveraging economic development from it is not unproblematic, especially if little is done beyond facilitating market-led redevelopment.

Revitalization built upon revalorizing property values and facilitating a middle-class remaking of areas adjacent to higher-order transit corridors and station areas will not produce social equity or mixed income communities over the medium or longer term. Instead, it is likely to accelerate reshaping Hamilton in locally specific ways that parallel the uneven development and patterning of social exclusion that has taken hold in Toronto since 1970.

■

So why do we keep building suburbs and reproducing suburbanism while either complaining about traffic congestion and long commutes or saying we want and need more urbanism across the city?

This is where the still significant pull of the "triple dream" of house, yard and community plays into the local struggles and negotiations that emerge around planning and development, whether urban or suburban. I see limited evidence as yet in Hamilton to suggest that much of the currently touted rebirth of urbanism in the city is fuelled by people wishing to live in new mid- and high-rise neighbourhoods of the sort that many urbanists promote and provincial and municipal "intensification" policies seem geared to produce.

That doesn't mean we aren't seeing mid- and high-rise construction, or that people don't already live in rental and condo towers in Hamilton. Nor is it to say that in larger centres like Vancouver and Toronto there isn't already ample evidence that people will live in denser forms of housing with less living space as a trade-off for living in vibrant urban neighbourhoods. Or to deny that it can be an attractive lifestyle choice. It is only to acknowledge that the current buzz about Hamilton seems to be driven by in-movers looking for ground-oriented housing (detached houses, semis, townhouses and row houses) that *they* perceive to be affordable.[13]

You might call it a thirst for the triple dream without the sprawl. If we begin to think in those terms, we might be better equipped to understand why "drive until you qualify" continues to be a thing. As previously mentioned, what is missing in our present housing mix in urban Hamilton is a fuller spectrum of housing options, including new market-affordable multi-unit housing such as stacked townhouses, that represents a modest increase in scale from its surroundings and incrementally intensifies the existing built fabric. Because residents place enormous emphasis on protecting the character of their neighbourhoods, with few exceptions we tend to get hyper-development in the core – and a few other select corridors and nodes designated for intensification – and new ground-oriented housing on greenfields out on the edge. The development industry seems happy to oblige. And why not? They respond to market signals and generally prefer to build what is tried and true – and profitable.

The result is a kind of pervasive suburbanism. On the edge, because what is being built is compact sprawl still largely oriented to practical dictates of the car, and in the centre, because many yearn for the triple dream without the sprawl. In their own very different ways, both will need to be reworked if a different, more equitable and economically, socially and environmentally sustainable future Hamilton is to be realized. To get there will require a deep understanding and appreciation for the social and political history of the city, recognition of the multiple sites of contestation and negotiation that shape day-to-day governance and decision making and a greater sensitivity to whose voices dominate and interests prevail in the layered politics of major city-building initiatives.

Endnotes

1   Dolores Hayden, *Building Suburbia: Green Fields and Urban Growth, 1820–2000* (Toronto: Random House, 2003), 8.

2   The emergence and course of the North End Urban Renewal Scheme is well documented in Margaret T. Rockwell's unpublished M.A. thesis "Modernist Destruction for the Ambitious City" (McMaster University, 2004), while the harbour drudging scandal, downtown renewal and Hamilton's machine politics are given an excellent analysis in *Their Town: The Mafia, the Media and the Party*

Machine, edited by Bill Freeman and Marsha Hewitt (Toronto: James Lorimer, 1979). We can add to these the recently published *The People and the Bay: A Social and Environmental History of Hamilton Harbour* by McMaster University professors Nancy Bouchier and Ken Cruikshank (Toronto: UBC Press, 2016), which provides a critical history of Hamilton's complicated and changing relationship with its waterfront and the people who live, work and play there. My understanding of what happened and why it still matters today is informed by these; the public library's local history collection, in particular scrapbooks of old *Hamilton Spectator* news clippings; and other writings about Hamilton.

3   Marjorie Freeman Campbell, *A Mountain and a City: The Story of Hamilton* (Toronto: McClelland and Stewart, 1966), 286.

4   In "Modernist Destruction for the Ambitious City," 78, Margaret Rockwell quotes Hamilton Urban Renewal Committee chairman Kenneth Soble as saying that "despite public meetings, mass mailings and an information office, the North Enders could not understand urban renewal was an attempt to preserve a neighbourhood, rather than flatten it."

5   Jane Jacobs, *The Death and Life of Great American Cities* (New York: Random House, 1961), 357.

6   Bill Freeman and Marsha Hewitt, eds., *Their Town: The Mafia, the Media and the Party Machine* (Toronto: James Lorimer, 1979), 35.

7   Marshall Berman, *All That is Solid Melts Into Air: The Experience of Modernity* (New York: Simon and Schuster, 1982), 326.

8   Campbell, *A Mountain and a City*, 271.

9   David Proulx and Joe Urban, *Pardon My Lunch Bucket: A Look at the New Hamilton . . . with a Bit of the Old Thrown in* (Hamilton: City of Hamilton, 1971), no pagination.

10   Samantha Craggs, "Hamilton city councillors will try to redraw ward boundaries themselves," CBC Hamilton, October 27, 2016, http://www.cbc.ca/news /canada/hamilton/hamilton-city-councillors-will-try-to-redraw-ward-boundaries -themselves-1.3824643.

11   Richard Harris, Jim Dunn and Sarah Wakefield, *A City on the Cusp: Neighbourhood Change in Hamilton since 1970*, (Toronto: Cities Centre, University of Toronto, 2015), http://neighbourhoodchange.ca/documents/2015/04/neighbourhood-change -in-hamilton-since-1970.pdf.

12   Teviah Moro, "Revolutionary rallying cry for tenant rights in Hamilton," *Hamilton Spectator*, August 4, 2018.

13   Stuart Berman, "The New Hamiltonians," *Toronto Life*, June 21, 2017, https:// torontolife.com/real-estate/the-new-hamiltonians/.

Reclaiming Hamilton Through Artistic and Environmental Interventions

Jessica Rose

t's a cool night in early June, and the sun is setting over Corktown Park near Hamilton's downtown core. The basketball court is empty, but an informal game of soccer between children and their parents has just begun. The Rail Trail Dog Park is still busy, and, most notably, volunteers are lining the Lower Escarpment Rail Trail between Corktown Park and Wentworth Street with candles in paper bags.

Called Fireflies at Night, this simple action illuminates a small part of Hamilton's trail network, offering pedestrians and cyclists an opportunity to see their surroundings differently, engaging with them in a new way. It's the final intervention of 100In1Day Hamilton, an annual celebration of active citizenship, which urges residents to activate one hundred innovative, thought-provoking ideas that transform their city all on one day. Hamilton is one of twelve cities in Canada to take part in this global movement, which started in Bogotá, Colombia. The goal is to change how people collaborate and interact with their cities by creating activities that put people first, each aligning with one of multiple themes, such as public space recovery, sustainability, art and culture, and solidarity.

According to 100In1Day Hamilton, "The actions of inspired citizens form the backbone of 100In1Day as a social-transformative model seeking to redefine cities by bringing people together in public spaces." The movement is just one example of a citizen-led artistic or environmental initiative that is reclaiming and reimagining underutilized spaces in Hamilton, making the city a more people-friendly place to live.

In *Transforming Communities Through the Arts: A Study of Three Toronto Neighbourhoods*, the authors – Margo Charlton, Deborah Barndt, Katherine Dennis and Rosemary Donegan – found that "the arts are a key component in changing the physical and social make up of communities. Initiatives to claim, create and celebrate local public spaces counter a trend of more privatized control of public space, and reinforce the importance of place-based art that speaks from and resonates with community members." An initiative of the Toronto Arts Foundation, the study's goal was "to gain a better understanding of how residents engage with the arts at a community level, to explore barriers to arts access, and to identify ways to strengthen local arts engagement."

In his book *Street Reclaiming: Creating Livable Streets and Vibrant Communities*, David Engwicht wrote of how the neighbourhood streets and other public spaces instilled within community members a sense of place, encouraging trans-generational interactions and a tradition of spontaneity, where social, cultural and economic exchanges between people happen on a whim. However, in cities such as Hamilton, where cars rule the streets, people and organizations must create opportunities that help these once commonplace interactions thrive.

This chapter looks at only a few of the many successful initiatives in Hamilton that are creating safe and inclusive opportunities for people to come together, fostering a feeling of connectivity that can happen when people gather in one place. Each encourages exploration and engagement within our own city limits by reclaiming empty, ordinary or underutilized spaces, bringing together culture and revitalization in innovative ways.

BEAUTIFUL ALLEYS

"Cities have the capability of providing something for everybody, only because, and only when, they are created by everybody." – Jane Jacobs

"Logan! Tie your shoes. You're going to trip," says Brenda Duke, joint co-chair of GALA, the Gibson and Landsdale Area Community Planning Team, to a young boy teetering on the edge of a skateboard ramp. Duke is leading a Jane's Walk called "Alleys and Greenways of Gibson," and she's paused in Powell Park, a recently revitalized multi-use green space just south of Barton Street. Logan is just one of the many neighbours she stops to chat with along the way.

Jane's Walks build on the ideas of journalist and urbanist Jane Jacobs, using citizen-led walking tours to make space for people to observe, reflect, share, question and collectively reimagine the places in which they live, work and play. This particular Jane's Walk is an opportunity for Duke to tell a small, but highly engaged, group about Beautiful Alleys, a community-led project that renews and reclaims underutilized alleyways. The group turns these neglected areas into dynamic, greener public spaces with improved livability and better walking conditions, while also making them more hospitable to birds and butterflies. Though some might call Duke the project's leader, she quickly acknowledges that Beautiful Alleys is led and run by many volunteers.

"Our goal is to create safe, accessible use for people of all ages and abilities," says Duke, who adds that in her community, and many others in Hamilton, "alleys were often a place for negative activity and underused for their potential. We recognized the potential for various uses and encouraged people to reclaim these forgotten spaces." Hamilton is home to more than seven hundred alleyways – 37 per cent of which are in the GALA neighbourhood – representing an era when horse-drawn carriages, and later trucks, needed easy access to homes and businesses to deliver milk, newspapers and other goods. However, over time, they have been forgotten or neglected, becoming dumping grounds for trash, debris and needles.

In 2011, Duke began cleaning the alley behind her own home, which is located near the shuttered Gibson School at Barton Street and Birch. She engaged neighbours, who began tending to their own alleys, and the idea continued to catch on. Since Beautiful Alleys was officially born in 2015, the group has transformed around two hundred alleys.

"Beautiful Alleys is an ongoing project," says Duke, talking about the twice-annual cleanups that happen in the spring and fall, and many other citizen-led initiatives that the project lends support to. "We are mainly an organizational group. We provide the contacts, help with supplies, advise [citizens] on their vision, and help them take initiative and responsibility," she says. The project is made possible through the care of community members, many of whom carry a trash bag with them whenever they leave their home, just in case an alley needs tending.

"Any project that brings community together, builds community. It brings a sense of pride and people become invested in their neighbourhood and their city. It opens their eyes to all of the possibilities and broadens their scope," says Duke. "They might clean to get rid of the garbage but then they want to plant so they can look at flowers when they walk the dog. They see an abandoned street corner and want to improve it," she adds, excited about how the initiative spreads enthusiasm.

When you walk through the many alleyways that intersect the GALA neighbourhood, you'll find they're maintained with great care. You'll spot corridor gardens, solar lighting, rain barrels, birdhouses and benches. You will also find pollinator plants from the Hamilton Pollinator Paradise Project, a collaborative initiative between Environment Hamilton and the Hamilton Naturalists' Club. Pollinator Paradise works with communities to achieve its goal of building an uninterrupted pollinator corridor across the city by planting native plants such as milkweed and other wildflowers, and promoting biodiversity.

"We work closely with Green Venture, Environment Hamilton and Pollinator Paradise to provide that expertise," says Duke, who, during her Jane's Walk, points out irises she planted with origins from her mother's farm. "When I moved from the farm over fifty years ago, I brought a clump of purple iris from my mom's garden," Duke later explains. "As they grow, I split them and give them to friends, neighbours, and plant them in bare corners and in our community gardens. There are irises from that first clump all the way between here and Dundas and from one yard to the next. Every time I see a purple iris it reminds me of my childhood home and my mom."

When asked what's next for Beautiful Alleys, Duke shares her vision for a safer public space for all community members, especially for children travelling between Birch Avenue and Woodlands Park. The park is located on the north side of Barton Street East between Wentworth Street and Sanford Avenue North, just south of the former Westinghouse industrial complex. "As a group, our vision is to complete the last leg of our safe trail to travel from Birch to Sanford for the children in this neighbourhood. Our hope is to complete a makeover on the alley between Milton and Fullerton with artwork and enhancements that will keep our children and others off the busy Barton corridor," she says.

People-powered artwork in unexpected places, in the form of vibrant, eye-catching murals, is a cornerstone of the Beautiful Alleys project, which uses the alley-facing back walls of brick buildings and once-tired looking garage doors as canvases.

"The murals are the 'beautiful' in Beautiful Alleys," says Duke. "In addition to cutting down on unsightly graffiti, they add a visual impact that encourages people to use the alleys as alternate routes. The increased activity cuts down on illegal dumping. It is all connected."

A favourite mural among children, Duke says during her Jane's Walk tour, is a colourful mural of Superman by local artist Stephan Hossbach. It's found in the unofficially named Trocadero Alley, known also as "Lois Lane," which runs between Westinghouse Avenue and Sanford Avenue North behind the famed Trocadero Restaurant. The mural pays homage to the Trocadero's owner Lois, who is well known for keeping the alley clean. The Trocadero itself houses its own mural, which depicts a busy Italian restaurant, which, of course, is a nod to its seventy-five-year history as a Barton Street staple.

Murals, as public art, can be found all over Hamilton, created both through citizen-led initiatives and city initiatives. In 2018, the City of Hamilton completed the James Street South Mural Public Art Project process to select a mural that was installed on an exterior wall on James Street South, near the Hamilton GO Centre. The volunteer citizen jury selected the work *Gateway* by Vivian Rosas and Vesna Asanovic, which "showcases the creative spirit of Hamilton using bright, engaging vignettes of some of the differing cultural communities of downtown Hamilton, with a focus on: James Street, Durand, and the Escarpment/ Bruce Trail." Other notable murals include a number of large-scale works by Lester Coloma, who has been professionally hand painting murals since 1996, including his interpretation of the Aesop's Fable the Tortoise and the Hare, which revitalized an exterior wall of what is left of Hamilton's once-grand Tivoli Theatre.

"No mural can represent everyone in the community, and perhaps it should not. Instead, it is useful to think of a mural as a visual record of a collaboration between a group in the community and an artist," writes Ronald Lee Fleming in *The Art of Placemaking: Interpreting Community Through Public Art and Urban Design*.

Despite all that it has achieved, the Beautiful Alleys project faces obstacles, especially at the city level.

"Our biggest barrier is the City's attitude toward alleys. They have no clear plan on how to care for alleys and no budget," says Duke. "There are also too many hoops to jump through. If the problem is weeds, that's one department. If it's garbage, that's another department. The list goes on and on. We have some small success with a few departments, like waste management, but overall each problem or need is a battle."

Duke worries that the easiest solution might not be the best.

"They think that selling off the alleys [to residents for a nominal fee], taking away that public space will solve their problems, but that creates more problems," she says. "It takes away public access to bike or walking paths that are safer than city streets. It means children have to play on the street instead of behind their homes. There are so many possibilities and such potential, but you fight every day to make them listen to what the community wants."

Reclaiming Hamilton's alleyways isn't Duke's only passion. She is also the coordinator of the Powell Park Community Garden, which was recently extended to house nearly fifty raised-bed plots, including a number that are tended by children from nearby Cathy Wever Elementary School and Prince of Wales Elementary School and other youth-focused organizations. Other plots in the Powell Park Community Garden are tended by newcomers or seniors who miss caring for gardens of their own.

"The Gibson and Landsdale Area Community Planning Team took it over three years ago and it has grown from a neglected and vandalized area to a space where we can provide food security to the community," says Duke, who talks excitedly about the large newcomer population who gardens at the Powell Park Community Garden, using the garden as a social and family gathering place, often for many hours a day.

"Our newcomer families totally embrace what a community garden should be," she says. "They are farmers and as such, garden differently than many of us. The families come most evenings, after supper. The men garden, the women and children enjoy the park and socialize. And they bring cookies!" she adds, noting that learning about a variety of cultures is a favourite part of the community garden.

"There is a language barrier, but we work around it with sign language, drawings and translation from the children," says Duke. "We are very proud to be able to include them and bring them into the community by providing an outlet for their passion."

"I truly believe that a city is built on the strength of its communities," says Duke, who believes that citizens become engaged in their community when they are recognized, supported and feel like their opinions matter. For that reason she, on behalf of the Gibson and Landsdale Area Community Planning Team, prides herself on providing the knowledge, training and support that citizens need to make their own visions a reality.

"We do everything 'with' them, as opposed to 'for them or to them,'" she says.

RIGHT ON TARGET

"What defines the character of a city is its public space, not its private space."
– Dr. Joan Clos, Former Executive Director, UN Habitat

It's an unseasonably cold night in late April 2018, and visitors to the former Target store at the Centre on Barton are bundled up. An opening in the building, caused by construction, is letting cold air in, and the fifty thousand–foot space won't stay warm. Yet despite the near-freezing temperature outside, hundreds of people have gathered for a pop-up night market – one of more than a dozen events that have reimagined the commercial space since Right on Target, a community-focused initiative, began in 2017.

Erratic, uncontrolled energy characterizes every Right on Target event, whether the underutilized space is hosting a synth social, where synthesizer enthusiasts can bring their gear to jam; a night market; or Playground in a Box. A popular interactive pop-up event, Playground in a Box offers children and youth a place to gather to play freely, whether riding bikes and scooters provided by New Hope Community Bikes, building structures out of cardboard boxes with no clear instructions or, simply, running around with friends. Free of rules and formality, any given night at a Right on Target event can have dozens of activities happening simultaneously, all under the roof of one reclaimed space.

"People nowadays want a very controlled thing where temperatures are controlled. There's no wind or dust, and everything looks like a hotel," says Fatima Mesquita, a community organizer and development coordinator at Toronto's Scadding Court Community Centre, which has been integral to the creation of Right on Target. At Right on Target, "you are a citizen capable of making your own decision," she says. "We try as much as possible to not be a place for rules."

The Centre on Barton, located on Barton Street East between Ottawa Street and Kenilworth Avenue, was home to one of seven Target stores that opened in Hamilton and Burlington in 2013. However, the American discount retailer's life in Canada was brief, and by April 2016, all 133 Canadian stores had closed.

The failed Canadian expansion of Target left large, vacant buildings in malls and plazas across the country. Triovest Realty Advisors Inc., the commercial real estate firm that manages the Centre on Barton, saw potential in this empty space. It looked to other adaptive reuse models that were already happening for inspiration. This included Toronto's Scadding Court Community Centre's Business Out of the Box, an initiative that uses retrofitted shipping containers to provide affordable vending space to low-income business owners. Business Out of the Box provides "a platform for both communities and entrepreneurs to transform underutilized spaces in a neighbourhood into vibrant, lucrative and inclusive markets," while reducing barriers, such as a lack of access to capital and space, to business owners.

"What we wanted to create is the 'third place,'" says Mesquita. She is referencing urban sociologist Ray Oldenburg's idea that a "third place" is an informal public gathering space separate from the two usual social environments of home ("first place") and the workplace ("second place"). In his influential book *The Great Good Place*, Oldenburg argues that these places are crucial to democracy, civic engagement, relationship building and community vitality.

Among Right on Target's first steps was extensive community consultation. They conducted a hands-on feasibility study and visioning sessions where members of the community could actively engage with the space and brainstorm inclusive and temporary uses for the vacant building to meet the Crown Point community's needs.

"We wanted to find out the needs and the wants of the community," says Mesquita. Since Right on Target's first event in 2017, the space has been used in dozens, maybe hundreds, of meaningful and unexpected ways. These include PA Day programming to offer parents an affordable option for child care, free workshops presented by McMaster University's Centre for Continuing Education, vendor markets, DIY art projects, and craft beer and food options, to name only a few. In June 2018, the City of Hamilton used the space to host Bringing the City to the Community, the first information fair for the Hamilton Aboriginal Advisory Committee, and during Hamilton Pride, Right on Target hosted a Roller Derby: Learn to Skate event.

"How could you imagine, for an example, that Pride would have an event at the mall?" asks Mesquita, who says that one of the most exciting things to have happened in the former Target building is a partnership between Right on Target and the Hammer City Roller Girls, the first not-for-profit, skater-operated, flat track roller derby league in Canada. Right on Target offered the group "cheap, affordable, easygoing" rent. "They needed a space. We had the space," says Mesquita, who believes mutually beneficial relationships are the key to Right on Target's success. "It's really cool because it's really about empowering young girls," she says, noting that she's met many children who are now interested in roller skating who might not have otherwise been exposed to it without Right on Target.

Many large- and medium-sized cities have a well-established history of artists and community organizers taking over vacant spaces for temporary projects, fostering creativity and increasing civic engagement. Locally, there are a number of examples, including Hamilton Flea, which has reclaimed empty spaces, including Treble Hall and Lawson Lumber, to host a vintage marketplace, and Pop-Up Hamilton, which combined Hamilton's culinary scene with unexpected and underused spaces.

The Toronto Arts Foundation's *Transforming Communities Through the Arts* highlights just a few arts organizations that have emerged in unused or underused spaces in Toronto: "In the absence of cultural hubs, unofficial spaces emerge for artists to meet in parks and people's homes. In addition, arts organizations use available spaces: a retrofitted store front has become a centre for children's art programs in St. James Town; and an unused space in the basement of the Yorkdale Shopping Mall has become the headquarters for Art Starts, a community arts organization that serves neighbourhoods throughout the city." "It's always changing – the way we use the space. It's very organic," says Mesquita, who delights in seeing so many people feel proud of the space and how it is being used.

One could argue that this optimistic energy hasn't been felt since the early days of the Centre on Barton, first known as the Greater Hamilton Shopping Centre. It opened to much fanfare on October 26, 1955, on the land formerly owned by the Jockey Club racetrack. At the time, it was one of the first shopping malls in North America. In 1974, the centre was enclosed and became known as The Centre Mall, and in 2008, Triovest rebuilt the property to what we see today. The

Centre on Barton is home to sixty stores, mostly of the commonplace big-box variety that one might argue are cold and uninviting, including Walmart, Canadian Tire, PetSmart and Michaels.

"People really had a connection with the mall, and they feel betrayed by it," Mesquita says, adding that the mall had a very communal feel with a very active walking club and a cinema where many east enders began dating their partners. Inclusivity is of utmost importance for Right on Target, which is wheelchair accessible and prides itself on bridging age gaps and racial divides. One of the pillars, Mesquita says, is looking at people as more than simple consumers, and offering experiences that are affordable to all people.

"You don't have to be a consumer," says Mesquita, who says that it is important that all people, whether they have a disposable income or not, can have a good experience at Right on Target events, even the Night Market, where many free activities take place alongside vendors. This is especially important, she says, during the winter months.

"We don't have a community centre. We don't have a place for you to go in the winter where you can be a non-consumer," she says, noting that in the summer public spaces like parks and pools give kids cost-effective ways to play. "You can just 'be' in the summer," she says. "But when it's -35 degrees, there's no place to go. You need to have money, or you have to keep your kids inside."

One thing that excites Mesquita is the many ways the space is being used in unpredicted, unimagined ways. "There's an element of surprise, and there is variety," she says, recalling a recent experience when grandparents visited the space with multiple grandchildren.

"The grandmother and grandfather were just sitting there. The man brought a crossword. He concentrated on it. She was reading a book for children about science that she found there, and the kids were just everywhere," says Mesquita. "They were probably doing whatever they would have been doing at home.

The kids were running, and they were spending nothing." Another time, Mesquita recalls, a group of mothers arrived together at Right on Target. "They brought food, and suddenly, there was a full area that looked like a picnic," she says with a smile, adding that providing intergenerational programming is a crucial component to Right on Target. Teenagers also frequent the space during events, bringing their BMX bikes. Mesquita struck a deal with them, allowing them to use the space, if they help her maintain it.

In *Street Reclaiming: Creating Livable Streets and Vibrant Communities*, David Engwicht argues that "adult play" is not prioritized in an era of "strong work ethic" and car culture, "leaving little room for exuberant, uninhibited" play among adults. At Right on Target, collaborative, communal art projects, even those as simple as doodling with markers or chalk, prove that art making and play aren't only for children.

The arts provide an opportunity for connection – with neighbours, with our own history, and with the surroundings we call home. Arts programs break down barriers by addressing social isolation, helping us find others who share our creative spirit or desire to make a change. We are inherently social creatures and the arts are good connectors. Whether the practise itself is social – playing in a band, joining a knitting group or participating in a community arts project – or a solo activity such as painting, composing or writing, research participants shared how creative practices present ways of relating to others. (Margo Charlton et al., *Transforming Communities Through the Arts: A Study of Three Toronto Neighbourhoods*)

When asked about challenges Right on Target has faced, Mesquita says that "the City has been wonderful. They're being really flexible as possible, with limitations," noting that challenging zoning from the 1950s has been an ongoing process. She also says that there is something liberating about being in a temporary space with an uncertain future.

"We are guests in this space. We are temporary. We don't know how temporary. We don't know if we're going to morph into something else," she says. This temporary status means the project doesn't need to have "crazy goals." "It's all very flexible. We don't have goals to beat. We don't need to grow every month."

Mesquita says that the success of Right on Target is measured by connections – the business partnerships that have started there and the pride east-end residents feel toward the project. The organization is also bringing people from across Hamilton to the east end, many of whom hold stereotypes about the Barton Street area.

"The city doesn't come here, and suddenly we're breaking that pattern. Suddenly, you can change the perception," she says, laughing at the thought that some people think it's too dangerous to walk around Hamilton's east end. "For me as a Brazilian, that's a big joke!"

People from all over the country are curious about the Right on Target model, but to Mesquita, and others involved in the project, it's the pride Hamiltonians feel that is most exciting. Many of them are returning to the neighbourhood for the first time in years, even decades.

"One thing that's very common is talking with someone who lives on the other side of the city, and they say, 'Oh, I grew up here. My grandmother lives here. Or my grandmother used to live here,'" she says. There was an exodus of residents who worked in factories from the community when jobs disappeared.

When reflecting on Right on Target, Mesquita likens it to a village, where everyone brings their own unique skills and passions to one central hub. "Everybody has a role to play while they're here," she says. "We have a collective responsibility. Everyone takes care of each other."

Activating unused public spaces, especially in cases like Right on Target, can generate vibrant and meaningful interactions, but ultimately, as Fatima Mesquita mentioned often in her interview, they're temporary. On June 20, 2018, Right on Target left the following message on their popular Facebook page: "By July 10, our great experiment of a place created by everybody with something for everybody will be officially done, but before this happens we are here to tell all of you – partners, community members, friends, vendors, suppliers, neighbours – how incredible it was to have your support in this journey." Giant Tiger and GoodLife Fit4Less have since filled the space.

BUILDING MAGIC

"Culture is not only beneficial to cities; in a deeper sense, it's what cities are for. A city without poets, painters and photographers is sterile." – Rebecca Solnit

For more than eighty years, the Westdale Theatre's facade has faced King Street West, between Paisley and Marion, in Hamilton's affluent Westdale Village neighbourhood. When it was put on the market in December 2016 for $1.8 million, it was the only single-screen theatre left in operation in Hamilton, after gems like the historic Century Theatre on Mary Street had closed and been demolished. Hamiltonians with decades' worth of memories feared that the 593-seat Westdale Theatre would suffer the same fate. However, in early January 2017, it was purchased by the Westdale Cinema Group, a non-profit organization formed by a group of dedicated volunteers to acquire, renovate and operate the underutilized theatre.

The goal of the Westdale Cinema Group is to create a community-based cultural and economic hub, not only to screen independent and classic films, but to also provide much-needed exhibition space for music, literary readings, lectures and public meetings. When it reopened to the public in February 2019, the renovated Westdale Theatre boasted new washrooms, including a fully accessible one near the lobby; new seats, including wheelchair seating; an extended stage for live music and lectures; and state-of-the-art projection and sound equipment. The project also included fully restored art deco decor, architectural detailing and a facade restored to look as it did in 1935.

A community-led project, volunteers were integral to the cleanup and renovation process at the Westdale Theatre, but they also offered crucial insight into how the space might best be used. Two of those volunteers were artists Sanjay Patel and Trisha Smith who, together, own Smith & Patel, which hosts art, food and music events in Hamilton. Patel is a visual artist who has created over six hundred original works and has produced paintings to capture the energy at over two hundred live events. Smith is a singer and musician who has created her own interactive children's performance, Music with Miss T. Together, as Smith & Patel, they are tenants at Art Aggregate, a co-creating space on Nash Road that caters to artists, makers and other cultural innovators. Art Aggregate seeks to eliminate barriers contemporary creators often face when running an independent studio.

While reclaiming and revitalizing the Westdale Theatre was the utmost priority, Smith and Patel, among other visual artists, saw potential not only in the historic building, but in the objects still residing inside it, many of which otherwise might have been thrown away. The result of this was the Building Magic Exhibition, which featured art created from reclaimed and revived items from the Westdale Theatre, including pendants made using vintage Westdale Theatre tickets dating to 1945, jewellery that incorporated broken Vitrolite from the theatre's facade and a clock made of old projection bulbs. The exhibition helped raise much-needed funds for the cinema renovation project.

"You don't want to throw [these things] out because they represent another time and the memory of this theatre," says Smith, who says she and Patel rummaged around the theatre to find relics that could inspire a work of art. They settled on three aluminum wheels called film platters.

"These would normally lay flat and you would link up a bunch of movies together on one wheel so you wouldn't have to switch reels," says Patel, while he paints and talks in his studio at Art Aggregate. The reclaimed film platter spun, making it easier to paint.

"As soon as word gets out that things are being upcycled, it's like a feeding frenzy," says Patel, who picked the film platters for their flat, easy-to-paint surfaces. As part of the project, Smith and Patel also spent a Saturday with fellow artists having a communal paint party, where works of art were created using bits of a reclaimed movie screen.

The Building Magic Exhibition took place on June 8, 2018, during the James Street North Art Crawl. It was hosted by the Factory Media Centre, a not-for-profit artist-driven resource centre dedicated to the production and promotion of creatively diverse forms of independent films, videos and other streaming multimedia art forms.

"Everything from the projection screen, glass tiles, bulbs from the marquee and more have been salvaged and artistically re-purposed for purchase with all proceeds going to the renovation and restoration of the Westdale Theatre," said the exhibition's description. "We have a great roster of talented Hamilton artists and artisans working with the theatre's reclaimed materials and objects to give them a new life!"

As a commission-based artist, building relationships within the community is crucial to Patel, who says coming together with other artists and community members is especially important when you spend so many hours within the confines of a studio. Both Smith and Patel agree that community-focused arts are a big part of what they do. One of their projects has been bringing Art Battle to Hamilton. Art Battle is a live-painting competition where visual artists create work during three timed rounds while audience members watch their creative process. The competition takes place every month between September and June.

"For us, Art Battle is about meeting other artists in the community," says Smith. "The people who are actually working and acting in the city are some of the first people who painted with us. It's about nurturing that community and trying to bring more artwork to the city." Part of this is an effort to move art out of gallery spaces, which can sometimes be intimidating and feel unwelcoming and inaccessible to the general public.

In a May 2017 article posted on Medium.com called "Intimidation of Fine Art," a writer named only as Rhymes&Oils argues that we must reframe and reclaim art in response to an "intimidation of fine art" that has surfaced, encouraging artists and consumers to seek opportunities outside of traditional spaces.

Public art spaces can also broaden our knowledge and understanding of art. Perhaps it is not the fine art itself we find intimidating, but the establishments in which they are presented to us. . . . As for artists, it is our responsibility to push the boundaries. There needs to be a stronger art community; as a whole, as opposed to dotted clusters. Interact with your followers, show support to fellow artists. This is not a competition. Thus don't fear that you are in this alone; there is room for every artist to succeed. . . . If we work on building a stronger community, we can help brighten the spotlight on the craft.

Smith and Patel believe that events like Art Battle and others that bring together art, music and food outside the realm of a gallery give people an opportunity to engage with art in an honest, organic way.

"It's creating more opportunities for people to see art and not be so separated from it, and not be so afraid," says Smith. "It's about showing off this creative process that so few people get to see and so many people are intimidated by."

"Not many people get to see that, and that's what the real secret of Art Battle is – Letting people peer into the artist's life for that moment," agrees Patel.

≡

"The arts offer a powerful form of communication. Community-engaged arts can bring disparate groups together, revealing differences and tensions

but also creating a place of possibility to examine these contradictions. They can help us see a different perspective, shatter expectations, question the status quo, deepen conversations and have a transformative effect on participants and audiences." – Margo Charlton et al., *Transforming Communities Through the Arts*

These initiatives, both large – welcoming hundreds of people to an unused big-box store – and small – planting flowers in a sunny corner of a long-mistreated alleyway – are just a few examples of citizen-led artistic and environmental interventions happening in Hamilton. These groups and events are putting people first, reclaiming and reimagining underutilized spaces in our city and creating community-driven change in fun, organic ways, and that's no small thing.

"Arts and culture are powerful tools with which to engage communities in various levels of change. They are a means to public dialogue, contribute to the development of a community's creative learning, create healthy communities capable of action, provide a powerful tool for community mobilization and activism, and help build community capacity and leadership," states *Arts and Positive Change in Communities*, a report published more than a decade ago by Creative City Network of Canada

Initiatives such as Beautiful Alleys, Right on Target and countless others may contribute to beautifying our city and giving underutilized spaces a new and re-energized purpose; however, the benefits stretch beyond aesthetics. Community-driven interventions create opportunities for community members to engage with art beyond a gallery setting and provide the opportunity for education and play for all ages. Most importantly, they offer a unique opportunity for artists, agitators and all citizens to work together to impact the health of their neighbourhoods, with each person having an equally critical role to play.

The Stadium and the Memory of Hamilton

Matthew Bin

B ack in the 1950s, John Michaluk stared out the window of his grade seven science classroom at Prince of Wales Elementary School. He had a clear view of Civic Stadium, later renamed Ivor Wynne Stadium and more recently replaced by Tim Hortons Field. "I watched these guys practicing," he says, "and like every kid in Hamilton, I dreamed about being on that field."

That dream came true. Michaluk played four years for the Hamilton Tiger-Cats, including the legendary 1967 season. The Tiger-Cats won the 1967 Grey Cup after dominating the entire league. In the last six games they played that year, they didn't surrender a single touchdown, even during their 24–1 Grey Cup victory.

John Michaluk retired from football in 1969, and soon after that he started doing the game commentary on local radio station CHML. He had that job for twenty-two years. Michaluk knows Hamilton and football like few others. He was around for Hamilton's greatest economic days – and the greatest days for Hamilton football.

Standing at the centre of Hamilton's football culture today is Tim Hortons Field, a twenty-three-thousand-seat stadium that opened in 2014. The new stadium is on hallowed ground: it was first Civic Stadium, built for the inaugural Commonwealth Games (then British Empire Games) in 1930. From 1930 until the original stadium was demolished in 2013, the site hosted Tiger-Cats games continuously.

The stadium occupies a unique place in the fabric of Hamilton as a city and as a society. But whether it will endure or whether it stands as a monument to past glory never to be regained is in the hands of its citizens. In many ways, football has been the city's civic religion, with the football stadium the city's place of worship. Much of that is because football is so tightly wound up with working-class identity. But now that Hamilton is no longer Canada's archetypal working-class city, its beloved football team and the culture that surrounds it may be in doubt.

THE STADIUM

Tim Hortons Field occupies about six blocks in Hamilton's east end. It stands just north of Cannon Street, an artery that flows westward toward the downtown core. The bleachers expand east and west; the north and south ends of the stadium are open, without seats. Approaching from the sides, the light grey walls look as industrial and functional as the steel mills not far away.

The tall sides of the stadium loom far over the squat brick houses that line the streets around it. The neighbourhood was built as part of the interwar expansion, providing low-cost housing to the steelworkers who streamed into the rapidly expanding Stelco and Dofasco grounds on the shores of Hamilton Harbour, only a few hundred yards north.

The stadium's location is a remarkable rarity. In most cities in North America stadiums are built in key economic areas. They are typically situated downtown, often at the waterfront. Otherwise, they sit in the suburbs, where land is cheap and highway access is easy.

Not in Hamilton. The city bought the land where Tim Hortons Field stands from a local farmer in 1913. The stadium was, from its earliest days, deep within the Stipley neighbourhood. It was built to house the 1930 British Empire Games, and even at the time of that event, the stadium was encircled by houses on three sides. The porches and rooftops visible in photographs of the 1930 games are the same ones fans pass as they walk up to the stadium gates today.

The stadium was an anomaly in the neighbourhood. Dr. Nancy Bouchier is a professor at McMaster University who studies the economics of sports. "The stadium was originally built for athletics, for a very upper class event," she points out. At the time, amateur athletes were the people who could afford to train instead of work; they were typically better off financially than pro sportsmen.

But soon after the Empire Games wrapped up, Hamilton pro football came to the stadium. The team continued to practise at the Hamilton Amateur Athletic Association (HAAA) Grounds, a park just west of the city. This park had a long history with Canadian football – the HAAA Grounds had hosted seven of the first twenty-three Grey Cup championship games.

When the modern CFL was born in 1950, the Tigers joined with another Hamilton football team, the Wildcats, to create the Tiger-Cats. And that same year, the team took its place in the expanded and modernized Civic Stadium.

Perhaps the greatest moment in the lifetime of the historic stadium was the 1972 Grey Cup. With over thirty-four thousand seats, the newly renamed Ivor Wynne Stadium was the largest football venue in the country. The Tiger-Cats had another very strong team, mainly because they still retained many of the veterans from their three Grey Cup wins in the sixties. Tiger-Cats legends Angelo Mosca, Tommy Joe Coffey, Ellison Kelly and Joe Zuger all left the team or retired after that year.

Hamilton had won the CFL's Eastern Football Conference that year with eleven wins and three losses, an identical record to the Ottawa

Rough Riders. Hamilton beat Ottawa in the semifinal to earn its place in the final against Saskatchewan. The game was a tense affair, and was won on the final play by a field goal scored by nineteen-year-old rookie kicker Ian Sunter. Tens of thousands packed the Hamilton downtown for the victory parade.

Hamilton has hosted only one Grey Cup since, in 1996, and the venerable stadium was crumbling even then. A *Globe and Mail* article published shortly after Tim Hortons Field opened shared some players' memories of Ivor Wynne. "They recall walking under the stands, as water dripped from the ceilings, to the dingy and outdated weight room. Ivor Wynne's turf felt like thin old carpet. The locker room was small, and its shower room had unpredictable water temperatures and faulty taps. One exasperated lineman with some plumbing chops would often attempt repairs himself."[1]

Local businessman Bob Young purchased the Tiger-Cats in 2003, saving the team from dissolving after the previous ownership group evaporated. Young was willing to invest in the team – he covered millions of dollars in operating losses in the first years he owned it. But he reiterated what everyone knew: the team needed a new stadium. And although the municipal government would not be able to bankroll the new building, it became a possibility when the 2015 Pan Am Games in Toronto and the Golden Horseshoe needed a stadium to host soccer matches and track and field events.

The new stadium was built in part as a soccer venue for the games; this provided over a hundred million dollars in funding to the city from the provincial government. But the location of the new stadium was a prolonged controversy. Hamilton's city council wanted to build the stadium on the waterfront near the downtown. Tiger-Cats owner Young refused to consider this location, citing the lack of major traffic arteries nearby. Other sites debated at length were Confederation Park on the shore of Lake Ontario; the East Mountain, where housing developments are quickly expanding; and the rail yard off Longwood Avenue, overlooking Highway 403. Young even threatened to move the team to Aldershot, part of nearby Burlington – outside of Hamilton.

The stadium controversy caused a groundswell of public reaction, and it was a fixture in the editorial pages of the *Hamilton Spectator*. There are over a thousand hits for the phrase *stadium location* in the newspaper from 2009 to 2013. The debate was finally put to rest with the due date for the Pan Am Games. The city and the team finally settled on building the new stadium on the grounds of Ivor Wynne Stadium only days before the deadline.

Rick Zamperin called Tiger-Cats games on CHML for over a decade and continues to host the popular *Fifth Quarter* call-in show. He's known the fans and the team intimately for a long time and he feels that while neither the city nor the team really wanted the stadium to stay in the same place, it was the only place everyone could agree on. "The history, the memories, and the community were all there," he says. "We'll never know whether it was the best choice, but it was the one everyone could live with. And the choice was a big relief to everyone."

The stadium construction was problematic, with long delays due to faulty design and, ironically enough, faulty steel. Lawsuits have dragged on since it opened. But it's Hamilton's stadium now, and home to the Tiger-Cats for generations to come.

THE TEAM AND HAMILTON

For better or worse, Hamilton has a reputation as a grimy, ugly city. Most non-Hamiltonians see the city from the Burlington Skyway, on the other side of Burlington Bay, as they pass through the area on the highway. When the city's manufacturing was in its heyday, the dark smudge of industrial lands at the waterfront belched steam and smoke into the air, and the pall of a rust-tinged smog hung in the sky above the massive slag heaps. Hamilton was ugly and dirty. It was first and foremost a steel town.

Two major companies, Dofasco and Stelco, dominated the local economy. Growing up in the nearby town of Stoney Creek in the late 1970s, the fathers of most of the kids in my own class, many of whom were Italian and Yugoslavian immigrants, were steelworkers. The Dofasco Christmas party – and the lavish presents given to the children of the company's workers – was legendary.

Hamilton proudly embraced its Steeltown image, probably because steel created a buoyant economy for the better part of a century. Dr. Don Wells, professor emeritus in labour studies at McMaster University, sees Hamilton's east end in the steel era as a Fordist community. As the industrial revolution entered the twentieth century, the concept of Fordism was born, applying principles of mass production, standardization and consumerism not only to the factory but to workers' lives in general. In a Fordist community, the industrial and residential areas are closely intertwined. Society is centred around the factory as much as it is the neighbourhood.

The city's industrial community also led to a strong bias toward organized labour. "Hamilton was also the citadel of industrial unionism," Wells says. "There is still a strong identity in the community." The lunch pail–carrying, hard hat–wearing, unionized heavy manufacturing worker was synonymous with Hamilton.

That identity stretched onto the football field. Hamilton played in ten Grey Cup finals between 1957 and 1972, winning five of them. The team was known for its tough, hard-hitting defensive style rather than flashy offensive play. This attitude was personified in Angelo Mosca, one of the most popular and famous Tiger-Cats players of all time. The towering 6'5", 295-pound Mosca was widely thought to be the dirtiest player in the game. He is still treated like royalty by Tiger-Cats faithful.

Citizens' connection to the team ran even deeper with the Hamilton-born players on the team. On John Michaluk's 1967 Tiger-Cats squad, he and three of his teammates – Bob Steiner, Ed Turek and Bob Krouse

– all came from Central High School in Hamilton, taking up four slots on a thirty-one-man roster. The team sought out and hired talent from the local community, so there were always local boys to cheer on.

Football, as well as the football stadium, were integral to Hamilton. Wells recalls working in the steel plants himself. "Everyone went to the games," he says. "Not just the workers, but the owning classes as well. It portrayed a sort of cooperative capitalism. Owners and workers had a shared identification."

"The stadium was the place to be," Michaluk agrees. "Ladies would wear chrysanthemums. It was the whole city, coming out to the game."

Civic Stadium was interwoven into the fabric of the community in other ways. United Steelworkers Local 1005, Stelco's labour union, used Civic Stadium for its contract ratification meetings; no other venue in Hamilton could hold the fourteen thousand union members. It was also the venue for community events. "They held Marian Day there, too," Michaluk says. "All these Catholic school kids in their dresses, a big parade. And high school football championships were always played there."

The stadium was not just located in Hamilton, and was not just a stadium. It was a symbol of the city and its people, a meeting place, a forum in the classical sense of the word.

Football was a key way Hamilton celebrated itself, but as the twentieth century drew to a close, there was very little to celebrate. In the early 1980s, the domestic demand for steel plummeted. Cheaper offshore steel began to flood the market. Manufacturing in Canada became unsustainable. The arrival of mass computing and electronics forced a shift to technology-related industries, where the Canadian workforce could be competitive.

Hamilton was left behind.

The steel industry in the city shed two-thirds of its jobs by 1990. Unemployment worsened, and the east end became a symbol not of working-class prosperity, but of the utter ruin of the North American manufacturing sector. Hamilton was no longer built on steel, and its steelworker families became a rarity instead of the norm.

The economy of central Hamilton was devastated. Barton Street, James Street North, Ottawa Street – these were vibrant commercial economies up to the 1970s, but were hollow wastelands by the 1990s. Changing consumer and retailing models were also unkind to local commercial areas and locally owned neighbourhood shops. Although the recent years have seen a renaissance in some of these areas, the boarded-up storefronts sprinkled along them show that they have not yet regained everything they have lost.

The Fordist community of Hamilton's east end disintegrated along with the steel industry. The monoculture that the single major industry created in Hamilton gave way to a more fragmented neighbourhood. Hamiltonians increasingly looked to other areas – Toronto, mainly – for work.

The decline of the steel industry was mirrored by a decline in the Tiger-Cats fan base. The 1980s saw the Tiger-Cats' worst years at the gate. The CFL instituted a blackout rule in the 1970s: if a team didn't sell out their stadium, they could force the CFL not to air the games locally on television. The idea was to encourage fans to view the games in person. In fact, attendance dwindled, and fans began to lose their connection with their home team.

I remember the era myself, sitting in the basement with my father, listening to CHML on the family's transistor radio, my father explaining patiently why we couldn't see our Tiger-Cats on the television.

The blackout policy, the economic downturn and unsteady Tiger-Cats ownership all contributed to dwindling attendance: the team averaged over thirty-two thousand fans in attendance in the 1972 season, which was nine thousand more than the league average. That figure plummeted below fifteen thousand in 1985, despite a Grey Cup appearance the year before. The decades of prosperity, for both Hamilton and its team, were over. Although the team was highly successful on the field

– they went to the championship game five times in the 1980s, winning the Cup in 1986 – attendance slid to a low of less than fourteen thousand by 1991.

The team lost its connection with the city in other ways, too. The team's ownership was more separate from the city: Toronto hockey magnate Harold Ballard owned the team from 1978 to 1990. Players were less and less frequently drawn from the local talent pool; the local boy became an anomaly on the roster.

Today, not a single Hamiltonian is on the Tiger-Cats roster. Mike Morreale and Rob Hitchcock were both local stars on the team, but played for the Tiger-Cats more than a decade ago. No Hamilton-born player has since played a central role for the team.

This isn't solely the team management's fault. The modern CFL includes high player turnover from year to year and a large contingent of American players (fully half of a team's roster can be from the USA). The Tiger-Cats aren't doing anything differently from other teams in the league. But they aren't going out of their way to hire local talent, either. And John Michaluk, who played his entire CFL career in his hometown, sees this as a problem. "This is not in the best interest of endearing fans to teams, building loyalty, creating stars, and making fans proud of their heroes."

Non-football fans often see the CFL as a dying league, a relic of bygone days. Attendance and television ratings have sunk in recent years, but the league has never been as prosperous as it is today. The TV rights deal with the TSN cable network is worth $40 million a year, a contract that is guaranteed until 2021. Only in comparison with the USA's much bigger NFL could the CFL be considered anything but a success.

But the neighbourhood around Tim Hortons Field is far different from the neighbourhood that surrounded it a couple of generations ago: same houses, different people.

AT THE STADIUM

Walk the perimeter of the stadium grounds on a game day in summer, a half-hour before kickoff.

As you approach the stadium, the first things you'll notice are the Tiger-Cats flags and banners adorning porches, even several blocks away. "The neighbourhood really supports the stadium," Rick Zamperin says. As the host of a call-in show after every Tiger-Cats game, he knows the fan base well. "The local neighbourhood really supports them. They feel really close to the team."

Some of the flags come from the team's merchandise store, which is attached to the stadium. Some look more homemade. A wooden sign is staked into the garden in front of one house, declaring THIS IS TIGER TOWN, hand-lettered in yellow and gold paint.

Disused parking lots are roped off and cars are waved in by attendants in orange safety vests. Ten minutes' walk from the stadium, parking is five dollars; closer, you'll pay ten dollars or more. Right across from the stadium, at the corner of Beechwood and Prospect Streets, one enterprising family has parked stadium goers' cars on their lawn for twenty dollars apiece. At last count they could fit ten cars.

Approaching every gate, two or three men stand just across the street, chattering at anyone in earshot. "Tickets. Got tickets? Need tickets? Buying and selling." For early season games they're only selling; on Labour Day, or late in the season with playoffs on the line, business is brisk in both directions. As throngs walk up to the gates, car traffic crawls. Pedestrians don't even look as they cross the road toward the stadium.

In good years, you'll hear chanting and yelling on the street. If Toronto is in town you can also count someone to yell a full-throated "Argos suck!" every few minutes. Inevitably someone will start up the traditional team chant, first yelled for the Tigers in 1921:

Oskee wee wee
Oskee wa wa
Holy Mackinaw
Tigers, eat 'em raw!

Many of the locals don't go to the games; they'll sit on their porches, often with a beer in hand, watching the ticket holders pass by. By kick-off they'll mostly be inside watching the game, although some bring a television out to the porch in the warmer months.

But this part of the city – like many parts of Hamilton – is relaxed and congenial. If you show up late and park further away, you'll pass people working in their backyard, and if you're wearing a jersey they might make a friendly comment: "Who're they playing today?" or "Think they'll get a win?"

In the stands, though, you'll see the Hamilton of a couple of generations ago: mostly white, mostly male and predominantly over forty. The team encourages a family-friendly atmosphere, with games and free face painting for kids. But this isn't the focus of the game day experience. Beer, food and merchandise sales dominate the concourses.

There's a remarkable feeling of togetherness in the stands. I once remarked that I didn't know anything about one of the players on Hamilton's wall of honour; I was treated to a long narrative about Tommy Joe Coffey from a nearby fan who had watched him play from that same seat.

The crowd erupts at every home team touchdown, of course. At one end of the stadium, though, high up on a pedestal, sits a massive brass factory whistle, and its deafening howl fills the stadium. Even now, the team reaches back to the blue-collar roots of the city.

After a win, in good seasons, the air turns electric. As fans flood the streets, triumphant cheers – the ever-present *Oskee wee wee* – break out spontaneously. Barton Street, Cannon Street and King Street, the three east-west arteries nearest to the stadium, turn into parking lots as several thousand cars take to the streets at once – but the honking horns are shouts of victory. Strangers high-five each other as they pass.

When you go to Tim Hortons Field for a Tiger-Cats game, you feel like you have found the living, breathing centre of the city. No city is its industry or its geography; a city is always its people. Here in Tiger Town is where the people of Hamilton live. The soul of Hamilton, it's often said, will always be steel, and Hamilton's heart is here.

HAMILTON TODAY, AND TOMORROW

But that's only one side of Hamilton.

When steel left the city, the city changed. The manufacturing sector is a pale shadow of its former self. The community that grew up on the northeast side of the city in a unionized, job-for-life economy is similarly a remnant of the past.

The character of football has also changed. A trickle of medical evidence about the effect of contact sports on players' brains began a decade or more ago. That trickle has since become a torrent, leading to questions about whether anyone – youths or adults – should be subjected to the severe damage that a football career inevitably causes. Whether football survives in its current form is very much in question.

Public figures of all kinds are held up to a different kind of scrutiny, too. In the middle of a disastrous eight-loss start to the 2017 season, Hamilton hired a successful American college coach, Art Briles. Public outcry swelled: Briles had been disgraced at Baylor University, where the football team worked for years to cover up rape accusations against its players. With such a forceful and immediate response from an angry public, the team cancelled the hiring before the day was out, and both Tiger-Cats owner Bob Young and league commissioner Randy Ambrosie soon released apologetic statements.

The character of Hamilton's population is different as well, not only because of economic realities, but because of other social shifts.

At the most surface level, one change is obvious: the car. Many Hamiltonians work outside of the city, and fans drive to the games instead of walking. The cohesive community that lived, worked and played together is gone. Even Hamilton as an urban centre has changed: it's been absorbed into a new regional economy, just one element of an economic-commercial-commuter zone that did not even exist forty years ago.

Other shifts in social dynamics have had a deep effect on the community as well, according to Dr. Wells. "People's identities seem less focused on overarching community identities," he says. "People are defined more by consumer tribes, and their identities are more fragmented and transitory."

Without this strong community identity, what can a team connect to? Even if Hamiltonians still identify with the team, the stadium isn't woven into the societal fabric in the same way. Is the team now just a business trying to turn a profit by cynically recalling images of Hamilton's past glory? It's possible. But does it matter?

It still matters to me – I have season tickets, and I still follow the team religiously. But I grew up in a family whose roots in Hamilton stretch back more than a century. Like many fans, I'm white, male and old enough to remember the city in the age of steel. There are plenty of others like me, and we fill the stadium for every Tiger-Cats game. But we're not the future of Hamilton. We are its memories.

The Tiger-Cats, the stadium, the neighbourhood – the city itself. These are all monuments for an era, an economy and a society that no longer exists. Hamilton now prides itself on being a diverse city with citizens from all over the globe. It is looking forward to the post-steel future, with health care research, technology, the arts and tourism all increasing in the wake of steel's decline.

Everything the Hamilton Tiger-Cats symbolize is a remnant of its history, not a reflection of its present or future. The brand new stadium towers above a much-changed neighbourhood, in the working-class part of a much-changed city. But it continues as a symbol of Hamilton, and maybe it always will. It might no longer reflect what Hamilton actually is, but it remains the perfect expression of how many of Hamilton's citizens want to see themselves: as the tough, hard-working, prosperous people they once were.

Endnotes

1   Rachel Brady, "Tim Hortons Field serves as turning point for the Ticats' pride," *Globe and Mail*, November 21, 2014, https://www.theglobeandmail.com/sports/football/new-stadium-serves-as-turning-point-for-the-ticats-pride/article21714265/.

Acknowledgements

Sometime in 2015 I met up with an old friend Stephen Dale, an Ottawa-based freelance writer specializing in politics, environment and culture, who was born in Hamilton and spent his formative years there before moving away as many young people do. In his case it was to pursue a successful career in journalism in both print and radio, which included the publication of four books and the production of radio documentaries for CBC *Ideas*. He has never forgotten his roots, though, and continues to visit friends and family. One day we ruminated over the significant transformative changes happening in Hamilton that were moving it away from a depressed post-industrial state. What had been dismissed as the "the Hammer" was coming to life and becoming the envy of Torontonians to the east, struggling to cope with their metropolis's almost insurmountable challenges of congestion and exorbitant housing costs.

So, Stephen and I met with another Hamiltonian and freelance editor Sarah Hipworth to talk about pulling together a non-fiction collection of articles or essays with this theme in mind. Within the trio I was the relative newcomer to Hamilton who was just getting his feet wet writing several articles for various local publications on political and historical machinations in the city. In the process I came into contact with Hamilton's redoubtable political bloggers and activists, such as Ryan McGreal, Shawn Selway and Joey Coleman who were showing a serious interest in participating in this project and also had suggestions of potential contributors.

A few of us met with publisher Noelle Allen at the James Street North storefront office for her company, Wolsak & Wynn, just to get an indication if a project like this might appeal to her. She surprised us by immediately giving us the go-ahead to pursue the collection. At one point I ended up taking stewardship of this project, having more time on my hands to find contributors, organize the endeavour and write both my own article on the city's car culture and the introduction. Unfortunately, Sarah faced some pressing personal matters that drew her away. Stephen Dale, as a freelancer, also had other projects on the go but he still had time to carefully go over the contributions and provide crucial feedback for the writers before Wolsak & Wynn undertook its editing process.

The work involved in putting together *Reclaiming Hamilton: Essays from the New Ambitious City* would not have been possible without the help of my wife, long-time editor Cathy McPherson, for her input and ideas on some of the assignments including my own. Also, I wish to thank Aha Blume for her professionalism and care in the transcription of recorded interviews, which can be a time-consuming task. In the process of looking for contributors I ran into a variety of politically knowledgeable people in Hamilton including Don McLean, the writer and reporter behind the Citizens for City Hall website, and Dave Kuruc, the owner of Mixed Media and King West Books. They were among the first people I met after moving here who gave me the lowdown of what to consider in a fuller understanding of local politics and concerns.

We were not able to write about some significant issues facing a major Canadian city such as Hamilton, but I hope our book will encourage Hamiltonians to reflect and critically examine their city to make it a better place to live, play and work.

PW

Contributor Biographies

Matthew Bin is an author and IT consultant, born and raised in Hamilton and currently residing in Oakville with his wife and beagles. He has published non-fiction books and articles on Canadian military history, international soccer and business, as well as military, horror and science fiction novels. In his spare time he is a licensed marriage officiant, artisanal pasta maker, and bassist and backup shouter in a punk rock band.

Nancy B. Bouchier, professor of history at McMaster, explores issues of locality, gender, social class and the environment in the history of sport and physical activity. She is author of *For Love of the Game: Amateur Sport in Small Town Ontario 1838–1895*.

Ken Cruikshank, professor of history and former dean of Humanities at McMaster, works on the history of business and of the administrative state in Canada and the United States, particularly between the 1880s and World War II. He is the author of *Close Ties: Railways, Government and the Board of Railway Commissioners, 1851–1933*.

As long-time research collaborators, Ken and Nancy have focused on the state, the environment and recreation in the history of Hamilton Harbour. In 2016 UBC Press published their *The People and the Bay: A Social and Environmental History of Hamilton Harbour*, which won the Canadian Historical Association's 2017 Clio Prize for Ontario regional history.

I'm **Joey Coleman**, a Hamiltonian who works as an independent crowdfunded journalist, is engaged with open data, involved in my neighbourhood association, a pinball player and am blamed by City Hall for increasing civic engagement with my work over at www .thepublicrecord.ca.

Kerry Le Clair is a Hamilton-based editor, community organizer and activist with a background in human rights, Indigenous solidarity and environmental racism work. She loves Hamilton for what it is and what it could be, and as such, continues to celebrate and castigate the city as needed.

Robert S. Fiedler completed a Ph.D. at York University where his research focused on suburban change and the politics and planning of postwar suburbanization in Toronto. He is originally from Vancouver and moved to Hamilton in 2011 after living in Toronto for five years. He lives in the North End with his spouse and children.

Kevin MacKay is a writer, community organizer, union activist and social science professor. He has lived in Hamilton for over thirty years and for the past fifteen years he has acted as Executive Director of the Sky Dragon Community Development Co-operative. In 2017 Kevin published *Radical Transformation: Oligarchy, Collapse, and the Crisis of Civilization*, with Between the Lines. He is currently working on a second book, *A New Ecological Politics*, with Oregon State University Press.

Ryan McGreal is the editor of Raise the Hammer (raisethehammer. org), a website focused on civic affairs in Hamilton, Ontario. He is a founding volunteer with Hamilton Light Rail (hamiltonlightrail.ca), a citizen group dedicated to bringing light rail transit to Hamilton. His writing has been published in the *Hamilton Spectator*, *Hamilton Magazine*, *The Walrus*, *HuffPost* and Behind the Numbers.

Seema Narula is a high school teacher, writer and sometimes DJ. She started her blog This Must Be The Place in 2011, where she documented her exploration of the city uncovering old gems and new places.

In 2016 she was nominated for the Hamilton Arts Award as an emerging artist in the category of writer. She has written for publications such as *The Guardian*, the *Hamilton Spectator* and Tourism Hamilton.

After writing this chapter, Seema has since become a member of the Coalition of Black and Racialized Artists (COBRA).

You can sometimes catch Seema DJing dance parties around the city or traipsing around various haunts with her kids in tow.

A graduate of Carleton University's School of Journalism, **Jessica Rose** is a writer, editor and book reviewer whose work has appeared in publications across Canada. She is a founding editor at *The Inlet*, the book reviews editor at *THIS*, a senior editor at the *Hamilton Review of Books* and was a long-time writer for *Hamilton Magazine*. She is the marketing manager at gritLIT: Hamilton's Readers and Writers Festival, sits on the Hamilton Arts Council's Literary Arts Committee and is a board member at the Adult Basic Education Association. She has nearly fifteen years of experience writing and editing publications for children.

Shawn Selway has a BA in Religion from McMaster and an Industrial Mechanic license from the Province of Ontario via the Steel Company of Canada basic works in Hamilton, Ontario. He is a moderate technological determinist broadly interested in questions of material culture and the attendant paradoxes. Accordingly, he finds himself writing about municipal planning issues for the local civic affairs blog, and about superseded industrial equipment for the clients of his consultancy in the conservation of historic machinery. He is the author of *Nobody Here Will Harm You*, a book about mass medical evacuation from the Eastern Arctic during the second half of the twentieth century.

Margaret Shkimba is a writer and contributing columnist to the *Hamilton Spectator*. A mother and grandmother, she lives in Hamilton with her partner, Ray, and her two hound dogs, Bonnie and Clyde.

Sarah V. Wayland is senior project manager for the Hamilton Immigration Partnership Council. From 2013 to 2018, she was the creator and leader of Global Hamilton, the City of Hamilton's immigrant attraction and retention initiative. A dual US-Canadian citizen, she earned her Ph.D. in political science from the University of Maryland. She immigrated to Canada in 1994 and settled in Hamilton with her family in 2001. From 2005 to 2014, she served on the board of Hamilton's largest settlement agency, including as secretary and president.

Paul Weinberg is a veteran journalist and freelance writer whose work has appeared in a wide range of newspapers, magazines and websites including the *Globe and Mail*'s Report on Business, *Toronto Star*, *Hamilton Spectator*, the *Monitor* (Canadian Centre for Policy Alternatives), *Canada's History*, rabble.ca and *NOW*. He is also the author of *When Poverty Mattered: Then and Now*, which was published by Fernwood in October 2019. He lives in Hamilton, Ontario.